Encyclopedia of Stress

RELATED TITLES OF INTEREST

Controlling Stress and Tension, Fifth Edition
Daniel A. Girdano, George S. Everly, Jr., and Dorothy E. Dusek
ISBN: 0-205-26388-7

Job Stress
James H. Humphrey
ISBN: 0-205-27202-9

Practical Stress Management: A Comprehensive Workbook for Managing Change and Promoting Health
John A. Romas and Manoj Sharma
ISBN: 0-205-16301-7

For more information or to purchase a book, please call 1-800-278-3525.

Encyclopedia of Stress

F. J. McGuigan

Institute for Stress Management
United States International University

Allyn and Bacon

Boston ■ London ■ Toronto ■ Sydney ■ Tokyo ■ Singapore

*This encyclopedia is dedicated
to my many stress management students
over the years who made this book possible.
They extended my horizons considerably
in this important human endeavor.*

Publisher: *Joseph E. Burns*
Series Editorial Assistant: *Sara Sherlock*
Manufacturing Buyer: *Megan Cochran*

Copyright © 1999 by Allyn & Bacon
A Viacom Company
160 Gould Street
Needham Heights, MA 02494

Internet: www.abacon.com

Library of Congress Cataloging-in-Publication Data

McGuigan, F. J. (Frank J.)
     Encyclopedia of stress / F. J. McGuigan.
         p.   cm.
     Includes bibliographical references and index.
     ISBN 0-205-17876-6
     1. Stress (Psychology)—Encyclopedias.   2. Stress management—
Encyclopedias.   I. Title
BF575.S75M235   1999
155.9'042'03—dc21   98-28926
                                                                                  CIP

ISBN 0-205-17876-6

Printed in the United States of America

10 9 8 7 6 5 4 3 2 1   02 01 00 99 98

CONTENTS

PREFACE

This encyclopedia is a reference work for the broad field of stress, including stress-related disorders. The book addresses an obvious need, as interest in the subject has never been higher. Indeed, stress is commonly accepted as the "twentieth-century disease."

Statistics indicate sizable increases in stress-related disorders. For instance, there has been a phenomenal increase in workers' compensation claims for stress-related disorders, with associated skyrocketing costs. In California alone, employers have paid more that one billion dollars annually just for medical and legal fees. Moreover, 90 percent of job stress lawsuits are successful, with average awards of over $15,000. A Gallup poll of corporate personnel and medical directors indicated that up to 25 percent of the nation's business workforce suffers from anxiety disorders and other stress-related illnesses. Furthermore, very few of those sufferers receive treatment. Eleven percent of all workers' compensation claims are due to occupational disease attributed to job stress. On-job depression and anxiety are common symptoms; about 34 percent of 19 million patients annually visiting private psychiatrists were diagnosed with depression and 16 percent were diagnosed with anxiety disorders.

From a slow beginning, the topic of stress has become a dominant one nationally and internationally. People have begun to realize that any substantial change in their routines, which may be changes for the better or for the worse, make intensive demands on their physical and emotional resources. The kinds of stress to which people are exposed cover all activities throughout the twenty four hours of each day. Be they in the workplace, in the home, or in complex relations with other individuals, the stresses of life (stressors) can take tremendous tolls on the human body. Stressors during sleep are even more disastrous than are waking stressors, as indicated by the relatively large number of heart attacks and ulcer activations during sleep.

To meet the needs of individuals who are victimized by a wide variety of stressful events, this encyclopedia provides entries that will help them to understand their problems. Insofar as possible, the entries suggest how one can help oneself with each stress disorder. The book emphasizes the need for information about stress and builds on the interests that people have in the general area.

How to Use This Encyclopedia

A few words about how to use this encyclopedia: First, the reader can obviously look up the appropriate topic alphabetically throughout the book. However, by consulting the index, not only can a rapid overview of stress topics be achieved, but also cross-references are readily available. Second, note that within entries certain topics are in boldface—such as **Anxiety**—which means that the reader should consider looking up each of those entries in the encyclopedia as a cross reference to the immediate topic of interest. Third, at the end of each entry, there is a bibliography that makes available to the reader additional information on the topic of interest.

How This Encyclopedia Was Constructed

The first task was to select topics that were particularly relevant to potential readers of this encyclopedia. For some five years I asked my students in my stress management classes in psychology and in the School of Business to research the literature for topics that they perceived to be especially important and of high interest value. These topics were validated by the publisher and by the author. A search through recent books in the field of stress yielded additional topics that were added. Reviewers yielded yet additional topics that might be pursued by readers of the book. The goal always was to present scientifically well-validated empirical information in a systematic way for those who wanted to easily find topics of particular concern. After all of this information was processed, a final version of the manuscript was written.

The aim of the book is to provide information on stress topics, but no effort was made to include contemporary experts; rather, those experts are represented in the bibliographies and the discussions throughout the encyclopedia. Two exceptions could not be avoided: The first is Edmund Jacobson, who produced the seminal work on stress management, first published in 1929, revised in 1938, and entitled *Progressive Relaxation,* which remains the "bible" on stress management methods. The other is Hans Selye, whose seminal work on the nature of stress was first published in 1956. However, it was not until some years later that Selye became aware of the difference in physics between the words "stress" and "strain." Had he not made that distinction, this would be an encyclopedia of strain, not of stress.

Acknowledgments

I would like to acknowledge gratitude to Mary Macken, whose dedication to detail and thoughtful suggestions greatly assisted in the development of this manuscript.

Thanks also to reviewers Dr. Lex Merrill, Naval Health Research Center, and Charles Spielberger, University of South Florida, for their suggestions and advice.

Finally, as noted in the dedication, I owe a considerable debt to my students over the years who helped me learn about many of the topics covered herein; I would like to have made them all coauthors. Also, a great appreciation is expressed to my assistants Patricia Moore and Louise Winheld for helping to edit, type and assist in the writing in many cases.

F. J. M.

INTRODUCTION

With its many interpretations, the various meanings of stress permeate society in the numerous ways elaborated throughout this encyclopedia. These many dimensions of stress have demanded our attention exponentially within the last several decades. It is a cliche, yet an instructive one, that stress has been dubbed the "twentieth-century disease," which well justifies the efforts herein to prevent and/or to control it.

In the entry entitled "Stress, Defined" on page 216, three definitions are developed: (1) a *stimulus*, an environmental event (a stressor); (2) a reaction of the body to stressors involving the numerous internal systems and organs; and (3) an interactive state in which stressors and bodily reactions affect each other. Yet, because of the many uses of the terms, there are other definitions that the reader may encounter. This encyclopedia takes a broad view and suggests that the reader employ the interpretation of the term "stress" that he or she considers appropriate in each context. Often, one of the three definitions stated above can be used to interpret the meaning of the term in the specific contexts in which society uses it.

One caution, though, is that researchers have found that the word "stress" is repeatedly used in descriptions of the various emotional states that one can experience. Similarly, discussions of anxiety have been found to include the word "stress" about as frequently as the word "anxiety" is itself used. A word used in such diverse ways can become meaningless; yet, whatever its uses, stress is a phenomenon not common a century ago. Hopefully, this volume will help explicate the term to approach a commonly accepted, scientifically based definition.

For now, however, regardless of the interpretation that one chooses, there is an enduring model that will assist in understanding any topic covered herein. Any stressor immediately evokes a widespread bodily reaction, traditionally referred to as the "startle reaction pattern." It is commonplace to point out that the startle pattern (which consists in part of a person rising on the balls of his or her feet, hunching forward, tensing striated muscles throughout the body) prepares one for fight or flight—to attack the stressor or to flee from it. Once a stressor—an environmental threat—evokes such neuromuscular events, including especially the extensive tensing of the striated muscles of the body used to prepare one to act, complex internal reactions follow. Thus, the startle pattern includes not only the neuromuscular events required for immediate response to the emergency, but also extremely complex additional reactions involving smooth muscles (those surrounding the blood vessels, those of the intestinal tract, etc.), hormonal secretions, and other chemical events. All of these phenomena can combine to create the subjective feeling of "being stressed."

It is thought that our ancient ancestors benefited from the startle reaction pattern as they survived the dangers of the jungle. Today we also benefit from the startle reaction pattern as we face the stressors of the contemporary "cement jungle"—the worries, problems, and threats of everyday life. However, in facing most contemporary stressors, our reactions are not so exaggerated, but are usually covert. That is, while one may not overtly respond to a stressor, the muscles of the body still tense—even though another person may not be able to observe those small-scale tensions. Just how a person reacts to a particular stressor depends on many factors: the characteristics of the stressor; the individual's repertoire of coping techniques; how he or she perceives the situation in the light of previous experiences; his or her capacity to tolerate anxiety, which may involve a genetic or personality disposition; and so forth.

Regardless of which of those characteristics influence the response to stressors, there is extensive tensing of the muscles of the body in the startle pattern, which is momentarily beneficial in meeting the immediate threat. However, in some people those muscles often fail to relax when the danger is resolved. Far too frequently members of contemporary society involuntarily, unconsciously maintain such extra muscular tension when it ceases to be beneficial. Failure to relax the muscles appropriately following a stressful life situation can result in a variety of pathological conditions. One's genetic predisposition and behavioral characteristics can also predispose the individual to exaggerate the body's reaction during and after stressful experiences, and thereby contribute to damaged health. Such prolonged muscular tension can wreak havoc on the body. Research has shown that as one repeatedly reacts to stressful events, the disastrous effects on the body accumulate so that the individual becomes increasingly susceptible to physical illnesses, emotional problems, behavioral disorders, and accidental injuries. When a human being perceives danger (whether real or imagined), the startle reaction triggers complex hormonal events; these include the release of adrenocorticotropic hormone from the pituitary gland, epinephrine, and various other hormones from the adrenal gland that speed up heart rate and raise blood pressure; there is also further increase in muscle tension. These effects are all part of the "fight or flight" response of the body to a threatening environment. As illustrated in the accompanying figure, chronic overtension of the striated muscles overdrives the central nervous system (the brain and spinal cord), which in turn leads to maladaptive functioning of other systems of the body. (Such excessive striated muscular tension is one aspect of what people refer to as "stress" or being "stressed.") If tension is excessive and chronic, any of diverse psychiatric disorders (anxiety, phobias, depressions, etc.) and psychosomatic disorders (headaches, high blood pressure, constipation, etc.) may follow.

Consequently, one who wishes to prevent or alleviate the variety of stress–tension disorders and diseases needs to learn how to judiciously employ (reeducate) the striated muscles. The overtension that has produced a pathologic condition should be treated in therapy, which involves, in large part, reducing excessive muscular tension and bringing it under volitional control. As a result, there are many references to treatments of stress–tension disorders through relaxation techniques, for they are the best ways in which we can "handle our stress."

Psychology, psychiatry, and related disciplines over the years have had great difficulty in scientifically addressing subjective feelings. I certainly do not deny

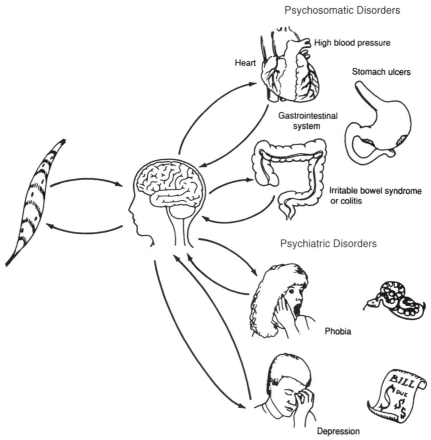

Overtension of the striated muscles can lead to a variety of psychiatric and psychosomatic disorders. Therapy is to reverse the process through relaxation.
(*Source:* Drawing courtesy of the author.)

that there are such phenomena, and a major portion of my work has been to scientifically explicate mental processes and, indeed, the entire concept of mind (McGuigan, 1994; McGuigan, 1998). The point here is that I frequently refer to "physical," "physiological," "organic," "materialistic" phenomena and the like, and I also necessarily refer to "psychological" phenomena. In no sense do I mean that psychological phenomena are not physicalistic: Psychological variables are physical in nature and psychological phenomena *are* generated in some way by systems of the body. But what is the difference between them?

One way of distinguishing between physical and psychological phenomena is to hold that the latter are simply those that are measured by psychological methods (versus those stated through physics, chemistry, physiology, etc.). For instance, psychologists have developed marvelous measures of psychological phenomena such as anxiety, anger, rigidity, and emotionality. In short, when we use the term "psychological," we are referring to physical events that are measured with the unique tools of psychology; these include psychophysiological methods, too, such as electroencephalogic measures of brain activity and electromyographic measures of covert behavior.

Bibliography

McGuigan, F. J. (1992). *Calm down: A guide for stress and tension control* (2nd ed.). Dubuque, IA: Kendall/Hunt. Accompanied by *Principles and practice of progressive relaxation: A teaching premier by Edmund Jacobson, M.D., Ph.D., and F. J. McGuigan, Ph.D.* (4 audio cassettes).

McGuigan, F. J. (1994). *Biological psychology: A cybernetic science.* Englewood Cliffs, NJ: Prentice-Hall.

McGuigan, F. J. (1998). A neuromuscular model of mind with clinical and educational applications. *The Journal of Mind and Behavior, 18,* 351–370.

A Absenteeism–Autogenic Training

Absenteeism

Description

Absenteeism occurs when workers are excessively absent from their jobs. It results in loss of productivity amounting to billions of dollars annually in the United States alone. Absenteeism is repeated by one person or it may be common among a number of individuals, and may be referred to as **Burnout.** It is also a very serious health-cost burden.

Causes

The varied causes of absenteeism include accidents, sickness, and "just not wanting" to come to work (burnout). When a worker reports not feeling well this may be interpreted variously, and a company interviewer can probabilistically diagnose the reason for the absence. No doubt severe stress and results of prolonged exposure to stressors are major factors in absenteeism; this is so in part because stressors lower the immune response and expose the body to other health risks, such as accidents.

Treatment

One could start with making managers and workers aware of the problem (if relevant personnel are not aware of important stressors faced daily by employees, obviously it is unlikely that causes for absenteeism can be identified). Once stressors are identified, a program to teach workers the long-term benefits of coping with those stressors could reduce absenteeism. Such a program could well pay for itself many times. The side rewards could be a reduction in medical costs and worker compensation claims, as well as increased productivity for the organization.

S E E   A L S O :

Burnout
Executive Stress
Workplace Stress

BIBLIOGRAPHY

Cooper, C. L., & Rousseau, D. M. (Eds.). (1995). *Trends in organizational behavior* (Vol. 2). Chichester, England: Wiley.

Klarreich, S. H. (1990). *Work without stress: A practical guide to emotional and physical well-being on the job.* New York: Brunner/Mazel.

Quick, J. C., Murphy, L. R., & Hurrell, J. J. (Eds.). (1992). *Stress and well being at work: Assessments and interventions for occupational mental health.* Washington, DC: American Psychological Association.

Addictive Behaviors

Description

An addictive behavior is a repeated compulsive, uncontrolled response, especially self-administration of drugs beyond medical needs. This type of behavior often fits a positive feedback model wherein the behavior is repeated until the abuser's system goes out of control (e.g., with continued ingestion and consequent pleasurable feelings, a cocaine addict may die, an alcoholic may black out, and a gambler may run out of money or collateral).

Five theoretical stages in the addiction cycle have been suggested. They are initiation, continuation, transition or escalation, cessation, and relapse. At each progressive stage, the individual's problem-solving abilities are further impaired, and while each stage may be embraced with renewed hope for a solution, those hopes can be quickly dashed, and feelings of powerlessness and hopelessness return with increased strength.

Causes

Addictive behavior may be understood in terms of such variables as euphoria/pleasure-seeking; drug knowledge, values, beliefs; cognitive factors; coping and tension-anxiety reduction; interpersonal variables (social, cultural, family issues); personality factors; and social/environmental factors. Each of these factors may act as a stressor and/or a causal factor in propelling the individual through progressive stages of the addiction cycle. Both stress and the addiction cycle can have their own forms of expression.

Treatment

The viciousness of the addiction cycle is characterized by the way an individual gets caught up in mini-feedback loops that fall between addiction stages (such as a problem drinking loop, or compulsive drinking loop). These loops are difficult to break because they encompass more of the individual's core behaviors and because they have the quality of closed feedback systems.

For a therapist to break a loop may well require encouraging the client to regress to a prior stage and probably to experience increased stress. (Presumably the client moved from one stage to the next as a means of reducing stress from the prior stage.)

Some benefits have been achieved though the additional use of mutual help groups. Mutual help supplies something different and complementary to what professionals offer. Addictive personalities frequently need both kinds of help: medical and psychological help as well as help in creating or discovering a sense of connectedness with people who know and care and help in combating the feeling of vulnerability and powerlessness that often overwhelms addicts.

SEE ALSO:

Alcohol Abuse in the Workplace
Alcoholism
Compulsive Behavior
Drug Abuse in the Workplace

Gambling
Obsessive-Compulsive Behavior
Tobacco Use

BIBLIOGRAPHY

Glaniz, M., & Pickens, R. (Eds.). (1992). *Vulnerability to drug abuse.* Washington, DC: American Psychological Association.

Gottheil, E., Druley, K. A., Pashko, S., & Weinstein, S. P. (Eds.). (1987). *Stress and addiction.* New York: Brunner/Mazel.

Peele, S. (1991). *The truth about addiction and recovery: The life process program for outgrowing destructive habits.* New York: Simon and Schuster.

Aging

Description

Life expectancy for newborn babies in the United States in 1993 was a record 78.3 years for females and 71.3 years for males. If increases in life expectancy continue at this rate, the average American can expect to live into his or her eighties by the year 2050.

As a consequence of living longer, the number of people over 65 years of age in the United States has greatly increased. Coupled with a reduced birthrate, the proportion of elderly people has increased sizably. One prediction is that there will be 35 million people over 65 years of age in the United States by the year 2000. There is, therefore, increasing concern about our aging population and the aging process.

The changes that are common among us as we age constitute the primary aging process. Some examples of the physiological and anatomical aspects of these "normal" aging changes follow: As aging increases, the amount of REM (rapid eye movements that occur during dreaming) and deep sleep decreases. There is a decrease in the amount of water in the body so that when drugs, such as lithium, are ingested, they become relatively more concentrated; as a consequence, the effects of drugs change with age. Similarly, the fat/muscle ratio increases so that there is more fat per unit of muscle; therefore, drugs stored in fat have a different effect than they do in the young. As one grows older, blood pressure typically increases, the vital capacity of lungs decreases, hearing acuity decreases, kidney function decreases, and the mass of skeletal muscle decreases leading to a decrease in muscular strength.

Auditory abilities, including the ability to perceive speech, commonly decline as one ages, as do such visual abilities as acuity, stereopsis (depth perception), and peripheral vision. There are also declines in the sensitivity of other sensory systems including those for taste, smell, and balance.

Changes in the respiratory system also occur with aging. Forced vital capacity, the maximum amount of air that can be forced out of the lungs, decreases with aging probably because the alveoli (air sacs in the lungs) become less effective in exchanging oxygen with the capillaries of the bloodstream. The decrease in the strength of the respiratory muscles also contributes to a decreased lung volume. Various structural changes result in a decreased ability of the lungs for expiratory flow rate and contribute to a decreased ability for muscular exercise.

The aged often have problems with their bones. Rather than being solid structures, bones are porous, living tissue containing marrow that manufactures blood cells. Bones also store calcium, which is required in small amounts by all body cells. Bones are hard and strong, in large part because of the calcium phosphate that they contain. They, like all cells of the body, are continuously changing, so there is always a need for calcium.

If calcium is insufficient, one result is osteoporosis, which is more common in women. With osteoporosis the skeletal system grows increasingly fragile and the female may develop what is known as a "dowager's hump," whereby the woman's head moves forward and her shoulders enlarge. Loss of height also typically occurs because the spinal vertebrae collapse and become bunched together, known as "crush fracture."

One of the greatest dangers of an unhealthy skeletal system in people over 65, particularly for women, is hip fracture. The forearms and spinal vertebrae are also very vulnerable to fracture.

The knee is another typical location for evidence of the aging process. One thing that happens is that the ligaments and tendons that hold the joints together weaken and stretch because the cartilage that cushions the contact between the bones deteriorates.

Of the cognitive changes that people observe in the elderly, a decrease in the effectiveness of remembering is among the most obvious. But there are different kinds of memory: "Intentional memory" declines with age, but "unintentional memory" does not. An example of intentional memory is the attempt to recall a person's name. An example of unintentional (spontaneous) memory occurs when the name "just pops into one's head" for no apparent reason.

Secondary aging processes include unique kinds of illnesses that contribute to aging; that is, pathological disorders take a toll on our bodies, causing us to age more rapidly. Normal aging is free of the pathological disorders of secondary aging processes and occurs as a result of primary aging processes.

Causes

Decreased activity of the central nervous system and subsequent loss of motor neurons (nerve cells) contribute to atrophy of muscle. Aging in part, then, occurs because the disuse of muscle and of neural tissue as they fail to interact leads to a deterioration of both. As one recognizes that one's body is deteriorating, it is common to increase worry about avoiding injuries, surviving the common stresses of life, and even one's longevity.

The *Chronicle of Higher Education,* May 15, 1991, reported that researchers have discovered that stress triggers the release of two hormones, epinephrine and cortisol. These hormones previously have been implicated in coronary artery disease and high blood pressure in humans. Elevated levels of these hormones have also been found in persons with **Alzheimer's Disease.** Research studies underway seek to determine if Alzheimer's might occur in people who are particularly susceptible to the effect of stress hormones as they age.

Treatment

The normal aging process has shown to be retarded by maintaining physical fitness (good endurance, motor performance, flexibility, and freedom from tremors) and successfully coping with the stresses of life.

Degeneration of the musculature can generally be counteracted through physical exercise. Continual aerobic and other exercise deters declines in vital capacity and cardiac efficiency. And with continual use of cognitive functions we can retard mental degeneration.

To deal with stress, one should properly relax the body when it strikes. The most effective way to achieve that desired state of physical tranquility is through **Edmund Jacobson's** method of **Progressive Relaxation.** Dr. Jacobson estimated that in learning to relax, we can add 20 years on to our lives. Through this method we can learn to control the systems of our bodies so as to rationally regulate ourselves to adjust to the stressful situations that we meet in life.

S E E   A L S O :

Alzheimer's Disease
Progressive Relaxation

B I B L I O G R A P H Y

McGuigan, F. J. (1994). *Biological psychology: A cybernetic science.* Englewood Cliffs, NJ: Prentice-Hall.
Ory, M. G., Abeles, R. P., & Lipman, P. D. (Eds.). (1992). *Aging, health, and behavior.* Newbury Park, CA: Sage.

Salthouse, T. A. (1991). *Theoretical perspectives on cognitive aging.* Hillsdale, NJ: Erlbaum.
Zarit, S. H., & Knight, B. G. (Eds.). (1996). *A guide to psychotherapy and aging: Effective clinical interventions in a life-stage context.* Washington, DC: American Psychological Association.

Agoraphobia

Description

Derived from the Greek words *agora* meaning "the market place" and *phobos* meaning "terror and fright," agoraphobia is described generally as an irrational fear of open spaces where escape is not possible. It was first described by C. Wesphal, a German psychiatrist, in 1871. Wesphal wrote of the psychological impossibility of walking through certain streets or squares, or the possibility of doing so only with dread and anxiety. Because the fear of going out is one of the major aspects of agoraphobia, the name stuck, even though the fear of public places scarcely covers the huge variety of agoraphobic manifestations.

The symptoms of agoraphobia are so diverse that it has been suggested that this "disease" is not a single syndrome. However, a common, central group of symptoms is characteristic. The somatic sensations are similar to any **Anxiety** state, while the associated anxious thoughts are characteristically centered on ideas of fainting and losing control. The situations (symbols) in which symptoms appear tend to be those that hinder escape, such as public transportation, busy shops, or elevators. A pattern of avoidance develops, and the condition may progress to the extent that the person becomes wholly housebound.

Physiological symptoms may include such reactions as tachycardia, **Colitis,** tremors, cold sweats, vomiting, fainting, and nausea. Some other unpleasant reactions include dizzy spells, **Backache, Gastrointestinal Disorders,** toothache, coughing, **Headache,** spots and rashes, cramps, and even itchy ears.

Causes

Development of agoraphobia may be influenced by some kind of psychological trauma in the individual's past in which one was conditioned to avoid dreaded situations. Anxiety thereby becomes associated with some symbol that warns the individual to remain at home. Usually the patient is unaware of the real source of the conditional anxiety. (For elaboration, see **Conditioning, Classical and Instrumental [Operant].**).

Stress of all kinds has an important role to play in contributing to agoraphobic symptoms. It does not have to be only **Distress** such as results from severe sickness and operations, but may also be **Eustress,** which can also be destructive to the individual. Eustress can be caused by the joy of having a baby, the excitement of going on a lecture tour, and the like.

Continued tension of any kind, from frustration, economic worries, harassment, or overwork (especially when it is not done for one's own satisfaction and pleasure, but in circumstances involving a feeling of injustice and hardship), renders a person vulnerable, liable to become oversensitive and feeling victimized by anxiety.

Treatment

Suggested treatments for simple agoraphobia are **Progressive Relaxation, Systematic Desensitization,** and low doses of antidepressants and anxiolytic medication. If the symptoms are accompanied by **Panic Attacks,** beta blockers and serotonin may be added by a physician. In any event, the therapist may employ some form of psychotherapy to help the individual understand the nature of the condition and to assuage the possible "fears of insanity," and so forth.

SEE ALSO:

Anxiety
Backache
Colitis
Conditioning, Classical and
    Instrumental (Operant)
Distress (Negative Stress)
Eustress (Positive Stress)

Gastrointestinal Disorders
Headache
Panic Attacks
Phobic Disorders
Progressive Relaxation
Social Phobia
Systematic Desensitization

BIBLIOGRAPHY

American Psychiatric Association. (1994). *Diagnostic and statistical manual of mental disorders IV.* Washington, DC: Author.

Carter, M. M., Turovsky, J., & Barlow, D. H. (1994). Interpersonal relationships in panic disorder with agoraphobia: A review of the empirical literature. *Clinical Psychology Science and Practice, 1,* 25–34.

Frampton, M. (1974). *Overcoming agoraphobia.* New York: St. Martin's Press.

Magee, W. J., Eaton, W. W., Wittchen, H. U., McGonagle, K. A., & Kessler, R. C. (1996). Agoraphobia, simple phobia, and social phobia in the national comorbidity survey. *Archives of General Psychiatry, 53,* 159–168.

Michelson, L. K., Schwartz, R. M., & Marchione, K. E. (1991). States of mind model: Cognitive balance in the treatment of agoraphobia. *Advances in Behavior Research and Therapy, 13,* 193–293.

Vose, R. H. (1981). *Agoraphobia.* London: Faber and Faber.

Wade, S. L., Monroe, S. M., & Michelson, L. K. (1993). Chronic life stress and treatment outcome in agoraphobia with panic attacks. *American Journal of Psychiatry, 150,* 1491–1495.

AIDS and Stress

Description

The stressor of learning that one has a positive HIV (human immunodeficiency virus) test result evokes considerable **Tension** throughout the body. Not only is the individual with the virus affected, but his or her family and friends also experience additional related stressors. The emotional suffering can include fear of contracting HIV/AIDS (acquired immune deficiency syndrome), personal loneliness and isolation, psychiatric disturbances, personal and family losses, and severe stress to the entire family system. (One who is exposed to HIV may eventually develop AIDS.) These stressors put individuals at increased risk of contracting AIDS when seeking to alleviate the stress. Individuals may engage in behaviors that are potentially self-destructive because they are so focused on their problems that they don't take proper care of themselves (e.g., not seeking medical attention), don't concentrate appropriately for any given situation (e.g., driving or operating machinery with their mind elsewhere), and reckless in some of their behaviors (e.g., engaging in unsafe sex practices). Some other distressful reactions may include suicidal ideation, **Suicide** attempts, **Anxiety,** and Drug Abuse.

Further, there are individuals who, despite being at no higher risk than the general population, have developed an acute fear of HIV infection. Some of these people are ignorant of the vulnerability and risk factors for HIV transmission; others are intellectually aware of current knowledge on HIV, but are uncomfortable with anything but zero risk. Some of these "worried well" develop AIDS phobia that interferes significantly in their lives. AIDS, like any other illness, might become for these people a metaphor for the expression of underlying problems.

Causes

People diagnosed with any life-threatening or chronic condition face potential stressors such as debilitation, financial costs, and death. A major factor in **Distress** responses is the loss of control of one's behavior. There is a significant association between higher levels of depression and feelings that individuals have no personal control over their health. Other contributing factors to distressful reactions may be anxiety, lack of coping skills, low self-efficacy, and interpersonal conflict. Not only does the person learning of the diagnosis experience the immediate stress and fears associated with such traumatic news, he or she also can suffer the social stigma peculiar to HIV and AIDS: loss of relationship, family, or other support, discrimination, and even unsympathetic attitudes by many health care providers. Studies have found that low perceived social support is consistent with higher levels of depression.

Treatment

One effective way to reduce the effects of stress-related tension and gain a sense of control over physical and mental health would be through **Stress Management Methods,** especially **Progressive Relaxation.** The practice of progressive relaxation may decrease anxiety by producing significant lessening of distress through enhancement of the immunological response, especially when applied to the behaviors mentioned. This is important in that at-risk populations already experience multiple psychosocial stressors, one of which is fear of acquiring HIV and/or

AIDS. Thus, it is valuable information for individuals diagnosed with HIV that they can manage their distress through stress management training.

Treatment can include building social support for the individual. There is a need for HIV positive individuals to gain a sense of control with respect to health regimens and other life activities; the measures described here may help.

SEE ALSO:

Anxiety   Progressive Relaxation
Distress (Negative Stress)   Stress Management Methods
Drug Abuse in the Workplace   Suicide
Immune System Disorders   Tension Awareness

BIBLIOGRAPHY

Antoni, M. H., Baggett, L., Ironson, G., LaPerriere, A., August, S., Klimas, N., Schneiderman, N., & Fletcher, M. A. (1991). Cognitive-behavioral stress management intervention buffers distress responses and immunologic changes following notification of HIV-1 seropositivity. *Journal of Consulting and Clinical Psychology, 59,* 906–915.

Glaser, R., & Kiecolt-Glaser, J. (1987). Stress-associated depression in cellular immunity: Implications for acquired immune deficiency syndrome (AIDS). *Brain, Behavior, and Immunity, 1,* 107–112.

Kalichman, S. C. (1996). *Answering your questions about AIDS.* Washington, DC: American Psychological Association.

Kelly, J. A., Murphy, D. A., Bahr, G. R., Koob, J. J., Morgan, M. G., Kalichman, S. C., Stevenson, L. Y., Brasfield, T. L., Bernstein, B. M., & St. Lawrence, J. S. (1993). Factors associated with severity of depression and high-risk sexual behavior among persons diagnosed with human immunodeficiency virus (HIV) infection. *Health Psychology, 12,* 215–219.

Landau-Stanton, J., & Clements, C. S. (1993). *AIDS health and mental health, a primary source book.* New York: Brunner/Mazel.

McGuigan, F. J. (1992). *Calm down: A guide for stress and tension control.* Dubuque, IA: Kendall/Hunt.

Perry, S., Fishman, B., Jacobsberg, L., Young, J., & Frances, A. (1991). Effectiveness of psychoeducational interventions in reducing emotional distress after human immunodeficiency virus antibody testing. *Archives in General Psychiatry, 48,* 143–147.

Alcohol Abuse in the Workplace

Description

Alcohol is the substance most abused in the business world. Experts estimate that alcoholism afflicts at least 10 percent of senior executives, and of the billions of dollars that alcoholism costs the nation every year, business pays the lion's share in extra health care, lost productivity, and absenteeism.

A study conducted by Alexander & Alexander Consulting Group for McDonnell Douglas Corporation shows how expensive it is to ignore substance-abuse problems in the workplace. The company found that, in the previous five years, each worker with an alcohol or drug problem had been absent 113 days more than the average employee and filed $23,000 more in medical claims. Their dependents also filed some $37,000 more in claims than the average family.

According to the March 25, 1991, *Business Week,* around 18 million Americans have a serious drinking problem. The annual deaths due to alcohol number about 105,000. Of all hospitalized patients, 25 percent have alcohol-related problems. Alcohol is involved in 47 percent of industrial accidents. Half of all auto fatalities are due to driving while intoxicated.

The annual costs from alcohol use include lower productivity ($47.7 billion), premature death ($28.5 billion), road accidents and crime and law enforcement ($9.6 billion), and $6 billion for "other." Indications are that alcohol may permanently damage the liver, stomach, heart, and brain. More specific problems include heart disease, cirrhosis of the liver, periodontal disease, convulsive disorders, pancreatitis and acute chronic **Gastrointestinal Disorders.**

Causes

The causes of alcohol abuse in the workplace are as elusive as a widely accepted definition of alcoholism. Potential causes range from social influence to stressful organizational pressures. The workplace can strongly promote heavy alcohol use if workers feel alienated and if managers adopt a permissive or ambiguous attitude toward alcohol. But there is no doubt that alcohol consumption produces immediate feelings of pleasure and relief from stressors, all of which strengthen the drinking response.

Treatment

Since alcohol consumption is reinforcing, **Behavior Therapy** strategies can be applied to reduce the relative efficacy of the drinking response.

What else can an employer do to deal with alcohol abuse? There are many different strategies from which to choose. Four main categories are (1) Employee drug education and awareness programs; (2) Substance testing; (3) Surveillance techniques, including searches, cameras, and undercover operations; and (4) employee assistance programs (EAP). These strategies should be based upon a sound company policy on substance abuse. Education and testing may or may not be used with an EAP. In comparison to substance testing, an EAP is not controversial, intrusive, or untested, and it integrates efforts for a drug-free workplace.

The EAP relies upon a supervisor's observations and constructive confrontation as the catalyst to cause the troubled employee to seek help. The actual strategy is a series of confrontations based on poor performance and, if necessary, bringing about a job-related crisis in the deviate drinker's life while he or she still holds the job. This may force the employee to take responsibility for poor performance and to act to correct it. Once an employee takes responsibility for alcohol abuse, the EAP can be of assistance; however, the employee must voluntarily accept help. After he or she is admitted to a program, an assessment of the problem is made and counseling or referral to appropriate agencies is provided. Depending on the situation, this may or may not include hospitalization.

SEE ALSO:

Absenteeism
Addictive Behaviors
Alcoholism
Behavior Therapy
Burnout

Compulsive Behavior
Drug Abuse in the Workplace
Gastrointestinal Disorders
Workplace Stress

BIBLIOGRAPHY

Ames, G. M., Grube, J. W., & Moore, R. S. (1997). The relationship of drinking and hangovers to workplace problems: An empirical study. *Journal of Studies on Alcohol, 58,* 37–47.

Ames, G. M., & Rebuhn, L. A. (1996). Women, alcohol and work: Interactions of gender, ethnicity and occupational culture. *Social sciences and medicine, 43,* 1649–1663.

Bureau of National Affairs (BNA). (1992). *Alcohol and drugs in the workplace: Costs, control and controversies.* Washington, DC: The Bureau of National Affairs.

Caldwell, P. E., Cutter, H. S., & Henry, S. G. (1997). Impact on work on early recovery Alcoholics Anonymous affiliation. *Employee Assistance Quarterly, 13,* 1–16.

Delaney, W., Grube, J. W., & Ames, G. M. (1988). Predicting likelihood of seeking help through an employee assistance program among salaried and union hourly employees. *Addiction, 93,* 399–410.

Guppy, A., & Marsden, J. (1997). Assisting employees with drinking problems: Changes in mental health, job perceptions and work performance. *Work and Stress, 11,* 341–350.

Alcoholism

Description

Addiction is defined as a physiological or psychological overdependence on a substance. Originally, however, the term applied only to physiological dependencies—in which the substance altered the biochemistry of the organism, requiring continued and often increased use of that or another substance. Regardless, alcoholism is characterized by repeated excessive drinking that interferes with an individual's health and work behavior.

Four types of alcoholism are (1) compulsive drinking, in which abstaining from drinking produces anxiety about being sober; (2) habitual drinking, in which constant physical and psychological functioning is to varying degrees alcohol-dependent, yet the alcohol intake does not necessarily exceed social norms; (3) drinking to avoid withdrawal, in which alcohol is used as a "liquid barbiturate," causing physical, life-threatening difficulties (e.g., dehydration through vomiting and diarrhea, hallucinations) when one attempts to stop drinking; and (4) drinking to experience pleasure, in which alcohol is a psychological disinhibitor, enabling the drinker to express feelings (e.g., rage, dependency, sexuality, despair, childishness) that he or she may not be able to when sober.

Frequently an individual begins to drink at about 12 years of age. The amount of alcohol (ethanol) consumed often increases during mid-adolescence and stabilizes by 17 to 18 years of age. Overall, 10 percent of the population in the United States consumes 50 percent of the ethanol. Typical patterns of alcohol abuse include moderate to large amounts ingested daily, heavy weekend drinking, and binges—with abstinence of a week or a month.

Symptoms of alcoholism include restlessness, agitation, gross tremors, hyperactivity, tachycardia, **Hypertension,** disturbance of visceral functioning and diaphoresis; in severe cases hallucinations may occur.

Causes

There are both internal and external causes of alcoholism. Internal ones include predisposition (addictive diathesis); biological and genetic predispositions; and psychological reasons. The external causes include environmental and sociocultural ones such as a loss or threatened loss of a spouse or family member, one's job, or money; and, paradoxically, either success or failure.

The pattern, nature, and motivation of drinking differs between alcoholics and nonalcoholic social drinkers, and the differences throw light on the relationship of ethanol intake to stress. Drinking in response to the occurrence of stress is common. Under the effects of alcohol the person may be free of feelings of anxiety, depression, and incompetence. It would appear that many use alcohol to relieve a sense of personal inadequacy, and it has been suggested that this relief may result from a release from the inhibitory control normally exerted over behavior by the higher regions of the brain.

The essence of alcoholism as an addictive disorder lies in the compulsive urge to drink or take drugs in the presence of significant contraindication in an area of life important to the individual, such as physical or psychological health; one's job, career, or education; and social, intimate, or sexual relationships. The physiological symptoms of tolerance and withdrawal may or may not be present, although they usually are. Tolerance means that the body has physiologically adapted to a level of ethanol or other drug intake so that more is required to produce the same effect. Withdrawal stems from the same source, for once the body has become dependent on the ethanol or other substance, abrupt withdrawal produces a specific symptom.

The physiological symptoms constitute motives for the alcoholic to continue or even increase drinking to prevent the symptoms of withdrawal and/or to achieve the desired effect without necessarily being influenced by external stressful events.

Treatment

Treatment for alcoholism varies according to the model espoused regarding its etiology. Yet, a primary complaint of the alcoholic leading him or her to use alcohol is the noxious hypertensive muscular state attributed to stressors between prolonged periods of abstinence. Thus, any treatment model should consider including the direct management of overtension by the individual as with **Progressive Relaxation** therapy.

Behavior Therapy has been effective in some cases. If alcohol usage has created dependence, the individual may need to go through detoxification and counseling and to seek social support as, for example, with Alcoholics Anonymous. Other treatments for an alcoholic include the use of antabuse (to block alcohol receptors), ambulatory detoxification (abstinence with or without the help of a physician), milieu approach with medical problems, continuation of care after abstinence, and the involvement of family/significant others in the therapy.

SEE ALSO:

Addictive Behaviors
Alcohol Abuse in the Workplace
Behavior Therapy
Compulsive Behavior
Drug Abuse in the Workplace
Gambling

Hypertension, Essential (High Blood Pressure)
Obsessive-Compulsive Behavior
Progressive Relaxation
Tobacco Use

BIBLIOGRAPHY

American Psychiatric Association. (1994). *Diagnostic and statistical manual of mental disorders IV.* Washington, DC: Author.

Bratter, E. & Forrest, G., (1985). *Alcoholism and substance abuse: Strategies for clinical intervention.* New York: Free Press.

Conrod, P. J., Pihl, R. O., & Vassileva, J. (1998). Differential sensitivity to alcohol reinforcement in groups of men at risk for distinct alcoholism subtypes. *Alcoholism: Clinical and Experimental Research, 22,* 585–597.

McCance-Katz, E. F., & Kosten, T. R. (Eds.). (1998). *New treatments for chemical addictions.* Washington, DC: American Psychiatric Press.

Alzheimer's Disease

Description

Alzheimer's disease was first described by a German neurologist, Alois Alzheimer, in 1907. He originally diagnosed a woman in her fifties with presenile dementia. Today neurologists agree that dementia in the elderly is the same as, or similar to, that earlier diagnosed presenile condition.

The symptoms are usually a gradual decline in intellectual and physical abilities. Alzheimer's begins with memory lapses and progresses through an inability to recognize people or normally familiar things. There follows an impairment in language and motor abilities and a change in personality. The family, which generally provides care for the Alzheimer's patient, is under an increasingly taxing burden throughout the progression of the disease. Although reactions and adjustments differ among families, several typical reactions have been described and seem to be intensified as the disability progresses. The disease ultimately leads to complete helplessness and death.

Many problems that families experience reflect insufficient knowledge about the disease. The lack of information can affect the quality of the coping skills and problem-solving behaviors of the caregiver, and are reflected in the level of perceived stress as well as in the quality of care.

In many families, defenses against the stress of overwhelming demands and unwanted life changes create interpersonal crises. Often the stresses lead to a disturbance in the family homeostasis. Long-standing conflicts that have existed between family members may be exacerbated. Competitiveness or maladaptive coalitions within the family can emerge and lead to difficulties in decision making or care. In many instances, the problems of role-reversal lead to pathological identifications with the parents or reenactments of one's own perceived childhood situation. Overinvolvement, disengagement, or parent abuse by the children are sometimes experienced, and the afflicted parent may experience excessive guilt when he or she cannot perform as an "adequate parent." Family members may even feel responsible for eliciting the patient's pathological behaviors and can experience intense feelings of guilt or depression.

Nonspecific stressors to the disorder are also perceived. There is frequent identification with the victim by other family members, characterized by fears of inheriting Alzheimer's disease. Denial is a common reaction that helps defend the family against their sense of hopelessness, but it makes realistic planning and treatment difficult and additionally stressful.

Expression of these feelings and assistance in working out alternative coping mechanisms are necessary in order to avoid acting out hostile feelings against the patient or developing stress-related adjustment reactions. Supportive therapy from the clinician or other professional caregivers, or involvement in self-help groups or mutual support groups, may be especially useful in dealing with the stressors of this disease.

Because of the nature of Alzheimer's, the patient may not always be able to follow simple instructions; however, during the lucid moments when the patient is cognizant of his or her aberrant behavior and feels the stress of his or her actions, a **Stress Management Method** may help.

Dr. D. Silver, a California neurologist who has worked extensively with Alzheimer's patients, advised that nearly all forms of dementia today are classified as Alzheimer's. According to Dr. J. Carson, an internist, there is a feud of sorts regarding this practice. Internists believe that the diagnosis of "Alzheimer's disease" brings with it such vivid images of the worst kind of dementia and death that it increases the **Anxiety** and **Stress** in both the patient and caregiver. The patient who hears this diagnosis is likely to give up. The caregiver often becomes apathetic, and both the patient and caregiver often sink into depression. An approach by many neurologists, on the other hand, maintains that their responsibility is to accurately diagnose the problem and to advise the patient of that diagnosis no matter how stressful it may be.

Causes

The cause of Alzheimer's disease is obscure. Many patients are afflicted while still relatively young—in their fifties or even earlier—while others are not afflicted until late in their lives—in their eighties or nineties. The most accurate method of diagnosis in the living appears to be by observing the patient's behavior through neuropsychological tests, the slowing of brain waves, and perceptible brain changes as shown through a CAT scan. The only certain diagnosis is through a biopsy at the death of the patient, when the brain in microscopically examined; the brain of a person with Alzheimer's disease will have an abnormally large number of neuritic plaques and neurofibrillary tangles.

Treatment

Today there is no known cure for Alzheimer's disease. Several medications for halting it are being studied. Some of these medications have strong side effects, such as increasing the disorientation and negatively affecting the liver and kidney functions.

The caregiver would certainly benefit from being well-trained to bring some control over his or her own stressful job.

SEE ALSO:

Aging   Stressful Life Events
Anxiety   Stress Management Methods

BIBLIOGRAPHY

Haley, W. E. (1998). Alzheimer's disease: A general overview. In E. A. Blechman & K. D. Brownell (Eds.), *Behavioral medicine & women: A comprehensive handbook.* New York: Guilford Press.
Light, E., & Lebowitz, B. D. (Eds.). (1990). *Alzheimer's disease treatment and family stress: Directions for research.* New York: Hemisphere.
Lushin, G. (1990). *The living death: Alzheimer's in America.* New York: Potomac.
Mace, N. L., & Robins, P. V. (1981). *The 36-hour day: A family guide to caring for persons with Alzheimer's disease related dementing illnesses, and memory loss in later life.* Baltimore: The John Hopkins University Press.
Siegler, I. C. (1998). Alzheimer's disease: Impact on women. In E. A. Blechman & K. D. Brownell (Eds.), *Behavioral medicine: A comprehensive handbook.* New York: Guilford Press.

Anger

Description

Anger is an excessive emotional response pattern often exhibited aggressively in verbal and physical ways, especially when one is threatened or attacked. Facial grimaces and body positions characterize anger that is cross-cultural. Hostility, a long-lasting emotional state, is manifested by a desire to harm or inflict pain upon others. Anger is a more intense and momentary reaction than hostility.

In anger there is increased blood pressure, respiratory activity, heart rate, gastrointestinal contractions, and secretion of gastric acid. Extended periods of these body responses can be very unhealthy. An extremely angry person is at very high risk for contracting debilitating illness and even early death from excess **Stress** and **Tension.**

Perhaps the most destructive of all emotions, anger is at the root of much interpersonal conflict and unhappiness. It precipitates fights and is central in ruining many relationships. In addition to alienating other people, anger can destroy our bodies from within.

Causes

There are numerous causes of anger. In most cases when we experience anger it is habitually in rebuttal to one or more of the following perceptions:

1. *Infringement:* Someone or something has violated our psychological territory ("space") or detracted from our status or self-worth.
2. *Frustration:* When we are prevented from getting something important that we want or are compelled to experience something unpleasant, we often respond with anger.
3. *Wrongfulness and Intentionality:* Anger regularly flows from a perception of injustice or inequity.

The intensity of one's anger varies with the individual and the circumstances. Some people are easily provoked, others are apathetic, and some control themselves so as not to become angry (the latter are obviously more likely to live longer lives).

Treatment

In order to control reactions to stressful situations and better cope with anger, one might consider that the anger and arousal thereby precipitated may be the direct result of the way we perceive those events and, indeed, the world in general. If maladaptive, we can learn to change our perceptions of certain undesirable and often unpredictable events whereupon we can learn to change the ways in which we cope. For instance, it is possible to prevent feelings of anger if one can perceive events with proper perspective. By perceiving our experiences in rational, clear ways, we can often control the frequency and intensity of angry feelings. This takes appropriate practice and dedication. Dealing positively and constructively with anger can generally be achieved by taking time for oneself to learn an effective **Stress Management Method.**

SEE ALSO:

Cardiovascular Disease
Emotional Behavior, Destructive
Frustration

Stress Signals
Stress Management Methods
Tension Awareness

BIBLIOGRAPHY

Kassinove, H. (Ed.). (1995). *Anger disorders: Definition, diagnosis and treatment.* Bristol, PA: Taylor and Francis.
McGuigan, F. J., (1992). *Calm down: A guide for stress and tension control.* Dubuque, IA: Kendall/Hunt.
Schloss, P. J., Smith, M., Santora, C., & Bryant, R. (1989). A respondent conditioning approach to reducing anger responses of a dually diagnosed man with mild mental retardation. *Behavior Therapy, 20,* 459–464.

Anorexia Nervosa

Description

Anorexia nervosa is characterized by a debilitating fear of food and weight gain, even though there is normal body development. There are usually extreme dieting, vigorous exercise, bizarre eating patterns, and a distorted "self-image." The bizarre eating patterns include picking at and hiding food, cutting it into small pieces, and consuming only very specific foods. Weight loss due to severe restriction of calories and/or the use of laxatives and/or diuretics is common. Overexercising and constant denial of hunger are common. The anoretic person will frequently be deceptive about when or how much he or she eats and often will claim to be on a diet; the person also may try to hide his or her body by wearing extra layers of loose-fitting clothes. This person will often be obsessed with cooking elaborate meals but will not partake of them.

Physiological signs include a loss of menstrual periods in females, slow pulse, low blood pressure, depression or agitation, weakness, fatigue, intolerance to cold, insomnia, electrolyte imbalance, and a growth of fine, down-like hair on the upper extremities called "lanugo."

Causes

Theories abound as to why a person who has accessible food would choose to starve himself or herself, making this a very difficult disorder to understand and treat. The onset of anorexia is typically abrupt and may occur after a stressful life change or developmental period. **Compulsive Behavior** and desire for perfectionism is generally associated with the disorder. By refusing to eat properly, the person may gain a false feeling of control over events in life that perhaps are perceived as proceeding too rapidly.

Treatment

Although anorexia can be a life-threatening disease, many treatments are available. Some of the more successful therapies include, especially, **Behavior Therapy,** and other **Stress Management Methods,** as well as family counseling. **Progressive Relaxation** techniques are also widely used with anoretic patients to help them gain control of their bodies. Through practice, an anoretic can relax at moments when he or she feels in the most danger. Drug therapies include the use of tricyclic antidepressants and antipsychotic medication. Extreme cases require hospitalization.

In addition to their need for structure and a nonthreatening environment, anoretic patients demonstrate a strong need for stress reduction. Indications are that persons with anorexia typically suffer two and a half times the magnitude of life **Stress** experienced by their peers. Additionally, stress among anoretics has been found to be most often self-generated. Consequently **Distress** levels should be reduced or eliminated before anoretic thoughts and behaviors can be confronted effectively.

S E E   A L S O :

Behavior Therapy
Bulimia
Compulsive Behavior
Distress (Negative Stress)
Eating Disorders

Food Abuse
Obesity
Progressive Relaxation
Stress Signals
Stress Management Methods

B I B L I O G R A P H Y

Garner, D. M., & Garfinkel, P. L. (Eds.). (1997). *Handbook of treating eating disorders* (2nd ed.). New York: Guilford Press.
McGuigan, F. J. (1992). *Biological psychology: A cybernetic science.* Englewood Cliffs, NJ: Prentice Hall.
Thompson, K. (Ed.). (1996). *Body image, eating disorders and obesity: An integrative guide for assessment and treatment.* Washington, DC: American Psychological Association.

Anxiety

Description

Anxiety has been described as a distorted emotional reaction to certain stimuli, especially threats to one's security, identity, integrity, values, or habits. It contains qualities of apprehension, dread, distress, and uneasiness. Anxiety is sometimes distinguished from **Fear,** as anxiety is often not bound to a specific stimulus whereas fear is usually associated with an identified physical threat. The body usually reacts by producing excessive muscle **Tension,** increased heart and breathing rate, sweaty palms, and the like. Muscle tension is a natural reaction, part of the primitive startle response pattern that prepares us for fight or flight.

The esophagus, containing a combination of smooth and striated muscles, is especially responsive to fear and anxiety. It responds to threat by contracting into a mild spasm that can last for hours, days, or even months. In a prolonged condition of anxiety and fear, chronic muscle spasm can feel like a "lump" in the throat (globus hystericus). The term "anxiety" was introduced into the English language from the thirteenth-century French word *anguisse,* which meant a "painful sensation in the throat."

Anxiety is also represented in the eye muscles as one visualizes specific matters of concern. Many conditions of exaggerated anxiety are learned through the visual modality, and emotional responses can be acquired vicariously from observing the pain of others. When we become fearful, threats are visualized and past dangers can be relived. By tensing eye muscles, circuits are activated between the eyes and the brain that generate visual images that are components of our anxieties.

Muscle tension helps in meeting or avoiding danger and is thus protective and adaptive. However, if the tension becomes excessive and/or prolonged beyond the actual threat, it becomes pathological, possibly leading to neurosis or depression.

Symptoms of anxiety can also include heart palpitations, difficult or irregular breathing, dizziness, excessive **Fatigue,** trembling, twitching, restlessness, being easily startled, sweating, cold/clammy hands, high resting pulse and respiration rates, tingling of the hands or feet, upset stomach, diarrhea, loss of appetite, hot or cold spells, and frequent urination. In extreme cases of anxiety, fear may interfere with one's ability to concentrate; there may also be **Insomnia,** impatience, hyperattentiveness, feelings of helplessness, lack of control, and depression. Anxiety stresses the body by lowering resistance and depleting energy, which can lead to increased risk for a variety of health conditions.

Anxiety occurs slightly more often in women than in men, with adolescents and the elderly being more susceptible.

Causes

Organic Causes. An overactive thyroid gland or a vascular brain disorder may be a physical contributor to anxiety-related symptoms.

Stress Causes. Anxiety is usually thought to be a psychological condition caused by inadequate coping with stressors, as in reactions to environmental factors that are perceived as threats to our safety and security. Perceptions of personal inadequacy or pressures also give rise to anxiety.

Cognitive Causes.   Some authors have held that several cognitive distortions affect anxious people, such as: perfectionism (unreasonably high standards for the self); rejectionism (the practice of exaggerating a single rejection until it affects other aspects in one's life); negative focus (letting one negative situation obliterate positive aspects of life); "shrink thinking" (shrinking something good until its value evaporates); fictional fantasies (letting emotions substitute for the truth about what is happening); "should and ought legalisms" (being other-directed to things not really wanted); and saying "my fault" (assuming responsibility for negative events that were not your fault).

Treatment

Because anxiety can occur in the striated muscle, relaxation of the striated musculature can tranquilize one and relieve one's anxiety. Research has shown that, for instance, when the esophagus becomes relaxed, the individual reports that fear and distress disappear, relieving anxiety. To accomplish this, the patient first learns to locate the excessive relevant muscular tensions wherever they are in the body. With practice, one can cultivate an ability to internally observe the world under the skin. Then, one learns to relax tensions, whereupon the states of anxiety generated by the tensions are correspondingly eliminated. (See **Progressive Relaxation.**)

Physical activity such as swimming or brisk walking can be helpful, in addition to relaxation. In severe cases, a physician may prescribe an anti-anxiety drug for temporary relief.

Through the process of relaxation, one may reprogram thoughts and significantly reduce anxiety.

SEE ALSO:

Fatigue, Chronic	Progressive Relaxation
Hypochondriasis	Social Phobia
Insomnia	Speaking Anxiety (Public)
Panic Attacks	Tension Awareness
Phobic Disorders	Worry

BIBLIOGRAPHY

Beck, A. T., Emery G., & Greenburg, R. L. (1990). *Anxiety disorders and phobias: A cognitive perspective.* New York: Basic Books.

Handly, R. & Neff, P. (1985). *Anxiety and panic attacks: Their cause and cure.* New York: Scribner.

Kleinknecht, R. A. (1991). *Mastering anxiety: The nature and treatment of anxious conditions.* New York: Plenum.

Arthritis, Rheumatoid

Description

Rheumatoid arthritis is characterized by chronic inflammation of the joints, accompanied by **Pain,** stiffness, and localized redness. When severe, it may lead to physical impairment and deformity. Symptoms can contribute to reduced activity in many areas of life, such as employment, recreation, and social involvement. The inflammation is exacerbated by muscular spasm (cramp) and fatigue that may persist for months or years without significant symptoms. When symptoms do occur, they are apt to appear first in the neck and shoulder muscles, but also in the hip and lower back muscles. Eventually, connective tissue in the joints such as cartilage, tendons, and bursae can be damaged. Scar tissue forms, which can contribute to deformed and immobilized joints. Weakness, fatigue, weight loss, and a tingling sensation in the hands and feet may be noticed. The small joints of the hands and feet are commonly affected, but the wrists, knees, ankles and neck are also common problem areas. This disorder is not limited to the joints, and has been known to also affect the tissues beneath the skin, the heart, lungs, and blood vessels. Rheumatoid arthritis occurs most often in those 20 to 40 years of age, afflicting women more frequently than men. Only about 10 percent of sufferers are severely disabled by rheumatoid arthritis.

Causes

The exact causes are not clear; however long-term overtension of the muscles of the arms, shoulders, neck, chest, hips, back, and legs, used in the instinctive "fight or flight" response, leads to fatigue, spasms, and inflammation that induce excessive wear on the joints.

Heredity may play a role since at least 50 percent of sufferers have a familial history of arthritis. The **Immune System** can also be involved in acute cases.

Treatment

Symptoms may be relieved by using antirheumatic drugs to suppress inflammation and relieve pain and muscle spasm; however, the result may be a further weakening of the muscles. In some cases, the immune system may be treated with cytotoxic drugs or by blood therapy.

In a severe attack of rheumatoid arthritis, bed rest may be prescribed and removable splints may be used to immobilize the joints, after which exercise learned through physical therapy can be helpful. Only in severe cases, when other treatments have failed, is surgery used or joint replacement accomplished.

Once the pain has been relieved, treatment may also include **Progressive Relaxation** of those muscles used in the reaction to stress and the instinctive "fight or flight" response. Relaxation can help to cope with the pain and possible limitations of movement by relieving the tight muscles that pull on the joints. Long-term results can be achieved with a great deal of time and diligence by both the patient and therapist.

SEE ALSO:

Immune System Disorders
Pain
Progressive Relaxation

BIBLIOGRAPHY

Anderson, K. O., Bradley, L. A., Young, L. D., McDaniel, L. K., & Wise, C. M. (1985). Rheumatoid arthritis: Review of psychological factors related to etiology, effects, and treatment. *Psychological Bulletin, 98*, 358–387.

Davidson, P. (1989). *Chronic muscle pain syndrome: Understanding and treating fibrositis—the body's powerful reaction to deep-rooted stress.* New York: Villard Books.

McGuigan, F. J. (1992). *Calm down: A guide for stress and tension control* (2nd ed.). Dubuque, IA: Kendall/Hunt.

Wisocki, P. A. (1998). Arthritis and osteoporosis. In E. A. Blechman & K. D. Brownell (Eds.), *Behavioral medicine & women: A comprehensive handbook* (pp. 562–565). New York: Guilford Press.

Zautra, A. J. (1998). Arthritis: Behavioral and psychosocial aspects. In E. A. Blechman & K. D. Brownell (Eds.), *Behavioral medicine and women: A comprehensive handbook* (pp. 554–558). New York: Guilford Press.

Zautra, A. J., Burleson, M. H., Matt, K. S., Roth, S. H., & Burrows, L. (1994). Interpersonal stress, depression, and disease activity in rheumatoid and osteoarthritis patients. *Health Psychology, 13*, 139–148.

Assertiveness Training

The basic assumption underlying assertiveness training is that the individual has the right to make requests, express feelings, beliefs, and opinions, and set boundaries with other people, should that be his or her choice. It assumes that the social skills required to effect such behavior enhance the competency of an individual both personally and interpersonally. People who lack assertiveness may have difficulty in expressing emotions (particularly anger, sadness, or affection), in rejecting intrusive requests, and in communicating their thoughts.

Assertiveness training can also be part of a treatment plan for **Depression, Anxiety,** and **Social Phobia.** Overall, assertiveness training emphasizes basic human rights in interpersonal relations, whereby the individual learns to elicit fair, respectful exchanges from others and to reciprocate in kind.

Training courses in assertiveness training often use methods found in cognitive behavioral therapy, wherein the individual becomes aware of his or her own "thinking style" and learns to identify self-sabotaging thought patterns that induce feelings of anxiety, depression, anger, and resentment. The validity of these distorted patterns for the individual is examined and she or he is taught strategies to intervene and challenge such thoughts. The goal is to reduce, thereby, the incidence of negative emotions and the **Stress** they generate.

The development of interpersonal skills is also an important feature of such programs. At this stage, trainees select the situations and the people who cause them difficulty and examine the patterns of interpersonal exchange most frequently used both by themselves and by those important others. Then methods and strategies through which nonproductive interactions can be remediated are discussed. Next, the trainee selects a particular problem that she or he wishes to address. The aim is to teach the trainee to be specific when describing the problem, to develop assertive responses that avoid accusations and apologetic behavior. The trainee is also taught to be assertive on the spot and to counter a variety of manipulative responses from others.

The instructor may use a variety of techniques that include modeling appropriate responses, role play, and instruction until the participant thinks that he or she is able to be proactive and decisive in a variety of settings.

Frequently, people are not lacking in assertiveness in all areas of their lives, and most people have selective vulnerabilities. Through the use of discussion and questionnaires, problematic areas of the individual are identified.

SEE ALSO:

Anxiety   Social Phobia
Depression   Stress Management Methods

BIBLIOGRAPHY

Alberti, R. E., & Emmons, M. L. (1996). *Your perfect right: A guide to assertive behavior* (7th ed.). San Luis Obispo, CA: Impact.
Corey, G. (1991). *Theory and practice of counseling and psychotherapy* (4th ed.). Pacific Grove, CA: Brooks/Cole.

Asthma and Stress

Description

Asthma is a chronic respiratory condition marked by periodic attacks of wheezing and difficulty in breathing, especially in expelling air. This is due to the narrowing of the bronchial tubes (the airways to the lungs) so that the airways constrict. The main symptoms of asthma are difficulty in breathing, a painful tightness in the chest, and varying amounts of wheezing. At times the wheezing may be audible only with a stethoscope, but sometimes it is loud enough to hear across a crowded room. In severe cases, breathing may become so difficult that it may cause sweating, increased pulse rate, and severe anxiety. In extreme attacks the face and lips may turn bluish due to the diminishing supply of oxygen in the body. Additional symptoms may include chest **Pain,** neck/throat tighteners (see **Esophageal Spasm**), and **Fatigue.**

Creer (1982) characterized asthma according to three factors: (1) intermittence, which means that there are periodic attacks, (2) variability, which is a fluctuation in the severity, and (3) reversibility, which means that the airway obstruction can be reversed, a characteristic that differentiates asthma from some other chronic respiratory conditions. Since the person is usually not aware of these factors, reactions of **Stress** exist which, added to the physiological pathologies, may result in serious or even fatal attacks.

People over about 50 years of age are particularly at risk of asthma, often due to additional illnesses. Millions of Americans are estimated to have asthma today, and the numbers are rising, possibly due in part to increasing air pollution. Sometimes asthma strikes suddenly in people with no idea that they were asthma prone.

Causes

The constriction of airways is actually a smooth muscle spasm with tissue swelling, excessive mucus secretion, dried or wet mucus plugs, or a combination of these factors. These conditions may be caused by allergies, infections, environmental causes, and emotion-arousing stimuli, some with hereditary predispositions (Masel et al., 1984). Specific environmental causes include air pollution, airtight homes and sealed offices that may carry an excessive number of dust mites, carpet fumes, second-hand smoke, and other irritants, as well as viral infections. When the symptoms are seasonal, often pollen or spores are contributing causes.

Those most at risk are smokers and their children, and those with a family history of disease and allergies. Aging is a factor in that of the some 5,000 Americans who died from asthma in 1994, a 50 percent increase over the number in 1980, most were over 65 and did not properly treat the disease.

A vicious circle may result in that the initial symptoms of coughing, wheezing, and the like may produce a feeling of suffocation that can trigger an **Anxiety** attack; in turn the symptoms may intensify, increasing the anxiety even more. The chronic sufferer often develops a feeling of lack of control.

Other factors that may trigger an asthma attack include some forms of exercise and psychological stressors.

Treatment

If it is not treated, a normal attack usually ends naturally. However, asthma attacks can be relieved by treatment. Because asthma is most often caused by an allergy, the first step in controlling the disease is to try to identify the allergen, or irritant, responsible. This can be achieved through skin tests conducted by a physician. The individual can also keep careful records of the attacks (including frequency and severity) to help identify possible causes: What time of year and time of day do the attacks generally occur? What environment was the individual in just prior to the attack? and so forth.

Once an allergen has been identified, one can strive to avoid or limit contact with or exposure to the substance. Various medications have also proved to be helpful.

Relaxation at the time of an oncoming attack can help to prevent and relieve it.

SEE ALSO:

Anxiety

Esophageal Spasm

Fatigue, "Nervous"

Immune System Disorders

Pain

Progressive Relaxation

Stress Management Methods

BIBLIOGRAPHY

Busse, W. W., Kiecolt-Glaser, J. K., Coe, C., Martin, R. J., Weiss, S. T., & Parker, S. R. (1995). Stress and asthma. *American Journal of Respiratory and Critical Care Medicine, 151,* 249–252.

Creer, T. L. (1982). Asthma. *Journal of Consulting and Clinical Psychology, 50,* 912–921.

Davis, M. H., Saunders, D. R., Creer, T. L., & Chai, H. (1973). Relaxation training facilitated by biofeedback apparatus as a supplemental treatment in bronchial asthma. *Journal of Psychosomatic Research, 17,* 121–128.

Girdano, D. A., Everly, G. S., & Dusek, D. E. (1997). *Controlling stress and tension* (5th ed.). Boston: Allyn & Bacon.

Lehrer, P. M. (1998). Emotionally triggered asthma: A review of research literature and some hypotheses for self-regulation therapies. *Applied Psychophysiology and Biofeedback, 23,* 13–41.

Lehrer, P. M., Hochron, S. M., McCann, B., Swartzman, L., & Reba, P. (1986). Relaxation decreases large-airway but not small-airway asthma. *Journal of Psychosomatic Research, 30,* 13–25.

Lehrer, P. M., Sargunaraj, D., & Hochron, S. M. (1992). Psychological approaches to the treatment of asthma. *Journal of Consulting and Clinical Psychology, 60,* 639–643.

Masel, B. J., Fentress, D. W., & Spirito, A. (1984). Behavioral treatment of childhood illness. *Clinical Psychology Review, 4,* 561–570.

Schmaling, K. B. (1998). Asthma. In E. A. Blechman & K. D. Brownell (Eds.), *Behavioral medicine & women: A comprehensive handbook* (pp. 566–569). New York: Guilford Press.

Attention-Deficit Hyperactivity Disorder (ADHD)

Description

The term "hyperactivity" refers to a behavioral disorder that is more precisely named attention-deficit hyperactivity disorder, or ADHD. Perhaps as many as 3 percent of all children are characterized as showing some signs of ADHD, with boys greatly outnumbering girls.

The disorder is marked by such signs as excessive physical activity, including fidgeting; impulsive reactions, including rapid shifts from one activity to another; and inattention to and ready distraction from matters at hand. ADHD may be observed in children before the age of four, but its signs are often missed until the child begins to attend school. A low threshold for frustration predisposes such children to uncontrollable tantrums, and a short attention span and the inability to concentrate may result in failure at school even if the child displays a high intelligence quotient (IQ).

Diagnosis of ADHD can be difficult. A child may display various signs derived from the categories of hyperactivity, impulsivity, and inattention. In addition, the pattern may vary from day to day and even from hour to hour. The combined signs may range from an extremely mild pattern that is difficult to differentiate from the behavior of a normally exuberant child, to pronounced deficits in behavior. Sometimes only a single symptom is present, and therefore that child is not necessarily labeled as exhibiting ADHD. Studies indicate that in some cases the symptoms of ADHD may persist beyond adolescence into adulthood, leading to various forms of social maladjustment and possible criminal behavior. The great majority of hyperactive children, however, appear to outgrow their childhood symptoms.

Causes

The causes of ADHD remain uncertain. Various predisposing factors affecting the pregnant mother have been suggested, including trauma and the use of medications, drugs, alcohol, and nicotine.

Some physicians have proposed that the presence in foods of artificial colorings, flavorings, and antioxidant preservatives may augment ADHD symptoms, but the U.S. Food and Drug Administration has held that evidence for this is inconclusive. Studies do not support the notion that excessive sugar in the diet augments ADHD, although some studies suggest that carbohydrate-rich meals plus doses of sugar may have such an effect.

Treatment

ADHD has been treated by various psychotherapies, including, especially, **Behavior Therapy,** with mixed results. Two drugs, methylphenidate hydrochloride (Ritalin) and dextroamphetamine, are commonly prescribed for children diagnosed as exhibiting ADHD. These drugs can have side effects such as weight loss, irritability, insomnia, and nervousness, such effects being especially notable in children who have been misdiagnosed.

Physicians in general support the usefulness of drug therapy, but the issue has aroused controversy—particularly because ADHD is often hard to differentiate from the effects of other problems children may be undergoing, such as a stressful life, anxiety, and depression.

SEE ALSO:

Behavior Therapy
Student Control (Achieving Classroom Discipline)

BIBLIOGRAPHY

Barkley, R. A. (1997). Behavioral inhibition, sustained attention, and executive functions: Constructing a unifying theory of ADHD. *Psychological Bulletin, 121,* 65–94.
Farley, D. (1989, February). Helping children with attention disorder. *FDA consumer.*
Fisher, B. C. (1997). *Attention deficit disorder misdiagnosis: Approaching ADD from a brain-behavioral/ neuropsychological perspective for assessment and treatment.* Boca Raton, FL: St. Lucia Press.

Autogenic Training

Autogenic training is an approach used to reduce **Stress.** It may be thought of as a variant of **Hypnosis** and is based on autosuggestion (self-hypnosis) made by a patient in the waking state and on suggestions made by a trainer to a patient. It is thus reported to have many of the same effects as other suggestion procedures. This therapy comes from the work of J. Schultz in the 1930s.

Passive concentration is one of the cornerstones of this therapy—passive concentration on feelings of heaviness and warmth in extremities, in the body for cardiac and respiratory regulation, and cooling of the forehead. The first exercise (formula) of the standard series is performed in the therapist's office and then the trainee independently continues the exercises at home (after lunch, after dinner, and before going to sleep). Then, the trainee is asked to learn the training protocol for each new session. A new formula is not applied until the trainee is able to induce the state required by the preceding formula without difficulties. Regular practice of autogenic exercises has been associated with functional changes that are opposed to the effects of stress.

SEE ALSO:

Hypnosis
Stress Signals
Stress Management Methods

BIBLIOGRAPHY

Girdano, D. A., Everly, G. S., & Dusek, D. E. (1997). *Controlling stress and tension* (5th ed.). Boston: Allyn & Bacon.
Lehrer, P. M. (1996). Varieties of relaxation methods and their unique effects. *International Journal of Stress Management, 3,* 1–15.
Linden, W. (1993). The autogenic training method of J. H. Schultz. In P. M. Lerner and R. L. Woolfolk (Eds.), *Principles and practice of stress management* (2nd. ed.), pp. 205–229. New York: Guilford Press.
Luthe, W., & Schultz, J. (1969). In W. Luthe (Ed.), *Medical applications* (Vol. II). *Autogenic therapy.* New York: Grune and Stratton.
Schultz, J., & Luthe, W. (1969). *Autogenic therapy.* New York: Grune and Stratton.

B Backache–Burnout

Backache

Description

Back pain has been estimated to be the most costly work-related injury (economic losses of $16 billion annually) in the United States. Backaches are characterized by **Pain** and stiffness that can develop suddenly or slowly. This common disorder has been estimated to be experienced by four out of five people sometime during their lifetime. Pain may be highly localized or somewhat widespread; it may occur only at specific times, or may be continuous.

Three general types of backaches are: (1) low back pain; (2) coccygeal pain; and (3) **Sciatica.**

Low back pain is usually centered in the small of the back, developing suddenly, even overnight. The intensity may be sufficiently severe to retard bodily movement. Lower back problems constitute a primary cause of lost work time in adults under the age of 45.

Coccygeal pain is usually a nonspecific backache located at the base of the spinal column in the coccyx area. The pain is typically continuous but worsens when sitting.

Sciatica pain is characterized by a burning pain shooting through the buttocks, down the back of the thigh, which intensifies when bending, coughing, or sneezing.

Causes

Emotional **Stress** may cause the subjective experience of pain in the lower back (as it may elsewhere too). In response to stress, the back muscles may go into spasm as if to protect themselves. That spasm creates pain that, in turn, can further the muscle spasms, and so on in continuous cycles. Such emotionally caused pain can interfere with work, family life, and general health, any of which can prolong the spasm–pain cycle. Problems with back muscles, discs, and ligaments are often interrelated with stress-related **Tension.**

Job-related stress has been associated with reports of backaches. In a study of an aircraft manufacturer, workers who did not enjoy their work reported back problems 2½ times more often than workers who enjoyed their work.

Particularly in younger people, excessive, chronic muscular tension is a common cause of back pain, often increased by sitting postures that strain relevant parts of the body. Among older people, a common cause is deterioration of spinal disks and vertebrae, which induces pressure on nerves that in turn produces pain. Low back pain caused by problems with the discs presents possibly the most troublesome backaches. The discs are filled with a jelly-like substance and act as shock absorbers between the vertebrae. Physical stress can flatten, bulge, or rupture the disc and press on the nerves in the spinal column, causing severe pain.

Low back pain is usually the result of exertion to which the person is unaccustomed, which causes the muscles to spasm and/or ligaments to be sprained. Lifting, falling, prolonged and awkward movement, poor work habits, poor physical fitness, lack of regular exercise, obesity, and poor sleeping habits often contribute to low back pain. Injuries from sports, automobile accidents, and heavy lifting are also common causes.

Low back and leg pain can also be acquired through a condition called **Spondylitis,** in which the vertebra are not completely formed, affecting 2 to 3 percent of the population. The elderly can also experience osteoporosis and **Arthritis,** which can cause back pain. Coccygeal pain is often the result of an injury during a heavy fall on the buttocks or from childbirth.

Some relatively rare causes of low back pain include infections of the spinal connective tissue and malignant tumors spreading to the spinal column from other areas of the body.

Treatment

If pain is prolonged for several days, consult a physician to determine whether there is a physical problem such as misalignment or disc injury. When stressors of everyday life cause back pain, the discomfort often disappears without treatment. However, the pain is a signal of a problem that may recur.

Pain killers, muscle relaxants, or other medication (as prescribed by a physician) may interrupt the spasm–pain cycle, which can provide an opportunity for relaxation. Please refer to the section on **Progressive Relaxation** on how to relax the muscles so as to reduce or eliminate pain. Bed rest, hot or cold packs, and massage (by a professional) may also alleviate the pain and, perhaps, the stress.

To prevent lower back pain, relaxation is especially recommended. Other ways of prevention are physical exercises (as prescribed by a health care professional), maintenance of good posture, weight loss (if overweight), not wearing high-heeled shoes, sleeping on a firm mattress, and use of only one pillow that is relatively flat. When sitting for long periods or driving long distances, use a pillow to support the small of the back. When lifting objects of any weight, use leg muscles, not the back muscles.

S E E   A L S O :

Arthritis, Rheumatoid
Pain
Progressive Relaxation
Sciatica

Spondylitis
Stress Management Methods
Tension Awareness

BIBLIOGRAPHY

Deyo, R. A., Rainville, J., & Kent, D. L. (1992). What can the history and physical examination tell us about low back pain? *Journal of the American Medical Association, 268,* 760.

Hadler, R. M., (1997). Back pain in the workplace. What you lift or how you lift matters far less than whether you lift and when. *Spine, 22,* 935–940.

Baldness

Description

Baldness ("alopecia") is a natural process in which there develops total or partial loss of scalp hair. The condition may be permanent or temporary. In most women, there is a gradual, yet slight, loss of hair throughout life. Conspicuous hair loss in women seems to be more traumatic than when baldness occurs in men.

Causes

Mark Twain wrote, "Trouble had brought these grey hairs and this premature balditude." However, there is no evidence that baldness or hair loss is a direct result of stressful life—it is the loss of hair that may be a stressor.

Premature baldness may partly result from an imbalance of sex hormones. Occasionally a woman's hair thins, temporarily, just after giving birth. Sudden temporary hair loss sometimes occurs as a result of typhoid fever, influenza, pneumonia, or the like. Temporary baldness also may be caused by exposure to nuclear radiation or X rays or by the internal use of certain anticancer drugs. Gradual thinning of the hair may be caused by severe nutritional deficiency, tuberculosis, cancer, or disorders of the thyroid gland or pituitary gland. Physical trauma such as self-inflicted hair pulling, twisting, and breaking can obviously cause temporary hair loss, particularly in severe emotional disorders.

In males, baldness tends to be genetic, though the genes are carried by the female.

Treatment

Plugs of hair-containing skin from the back of a bald person's head are sometimes successfully transplanted on bare areas of the scalp; more painstakingly, individual hair follicles may be transplanted.

The hypertension drug minoxidil has been found to sometimes restore hair growth. It is expensive, must be used daily, and seems to work mainly on young men who only recently began to lose hair. Although originally not approved for such use because of concern over serious side effects, it was approved for sale as a hair restorer (Rogaine) in Canada in 1986, and the United States in 1987.

BIBLIOGRAPHY

Kunz, J. R. M., & Finkel, A. J. (1987). *The American Medical Association family guide.* New York: Random House.

McGrath, J. E. (1988). Behavioral psychology in medicine. In M. D. Dunnette (Ed.), *International handbook of industrial and organizational psychology.* Skokie, IL: Rand-McNally.

Price, V. H. (1994). Stress and hair loss: Myths and truth. *The Newsletter of the American Institute of Stress, 7.* Yonkers, NY.

Schnohr, P., Lange, P., Nyboe, J., Appleyard, M., Jensen, G. (1995). Grey hair, baldness and wrinkles in relation to myocardial infraction: The Copenhagen City Heart Study. *American Heart Journal, 130,* 1003–1010.

Wells, P. A., Willmoth, T., & Russell, R. J. (1995). Does fortune favour the bald? Psychological correlates of hair loss in males. *British Journal of Psychology, 86,* 337–344.

Behavioral Medicine

This field applies behavioral procedures, principles, and techniques for health-related problems that fall within the context of traditional medicine. Behavioral medicine involves a rich interplay among the principles of medicine, psychophysiology, physiology, biochemistry, and learning. Journals specialized for the field include *Annals of Behavioral Medicine, The British Journal of Medical Psychology,* and *Psychological Medicine.* There thus is considerable overlap among behavioral medicine, **Behavior Therapy, Progressive Relaxation,** and exercise medicine.

Neal Miller offered an example of how behavioral variables can be used to understand etiology and treatment for pathophysiological disorders. In this case, instrumental learning principles were applied for a woman who had been bedridden for months. Her problem was that when she was brought upright using a tilt table, she became faint, even when the raising was gradual. A behavioral analysis indicated that the nurse would raise the patient slightly on the tilt table and then leave the room. As soon as the woman complained of being faint, the nurse hurried back, reassured the woman, and lowered the table. Fainting behavior was thus actually being reinforced by the nurse so that, by operant conditioning, fainting became strengthened. The appropriate therapy was to reverse the procedure so that the woman was raised slightly on the tilt table while the nurse talked with her and reassured her. If the woman grew faint, the nurse lowered the table but left the room. Fainting was thus no longer reinforced, and in fact it was punished by the loss of contact with the nurse. The result was that the woman quickly recovered.

SEE ALSO:

Behavior Therapy
Progressive Relaxation
Stress Management Methods

BIBLIOGRAPHY

Dollard, J., & Miller, N. E. (Eds). (1982). *Biofeedback: Basic problems and clinical applications.* New York: North-Holland.
Hillbrand, M., & Spitz, R. T. (Eds.). (1997). *Lipids, health and behavior.* Washington, DC: American Psychological Association.
Lehrer, P. M., Woolfolk, R. L. (1993). *Principles and practice of stress management* (2nd ed.). New York: Guilford Press.
McGrath, J. E. (1988). Behavioral psychology in medicine. In M. D. Dunnette (Ed.), *Handbook of industrial and organizational psychology.* Skokie, IL: Rand-McNally.
McGuigan, F. J. (1994). *Biological psychology: A cybernetic science.* Englewood Cliffs, NJ: Prentice-Hall.
Resnick, R. J., & Rozensky, R. H. (Eds). (1996). *Health psychology through the life span: Practice and research opportunities.* Washington, DC: American Psychological Association.
Richter-Heinrich, E., & Miller, N. E. (1950). *Personality and psychotherapy: An analysis in terms of learning, thinking, and culture.* New York: McGraw Hill.

Behavior Therapy

As a result of many decades of research to develop laws of learning, we have arrived at powerful principles of **Conditioning, Classical and Instrumental (Operant).** They have been effectively applied for clinical purposes in behavior therapy, sometimes more generally referred to as behavior modification. The basic strategy is that many psychiatric and somatoform (psychosomatic) disorders that have been learned can be modified through relearning or new learning. Traditional "talk" psychotherapy, which only discusses problems and possible solutions, contrasts with behavioral approaches; the goal in behavior therapy is to apply learning principles to effectively change the ways the patient acts and thinks.

Mental (cognitive) disorders are viewed as physical phenomena that include small-scale muscular behaviors. Such covert behaviors can be systematically manipulated by learning principles to alleviate pathological conditions. Clinical conditioning procedures that have been successfully applied include covert sensitization, covert positive reinforcement, covert negative reinforcement, and covert extinction. Clinical relaxation is also used, as in the treatment of a phobia: The patient imagines fearful acts of increasing intensity, then relaxes the musculature to relax the fear away. In a classic case treated by Edmund Jacobson in the early 1930s (see Jacobson, 1976), a patient who feared heights was told to imagine a feather dropping and then to relax the muscles. Gradually, the patient proceeded up a scale to imagining looking down from tall heights. Eventually, the patient rented an office high up in a sky-scraper, having totally relaxed away the fears that were represented in his muscles.

As another example, to deal with learned aspects of depression, the behavior therapist helps individuals learn how to behave in order to increase reinforcements. The individuals can often learn that their reasoning is faulty, thereby reducing negative perceptions and thus the frequency and duration of painful emotional states. That accomplishment also increases the opportunity to experience and enjoy positive experiences. Behavior therapy has also been especially effective in the treatment of autism.

SEE ALSO:

Conditioning, Classical and
  Instrumental (Operant)
Jacobson, Edmund (1888–1983)

Progressive Relaxation
Stress Management Methods

BIBLIOGRAPHY

Jacobson, E. (1976). *You must relax: Practical methods for reducing the tensions of modern living* (5th ed.). New York: McGraw-Hill.
Lehrer, P. M., & Woolfolk, R. L. (Eds.). (1993). *Principles and practice of stress management* (2nd ed.). New York: Guilford Press.
O'Donohue, W., & Krasner, L. (Eds.). (1995). *Theories of behavior therapy: Exploring behavior change.* Washington, DC: American Psychological Association.
Wolpe, J. (1974). Relaxation as an instrument for breaking adverse emotional habits. In F. J. McGuigan (Ed.), *Tension control: Proceedings of the First Meeting of the American Association for the Advancement of Tension Control.* Blacksburg, VA: University Publications.

Biofeedback

Description

Biofeedback is a method by which people may learn to control internal events, such as brain waves, that they are not able to directly observe through regular sensory modalities. The first step is to sense the event, usually with electrodes that detect electrical signals generated when muscles contract, when brain tissue is active. Then the event of interest is amplified and transduced (changed to another form of energy); for example, the electrical signals generated when the brain and muscles are active are changed to external visual or auditory signals so that the event can be monitored by the learner. Consequently, when they are so transduced, one can see, hear, or otherwise monitor one's own covert muscle responses, brain waves, cardiovascular activity, galvanic skin responses, skin temperature, and so forth.

For training, one observes the continuous activity of an internal event as it is read out from a biofeedback system and efforts are made to modify it. For example, by monitoring activity of the muscles through an electromyograph, one can decrease muscle tension by relaxing. As with all therapies, one then seeks to generalize what is learned in the clinical situation to normal life situations. For instance, if one has learned to relax muscles through biofeedback, one should then learn to relax those muscles throughout everyday life.

Biofeedback has been used for many scientific and clinical purposes. Scientifically, efforts involve advancing our understanding of how bodily systems function and developing principles of volitional control over them. As such, biofeedback holds great promise, but so far it has been used mostly for clinical purposes such as relieving headaches or alleviating **Raynaud's Disease** (see the extensive applications made in *The Journal of Biofeedback and Self-Regulation*).

Stress and Tension Control

Biofeedback, by providing objective measurements of muscular bodily functions, offers much for tension control. Here, the purpose of biofeedback instrumentation is first to develop an ability to identify and then control muscular tensions in the various bodily regions. There are thus two basic steps to relaxation: (1) identifying when and where the tension manifests in the muscles of the body, and (2) letting go of that tension. The ability to identify tensions (**Tension Awareness**) is a learned skill that requires much practice and experience. Next, one seeks to continue tension control without the use of the system. Learning to identify and control arousal at early stages makes it much easier to reverse the build-up of stress tension.

Biofeedback Systems

Five major instruments of biofeedback that provide immediate information as to the status of biological conditions throughout the body, and as such, can be a useful supplement to the practice of stress and tension control, are summarized as follows:

1. The electromyograph (EMG) monitors skeletal (voluntary) muscle tension. Electromyography has been successfully employed in the treatment of **Headaches, Migraine and Tension; Insomnia; Anxiety; Asthma; Hypertension; Colitis;** menstrual distress, and so forth. Almost any muscle can be monitored, but the following three are commonly used in biofeedback:

   a. Frontalis: This is the forehead muscle that generates frowns and tightens as a response to worry or pressure.
   b. Masseter: This muscle tightens and clenches the jaw, especially when one is angry or frustrated.
   c. Trapezius: This muscle hunches the shoulders and tightens, as when one is alarmed or chronically anxious.

      These muscles are chosen because they are prominent in responding to stressors and can be measured without much interference from other muscles. They are good starting points in which muscle relaxation training can be generalized.
2. The thermograph monitors minute fluctuations in body temperature. These temperature fluctuations are measured by monitoring finger, hand, or foot temperature.
3. In galvanic skin response (GSR) training, a feedback dermograph measures electrical conductance or electrical potential changes in the skin. This instrument monitors small changes in the concentration of salt and water generated by sweat glands. One method is to conduct a normally imperceptible electric current over the skin; if and when sweat glands become more active, the system registers the skin's increased ability to conduct electricity.

4. The electroencephalograph (EEG) permits monitoring of brain waves. EEG has been used for the treatment of stress, insomnia, epilepsy, and the like, in conjunction with other biofeedback modalities.

5. The heart-rate monitor measures beats-per-minute and provides immediate feedback—for instance, on how relaxation influences heart rate. A lowered heart rate is often an important component in relaxation.

Other biofeedback systems include those that identify blood pressure responses during thoughts and feelings.

SEE ALSO:

Anxiety
Asthma and Stress
Colitis
Headache, Migraine and Tension
Hypertension
Insomnia

Migraine Headaches
Menstruation
Progressive Relaxation
Stress Management Methods
Tension Awareness

BIBLIOGRAPHY

Goldberger, L., & Breznitz, S. (1993). *Handbook of stress: Theoretical and clinical aspects* (2nd ed.). New York: Free Press/Macmillan.

McGuigan, F. J. (1994). *Biological psychology: A cybernetic science.* Englewood Cliffs, NJ: Prentice-Hall.

Stoyva, J. M., & Budzynski (1993). Biofeedback methods in the treatment of anxiety and stress disorders. In P. M. Lehrer & R. L. Woolfolk (Eds.), *Principles and Practice of Stress Management* (2nd ed., pp. 263–300). New York: Guilford Press.

Blood Pressure, Proper Measurement of

Blood pressure measurements result in such values as 140/86, where 140 is the systolic pressure and 86 is the diastolic pressure. The usual technique is to place the strap somewhat tightly about the upper arm. The sensor for listening is then placed on the inner surface of the arm just *below* the strap. (It should not be placed underneath the strap, as is often done, because pressure caused by that location of the sensor may artificially elevate systolic pressure—the highest arterial blood pressure of a cardiac cycle—by as much as ten points.) Then, with one hand, increase the pressure while monitoring the pulse at the wrist with the other hand. Diastolic pressure (the lowest arterial blood pressure of a cardiac cycle) is taken *on the way up* as the pressure within the strap is increased by pumping. Next note the systolic pressure. *An accurate reading of systolic pressure can only be taken on the way up.* The other hand monitoring the pulse can note that the pulse is eliminated when the value for systolic pressure is exceeded on the visual monitor. The procedure frequently employed of pumping pressure in the strap well above systolic and then getting the two readings on the way down also artificially elevates both readings. By increasing pressure with the excessive inflation, one increases arterial pressure itself above what it actually is.

Individuals who take their own pressure with a "drugstore" kit (a sphygmomanometer) should also note that the process of taking their own blood pressure can artificially increase it. One should continuously practice and, perhaps after a week or so, a relatively stable set of readings that are of greater accuracy can be obtained. A tendency toward hypochondriasis should be avoided by not worrying about one's self-taken blood pressure. Variations in pressure can be expected and should not be alarming. In fact, huge variations due to circadian rhythms can be expected, perhaps varying blood pressure as much as 25 percent, depending upon time of day. Accurate readings taken at home *can* be obtained and provide valuable information; for example, someone on medication can take his or her blood pressure at sample periods several times during the day, keeping records that can be reported to the physician. Medication dosage and time of dosage might thereby be systematically altered for greater effectiveness.

SEE ALSO:

Cardiovascular Disease
Hypertension

BIBLIOGRAPHY

McGuigan, F. J. (1994). *Biological Psychology: A cybernetic science.* Englewood Cliffs, NJ: Prentice-Hall.

Breathing Techniques

Some practitioners use practice in special breathing, as in deep breathing, for the purpose of decreasing arousal of the body. One set of instructions is to first establish deep, diaphragmatic breathing. Then, practice over a period of weeks is carried out to considerably reduce respiration rate to minimal respirations per minute. When meeting stressors, the learner then exhales, letting breath go slowly and deeply, the purpose being to reduce anxiety.

Those interested in this approach can find numerous variations. One particularly valuable example is in the work of van Dixhoorn (1999), wherein breathing techniques and exercise are combined in the treatment of cardiac patients.

SEE ALSO:

Stress Management Methods

BIBLIOGRAPHY

Lehrer, P. M., & Woolfolk, R. L. (Eds.). (1993). *Principles and practice of stress management.* New York: Guilford Press.
van Dixhoorn, J. (1999). Implementation of relaxation therapy within a cardiac rehabilitation setting, in D. Kenny, J. C. Carlson, F. J. McGuigan and J. L. Sheppard (Eds.), *Stress and health: Research and clinical implications.* Boston: Allyn & Bacon.

Bruxism (Teeth Grinding)

Description

Bruxism is the habitual grinding and clenching of one's teeth, most frequently at night during sleep, but also at moments during the day. If chronic, there is wearing down of teeth; in turn, bruxism may produce or exacerbate other bodily malfunctions such as **Temporal Mandibular Joint Syndrome (TMJ)** and **Pain** in the face, head, or neck areas.

Causes

It is generally presumed that this disorder is a result of "unrelieved stress" in the individual's life. More precisely, inadequate coping with stressors results in excessive, chronic muscular **Tension** throughout the body; for many, this is concentrated in the jaw muscles.

Treatment

One of the most effective treatments for bruxism is **Progressive Relaxation,** paying special attention to the practice periods of relaxing the masseter (jaw) muscles. Bruxism is one of the earliest tension problems to be eliminated through relaxation methods. Avoiding chewing gum and eating soft foods may help alleviate the pain of the sore muscles that are a result of the disorder.

SEE ALSO:

Pain
Progressive Relaxation

Temporomandibular Joint
Syndrome (TMJ)
Tension Awareness

BIBLIOGRAPHY

Alman, B. M., & Lambrou, P. (1992). *Self-hypnosis: The complete manual for health and self-change* (2nd ed.). New York: Brunner/Mazel.
McGuigan, F. J. (1992). *Calm down: A guide for stress and tension control* (2nd ed.). Dubuque, IA: Kendall/Hunt.

Bulimia

Description

Bulimia is an eating disorder characterized by rapid ingestion of large portions of food in a brief time span, often in secret, frequently followed by self-induced vomiting, use of laxatives, and abdominal stress. Those who vomit may go through this binge/purge cycle from twice a week to perhaps 20 times a day. Bulimic persons typically restrict their diet following a binge and often exercise excessively.

Bulimia is much more prevalent than **Anorexia Nervosa.** It differs from anorexia in that bulimic females typically have normal menstrual periods, and both males and females have normal sex drives and average normal body weight. However, like anoretic persons, they often tend to be depressed.

The duration of bulimia varies, lasting from a couple of weeks or months to many years.

Causes

Bulimia typically occurs in adolescence or in the twenties and is much more common in females and in the upper socioeconomic classes. One survey indicated that 13 percent of the college population exhibited the major symptoms of bulimia. Of this number, 87 percent were female.

Much research is currently being conducted into the causes of bulimia, but no one theory or explanation seems to be dominant at this time.

Treatment

Behavior therapy coupled with drug therapy has had some success.

S E E   A L S O :

Anorexia Nervosa   Eating Disorders
Behavior Therapy   Stress Management Methods

B I B L I O G R A P H Y

Fairburn, C. G., & Wilson, G. T. (Eds.). (1993). *Binge eating: Nature, assessment and treatment.* New York: Guilford Press.

Garner, D. M., and Garfinkel, P. L. (Eds.). (1997). *Handbook of treatment for eating disorders* (2nd ed.). New York: Guilford Press.

Wilson, G. T. (1997). Cognitive behavioral treatment of bulimia nervosa. *The Clinical Psychologist, 50,* 10–12.

Burnout

Description

Burnout is frequently characterized by emotional exhaustion, depersonalization, and reduced accomplishment in one's vocation. There is often a feeling that one's emotional resources are depleted, along with a build-up of frustration and tension when the individual cannot function consistently in meeting his or her expectations or those of others.

The worker who suffers from burnout may act cynically toward coworkers and clients, appear detached and emotionally callous, and distance himself or herself from others. The person with burnout tends to evaluate self negatively and become derogatory in sensitive situations.

The burnout-prone individual tends to be unassertive in dealing with people and fearful of involvement, as well as one who risks emotional exhaustion because of inability to control situations. This type of individual also tends to be impatient and easily angered and frustrated. Because they are more reserved and conventional in their behavior, they often lack the self-confidence needed to attain their goals.

Causes

Extended exposure to stress and frustration in a person's vocation, with lack of success and reinforcements, contributes to burnout. Specific factors include time management difficulties, lack of support systems, being over- or underqualified for the job, social and intrapersonal conflicts, life changes, and mental, emotional, and environmental stressors.

Demographically, the incidence of burnout is greater among younger workers than among older ones. Married individuals experience less burnout than single people, and those with children are even less likely to experience burnout. Part of this is due, no doubt, to the social support that is provided by the family in times of stress.

Treatment

Guidance in order to increase awareness of the nature of burnout may help a person. The person should be guided to objectively assess his or her behavior, the work demands, and personal strengths and weaknesses. The way in which a person reacts to stressors, not just the nature of the stressors themselves, is important in preventing or treating burnout. Support and communication systems should be evaluated and improved wherever possible in the workplace. A stress management program should be followed and an individual revitalization plan should be implemented that includes time management, exercise, good nutrition, and training in **Differential Relaxation.**

SEE ALSO:

Differential Relaxation
Executive Stress
Stress Management Methods

Stress Signals
Workplace Stress

BIBLIOGRAPHY

Chernis, G. (1992). Long-term consequences of burnout: An exploratory study. *Journal of Organic Behavior, 13,* 1–11.

Evans, B. K., & Fisher, D. G. (1993). The nature of burnout: A study of the three factor model of burnout in human service and non-human service samples. *Journal of Occupational and Organizational Psychology, 66,* 29–38.

Girdano, D. A., Everly, G. S., & Dusek, D. E. (Eds.). (1997). *Controlling stress and tension* (5th ed.). Boston: Allyn & Bacon.

Jackson, S. E. (1984). Organizational practices for preventing burnout. In A. S. Sethi & R. S. Schular (Eds.), *Handbook of organizational stress coping strategies.* Cambridge, MA: Ballinger.

Matteson, M. T., & Ivancevich, J. M. (1987). *Controlling work stress.* San Francisco: Jossey-Bass.

Rice, P. L. (1992). *Stress & health* (2nd ed.). Pacific Grove, CA: Brooks/Cole.

Smith, J. C. (1993). *Understanding stress and coping.* New York: Macmillan.

C Cancer–Crying

Cancer

Description

Cancer encompasses a large group of diseases, all of which are characterized by the uncontrolled growth and spread of abnormal cells. Cancer is not considered an infectious disease; rather, it is one in which the cells of the body fight against themselves. In cancers, normal cells are converted into malignant cells—those which grow, reproduce, and spread in an abnormal, unrestrained fashion.

Causes

Four hypotheses as to the causes of cancer are (1) a relationship of stress, tension, and negative emotions: Some research has indicated that attitudes of passivity, hopelessness, and self-effacement may render people cancer-prone; (2) an environmental theory, concerning the relationship between cancer, chemicals, poisons, and the like; (3) a virus theory that states that a virus takes over the functioning of a normal cell and induces changes in surrounding cells; and (4) a genetic theory that holds that there are oncogenes in organisms that, when activated as by environmental events, can result in specific cancers. The likelihood of developing cancer may also be dependant on the effectiveness of one's immune system functions.

Links between diet and cancer have been established. The amount of fiber intake has been related to colon cancer prevention. Sugar and starch intake has been linked to increased risk, as excessive carbohydrate consumption increases caloric intake, which increases the chances for obesity, which in turn is linked to carcinogenesis.

Three possible causes of "spontaneous regression" in cancer patients include good health, the influence of hormones, and the action of immune bodies. There is no evidence of a relationship between stress and disturbances of the immune system that may precede cancer. However, because stress does affect the immune system, the immune system may in turn affect the growth of tumors. One thought is that stressful events influence existing tumors through central and peripheral neurotransmitter activities and the secretion of hormones. (see **Chemicals of the Body and Stress.**)

During a stress response, the hormone cortisol is released and consumes fat and protein to ensure that the body has sufficient energy to fight threats. Immunosuppression occurs because when cortisol converts protein into energy, there is no longer enough protein to manufacture new cells. White blood cell counts drop dramatically during chronic stress, weakening the immune system. In this way, stressful events may affect other disorders, too. Through feedback circuits, stressors can influence the development of psychiatric illnesses, which in turn may influence the immune system, perhaps facilitating the development of cancer.

Laboratory research has confirmed that experimentally induced tumors in animals can be influenced by specific environmental and behavioral variables. It is now possible to predict to some extent how an already existing tumor will respond to stress. Stressors may influence viral tumors to grow faster.

Overtension may occur when cancer patients are faced with their own mortality, which may facilitate the cancer. Cancer patients often experience anger, anxiety, hopelessness, depression, and feelings of powerlessness, grief, guilt, and self-blame. They may suffer a sense of loss of well-being and strength, as well as diminished self-efficacy and control when faced with treatments. Patients who go through disfiguring operations, particularly women who lose a breast or who have gynecological cancer treatments, often experience a profound loss of personal integrity, femininity, and sexuality. Aversion to chemotherapy or radiation treatments may become conditioned, and patients often feel nauseated.

Treatment

Prevention measures often focus around diet. Recommendations from the American Cancer Society include avoiding obesity, cutting down on total fat intake, increasing daily consumption of high-fiber foods, including foods high in vitamins A and C, and limiting consumption of alcohol, salt-cured food, and smoked and nitrite-cured food. By reducing exposure to the many carcinogenic influences each day—such as cigarette smoking, second-hand smoke, automobile pollutants, and excessive sunshine—one can also affect the likelihood of developing cancer. Hans Eysenck (1991) has concluded that the combination (interaction) of cigarette smoking and stressors is especially critical in the development of cancer.

Host resistance to cancer depends in part on the strength of the immune system. Certain vitamins and minerals, particularly vitamin C and the mineral selenium, may have positive prevention effects. Eating a diet containing sufficient cereal grains and seafood ensures that one has a normal level of selenium. Taken in nonfood form at high doses, however, selenium becomes toxic.

Forms of cancer treatment by medical means include surgery, hormone therapy, radiation therapy, and chemotherapy. These treatments are aimed at controlling or eliminating the disease. Additionally, there are nonmedical treatments available, ones that incorporate "attitude and imagery." A positive attitude toward life has been thought by some to be correlated with positive treatment outcomes of cancer patients.

Psychological effects of cancer may be alleviated by the use of **Stress Management Methods.** Patients who have been trained in relaxation and imagery techniques have significantly decreased levels of tension, anger, depression, self-reported nausea, and physiological arousal. Relaxation and imagery techniques are often effective in decreasing stress reactions, psychological effects, and psychological responses in patients undergoing chemotherapy and radiation treatment for cancer. Patients undergoing chemotherapy and radiation treatment frequently become nauseated and may develop a conditional response (refer to **Conditioning**) to the treatment regimen with anticipatory nausea before treatment or when they encounter conditional stimuli (e.g., sights, smells, thoughts, and people) associated with the treatment. Reconditioning may solve such problems.

SEE ALSO:

Cancer and Suicide
Chemicals of the Body and Stress
Conditioning, Classical and
   Instrumental (Operant)

Immune System Disorders
Stress Management Methods

BIBLIOGRAPHY

Andersen, B. L., Kiecolt-Glaser, J. K., & Glaser, R. (1994). A biobehavioral model of cancer stress and disease course. *American Psychologist, 49,* 389–404.
Costa, P. T., & VandenBos, G. R. (Eds.). (1990). *Psychological aspects of serious illness: Chronic conditions, fatal diseases and clinical care.* Washington, DC: American Psychological Association.
Decker, T. W., Cline-Elsen, J., & Gallagher, M. (1992). Relaxation therapy as an adjunct in radiation oncology. *Journal of Clinical Psychology, 48,* 388–393.
Eysenck, H. J. (1991). *Smoking, personality, and stress.* New York: Springer-Verlag.
Laszlo, J. (1987). *Understanding cancer.* New York: Harper Row.
Lyles, J. N., Burish, T. G., Krozely, M. G., & Oldham, R. K. (1982). Efficacy of relaxation training and guided imagery in reducing the aversiveness of cancer chemotherapy. *Journal of Consulting and Clinical Psychology, 50,* 509–524.
Redd, W. H., & Andrykowski, M. A. (1982). Behavioral intervention in cancer treatment: Controlling aversion reactions to chemotherapy. *Journal of Consulting and Clinical Psychology, 50,* 1018–1029.

Cancer and Suicide

Description

While some studies indicate that suicide is no more frequent in cancer patients than it is in the general population, others find that it is up to 2 to 10 times more frequent. However, the actual incidence is probably underestimated, perhaps because families are reluctant to report death by suicide. Though they may not actually commit suicide, suicidal thoughts are common among cancer patients. Most cancer suicides occur at home, with overdosing with analgesics and sedatives the most common methods used.

Causes

Among the numerous causes of suicide is increased stress resulting from various bodily conditions and historical variables. Such risk factors include a history of previous psychiatric disorders, a family history of suicide, a history of suicide attempts, depression, substance abuse, the recent death of a friend or spouse, and limited—if any—social supports. The likelihood of suicide increases if the patient is in an advanced stage of the disease with a poor prognosis, is in a state of confusion, has inadequately controlled pain or bodily deficiencies such as inability to eat and swallow, or is experiencing exhaustion or fatigue. Men are clearly at an increased risk of suicide compared to the general population.

Treatment

The suicidal patient should be carefully assessed to determine whether the underlying cause is depression or an independent desire to escape the intolerable conditions of advanced cancer. Astute intervention should be properly made, particularly in the case of depression and hopelessness. First, a good rapport should be established with the patient to modify destructive attitudes, for example, so as to indicate that much can be done to alleviate emotional and physical pain. Contributing symptoms such as pain, depression, and delirium should be aggressively addressed.

SEE ALSO:

Cancer
Stress Management Methods
Suicide

BIBLIOGRAPHY

Breitbart, W., & Passik, S. D. (1993). Psychiatric aspects of palliative care: In D. Doyle, G. W. Hanks, & N. MacDonald (Eds.), *Oxford textbook of palliative medicine* (pp. 609–626). New York: Oxford University Press.
Henridsson, M. M., Isometsä, E. T., Hietanen, P. S., Aro, H. M., & Lönngvist, J. K. (1995). Mental disorders in cancer suicides. *Journal of Affective Disorders, 36,* 11–20.
Grabbe, L., Dem, A., Camann, M. A., & Potter, L. (1977). The health states of elderly persons in the last year of life: A comparison of deaths by suicide, injury and natural causes. *American Journal of Public Health, 87,* 434–437.
Valente, S. M., & Saunders, J. M. (1997). Diagnosis and treatment of major depression among people with cancer. *Cancer Nursing, 20,* 168–177.

Cardiovascular Disease

Description

Cardiovascular diseases include the wide range of disorders that afflict the heart and the blood vessels, the components of the circulatory system that pump blood throughout the body. The cardiovascular system as a whole has been considered a major component for the body's stress response. Disorders of this system include those that affect the heart itself, blood pressure, and the system of veins, arteries, capillaries. The results may be **Hypertension** (high blood pressure), arrhythmia, Arteriosclerosis, atherosclerosis, angina pectoris, heart attack, and heart failure.

Cardiovascular diseases account for almost one-third of all deaths in Western countries. Coronary artery disease may be caused by atherosclerosis, a thickening of the internal lining of the blood vessels that is linked with fatty substances, including cholesterol, in the blood. This obstructs the flow of blood that nourishes the heart muscle through the coronary arteries.

Arteriosclerosis is the hardening of artery walls, which interferes with the dilating and constructing of the arteries to regulate blood flow. This rigidity encourages the formation of blood clots, which can further affect blood flow.

Causes

Atherosclerosis is common among many people in North America, including children. Research indicates that this may be due to a diet consisting of large amounts of fatty and cholesterol-rich foods such as meat, butter, and eggs. There is a variety of risk factors that contribute to heart disease, including a family history of heart disease, excess weight, a lack of sufficient exercise, smoking, diabetes, high levels of low-density lipoprotein cholesterol in one's blood, constant stress, or various combinations of the above. The American Medical Association identified stress as one of the producers of essential hypertension, which is pathologically high blood pressure.

Stressful life experiences are prominent among stimuli that cause heart disease. Hypertension seems to be a serious medical problem associated with extreme stressful situations such as wars, fires, or natural catastrophes. For example, during the three-year siege of Leningrad in World War II, the incidence of hypertension increased from 4 to 64 percent. In most of the persons affected, the hypertension persisted even after the end of the war, and the majority suffered premature death from causes presumed to be related to heart disease.

Job stress can also contribute to premature heart disease. High heart attack rates occur on Wall Street. When the stock market has plunged, admissions to the hospitals' emergency cardiac care units have soared.

Inadequate coping with stressors increases the risk of heart problems by striking at the three main targets in the cardiovascular system: the arteries feeding the heart, the heart muscle, and the heart's electrical system (which functions in part with synapses that conduct electrical signals).

Chronic tension contributes to the development of cardiovascular disorders. When one reacts to the stresses of everyday living, there is necessarily an increase in skeletal muscle activity. This increased bodily activity in turn causes increased levels of cardiovascular response. (See the figure in the Introduction, p. xiii.)

Under stress, not only does blood pressure rise, but so may the amount of cholesterol in the blood. It seems that any type of stress, or physical or psychological trauma, causes the adrenal cortex to secrete cortisol, which results in the mobilization of fatty acids. These fatty acids pour into the bloodstream and are metabolized by muscles in "fight or flight" situations, but are left circulating when there is more anxiety than action. Eventually, the fatty acids may convert to cholesterol deposits of plaque. Later, the deposits contain fibrous tissue and calcium.

Plaque decreases the diameter of blood vessels. When an acute clot forms, it may completely block one or more of the coronary arteries; and when that particular portion of the heart muscle is deprived of its blood supply, a myocardial infarction (heart attack) may occur.

Fatty deposits (atheroma) accumulate on the inner lining of the arteries. Fats dissolved in the blood, such as cholesterol, may be precipitated out of solution faster in the presence of prolonged elevated blood pressure. Blood pressure increases during stress which the body responds to by constricting the muscles of the arterial walls, helping to supply necessary additional blood. The greater the duration of stress, the longer the increase in blood pressure; the longer the increase in blood pressure, the greater the amount of fatty deposits brought by the additional blood. There seems to be a connection between stress, high blood pressure, and atherosclerosis, and that connection may involve cholesterol.

Treatment

A combination of treatments is often indicated to decrease the chances of an individual's developing heart problems. Thus the following are usually recommended: diet low in cholesterol, in sodium, and in fat; and a lifestyle that incorporates regular exercise and relaxation.

Various drugs have been used to attempt to dissolve the blood clots that cause heart attacks. Even though they may be successful, the arteries may return to their earlier occluded state.

Behavioral control can help prevent excessive atherosclerosis, and thus prevent heart attacks, by reducing high-fat diets, particularly if begun early. This is because thickening of the walls of the arteries begins early in life and slowly progresses over decades. **Stress Management Methods** have also been helpful in accomplishing long-term behavioral changes; symptoms that have persisted beyond medical treatment have been thereby alleviated. The reduction in the reflex irritation and excitation of the areas afflicted can be accomplished through a reduction of neuromuscular activity in skeletal muscles.

Occasionally, when the situation is particularly serious, surgery may be required.

SEE ALSO:

Blood Pressure, Proper
   Measurement of
Cardiovascular Reactivity
Hypertension, Essential (High
   Blood Pressure)

Stress Management Methods
Stroke
Type A Behavior

BIBLIOGRAPHY

Allen, R., & Scheidt, S. (Eds.). (1996). *Heart and mind: The practice of cardiac psychology.* Washington, DC: American Psychological Association.
Blascovich, J., & Katkin, E. S. (Eds.). (1993). *Cardiovascular reactivity to psychological stress and disease.* Washington, DC: American Psychological Association.
Kunz, J. R. M., & Finkel, A. J. (Eds.). (1987). *The American Medical Association family medical guide.* New York: Random House.
Turner, J. R. (1994). *Cardiovascular reactivity and stress, patterns of physiological response.* New York: Plenum.

Cardiovascular Reactivity

Description

Cardiovascular reactivity is a psychophysiological construct referring to changes in cardiovascular activity that are related to psychological stress; for example, consistent psychological distress may cause high blood pressure. The construct refers to interrelationships among psychological and social factors, biological and physiological functions, and the development, as well as the course, of illness. Although individuals differ in the degree to which their cardiovascular responses are made to various psychological stimuli, some response patterns may be risk markers for, or causal factors of, cardiovascular disease. This suggests that greater cardiovascular reactivity to behavioral stressors may play some role in the development of sustained arterial **Hypertension** (chronic high blood pressure), which in turn may predict a later onset of cardiovascular disease.

Causes

Cardiovascular reactivity is caused by exposure to psychological stressors. There is thought to be a strong correlation between sizable responses to stressors and the later development of cardiovascular disease.

Treatment

Cardiovascular reactivity has been treated in two different ways: pharmacologically and behaviorally. Behavioral treatments include **Stress Management Methods** and dietary changes. Stress management is any behavioral (psychological) procedure offered or undertaken that deliberately attempts to alter beneficially any aspect of the general stress process; this includes altering the environment—the subjective, behavioral, and physiological responses to stressful experiences.

Four effective strategies have been used in controlling cardiovascular reactivity: aerobic **Exercise, Social Support, Biofeedback,** and **Self-Operations Control,** a synonym for **Progressive Relaxation,** which is an important intervention providing the individual with a sense of personal involvement and control over his or her condition.

SEE ALSO:

Biofeedback
Cardiovascular Disease
Exercise, Benefits of
Hypertension, Essential (High Blood
   Pressure)

Progressive Relaxation
Self-Operations Control
Social Support
Stress Management Methods

BIBLIOGRAPHY

Blascovich, J., & Katkin, E. S. (Eds.). (1993). *Cardiovascular reactivity to psychological stress and disease.* Washington, DC: American Psychological Association.
Turner, J. R. (1994). *Cardiovascular reactivity and stress: Patterns of physiological response.* New York: Plenum.

Chemicals of the Body and Stress

When one confronts an aversive stimulus, the natural response is to cope with the stressor. The resulting stress response is a highly complex one involving the central nervous system, the adrenal system, the cardiovascular system, the striated muscle system, and so forth. The hypothalamus at the base of the brain secretes corticotropin releasing factor (CRF). CRF then triggers a series of physiological and behavioral reactions by being transported through the blood and activating the pituatary gland to release adrenocorticotropin hormone (ACTH), also known as corticotropin. ACTH then activates glucocorticoid hormones (i.e., steriods) released by the adrenal glands, which are located on the top of the kidneys. As one responds, endogenous chemicals (those naturally occurring in the body) are secreted, along with increased activity of neurotransmitters, neuroendocrines, prolactin growth hormone, as well as peripheral norepinephrine and epinephrine; there are also changes in the immune system. Among the neurotransmitters in the brain are norepinephrine; epinephrine, dopamine, serotonin, and acetylcholine. Amines usually increase during stress, which then increases the supplies of neurotransmitters. These internal events have adaptive significance and help one to cope with stressors and help to protect against health risk.

We can thus see that chemicals play complex roles as we react to stressors. As one effectively controls one's behavior during stress by means of the striated muscles, these complex chemical processes can be returned to their normal state of homeostasis.

SEE ALSO:

Disease and Stress   Psychoimmunology
Immune System Disorder   Psychopharmacology
Jet Lag

BIBLIOGRAPHY

Benton, D., & Owens, D. (1993). Is raised blood glucose associated with the relief of tension? *Journal of Psychosomatic Research, 37,* 723–735.
Gordis, E. (1996, April). *Alcohol Alert.* Washington, DC: U.S. Department of Health and Human Services, National Institutes on Alcohol Abuse and Alcoholism, 32, 1–4.

Child Sexual Abuse, Stress of

Description

Child sexual abuse has been defined as sexual contact by an adult with an individual who is under eighteen years of age. Most incidents of abuse are either single events or occurrences of short duration. The majority of cases reported involve the abuse of girls, and it is suspected that the occurrence of sexual abuse of boys is underreported.

Children who have been sexually abused report more somatic and psychiatric symptoms such as anxiety, depression, anger, substance abuse, and conduct disorders than do their nonabused peers. Boys who are abused face additional risk of damage to a subjective sense of maleness, gender confusion, and stigmatization as a potential perpetrator. Adults who have been abused as children are more vulnerable to self-destructive behavior, personality disorders, and sexual dysfunction, as well as to medical problems—particularly gastroenterological and gynecological complaints.

Research on the coping strategies used by victims while being abused suggests that such strategies are influenced by age. Preschool children do not have the cognitive repertoire required to assess their predicaments; therefore, their coping skills are limited to denial and dissociation. Older children who have an increased ability to assess the appropriateness of sexual contact are at risk of blaming themselves for the adult's conduct, thus internalizing feelings of shame and guilt. This is particularly so in the case of incest. Other children involved in serious abuse try to deny the reality of their situations and in so doing reduce the probability that they will seek outside help. Adolescents tend either to rely on denial or engage in impulsive behaviors such as substance abuse, sexual promiscuity, or running away and, in this way, add to their risk of developing a pathology.

Causes

Many children do not develop any symptoms as a result of inappropriate sexual contact, and sexual abuse can be considered a risk factor but not a determiner of later pathology. Factors that are associated with high levels of symptoms are abuse by a parent or close relative, invasiveness, long duration of sexual contact, physical injury, and perceived or actual coercion. Such conditions increase the level of risk of developing symptoms in both the short and long term.

Recent research on girls who have been abused indicates the presence of biological abnormalities many years after the abuse has ceased. One study on girls whose abuse had ended up to a year prior to the investigation found elevated morning levels of plasma cortisol (a stress hormone produced by the adrenal glands) when compared with controls. Another study found higher levels of catecholamines in the urine of girls whose abuse had ceased many years prior to the investigation. Excessive levels of catecholamines for long periods of time cause the body to become stressed and hyperaroused. There is also some preliminary evidence that, among subgroups of girls, the stress of sexual abuse adversely affects the immune system, and that some abused girls reach puberty earlier than do nonabused girls. Thus, the severe stress of sexual abuse may lead to alterations in the biological functioning of victims that may be influenced by age, the severity of the abuse, and the individual's genetic constitution.

Another source of serious behavior disorder is false allegations of child sexual abuse ("false memory syndrome"). The child may make bizarre allegations against improbable people, causing great distress for all. This is a particular issue in cases that involve young children whose memory capacities are less well formed and who are more vulnerable to suggestion than older children and adults. Despite these limitations, current research indicates that some preschool children are able to accurately recall events important as forensic evidence. However, in cases where a young child testifies, it is important that information about the methods used to obtain the child's report be presented in court.

Treatment

An adaptive method of coping with abuse is to disclose and request help. However, disclosure is also a stressor for the child, at least initially. It can create or increase family conflict, initiate separation of parents, and/or the removal of the child from the home. Other stressors associated with disclosure are investigative/ therapeutic interviews, judicial proceedings, and unsupportive reactions from the nonoffending parent—thus isolating and scapegoating the victim. On the other hand, children who are securely attached to the nonoffending parent and who receive his or her support are less at risk of developing symptoms. The psychotherapeutic treatment modalities used with children after disclosure of abuse are play therapy with young children and cognitive restructuring with older children and adults. In play therapy the child theoretically gains emotional release and a sense of control and learns more adaptive social skills. Cognitive restructuring seeks to change the individual's interpretation of events. This form of treatment increases emotional distress in the short term but may be more adaptive in the long term. Adults who were abused as children seek to make sense of what happened to them, and those who succeed in doing so seem to have fewer symptoms.

Allegations of sexual abuse made by adults who think they have recovered memories of such abuse while undergoing therapy are controversial. This is particularly so in cases that use such techniques as hypnosis to facilitate recall. Frequently, such techniques have been used by therapists poorly trained in either psychology or in the ethical use of hypnosis, and the so-called "recall" is the result of the therapist's suggestions. Any claim of memory being recalled from infancy should be treated with skepticism, at best, since the psychological cognitive abilities necessary to lay down a memory trace are not developed until much later in childhood.

It is important that therapists do not abuse their positions and exploit the vulnerability of clients by planting such memories through leading questions or questionable use of hypnosis. If there is a deep-seated sense of being uncared for, that should not be translated into an allegation of abuse. It is also important that genuine experiences of sexual abuse by the client not be discounted.

SEE ALSO:

Sexual Dysfunction in Men
Sexual Dysfunction in Women

BIBLIOGRAPHY

Ceci, S. J., & Bruck, M. (1993). Suggestibility of the child witness: A historical review and synthesis. *Psychological Bulletin, 113,* 403–439.
De Bellis, M. D., Leter, L., Trickett, P. K., & Putnam, F. (1994). Urinary catecholamine excretion in sexually abused girls. *Journal of the American Academy of Child and Adolescent Psychiatry, 33,* 320–327.
Pope, K. S., & Brown, L. S. (1996). *Recovered memories of abuse: Assessment, therapy, forensics.* Washington, DC: American Psychological Association.
Spaccarelli, S. (1994). Stress, appraisal, and coping in child sexual abuse: A theoretical and empirical review. *Psychological Bulletin, 116,* 340–362.

Cognitive Behavior Therapy

Cognitive behavior therapy is based on the assumption that negative feelings and maladaptive behaviors are the result of distortions in thinking. This approach regards cognitions as covert behaviors that significantly interact with both emotions and overt behaviors and thus affect human functioning.

Disorders such as anxiety, phobias, and depression are considered primarily as thinking disorders that are caused when the individual focuses on certain negative aspects of the situation while ignoring or discounting other salient features. In this way, the individual loses objectivity and distorts reality. As a result of these distortions, the individual's ability to modulate behavioral responses to the situation is attenuated, placing him or her at risk of acting in a manner that is either over- or undercontrolled. Thus, the immature, demanding, and one-sided judgments that are used to assess a situation are reflected in the reaction to that situation.

Over time these distortions develop into *automatic thoughts,* that are involuntary, difficult to dismiss, and autonomous in that the thoughts are responding to internal stimuli and not to any actual external event. The particular constellation of cognitive distortions a given person may have depends on his or her experiences of having certain cognitive schemas paired with particular noxious stimuli, thus creating vulnerabilities within the individual when triggered. For example, if depressed individuals focus on loss or defeat, it negatively colors their concepts of themselves, their environment, and their future. As a result, they deprecate themselves, and they may see their external environment as harsh and ungiving and their future as bleak, without any hope of improvement. Consequently, they can feel helpless and hopeless and respond to the world by becoming inactive, withdrawing, and isolating.

The purpose of cognitive behavior therapy is to correct these distortions by reorganizing a person's "self-talk," thus, changing his or her behavior and the nature of reinforcement elicited from the environment. In this way, it enables clients to assess their own contributions to their problems and to learn healthy alternative behaviors.

A cognitive behavior therapist using the method advocated by Beck (1993) collaborates with the client to evaluate the contribution of his or her thoughts to current distress. The therapist uses a Socratic approach in disputing negative patterns of thinking so that the client learns to recognize, observe, and monitor his or her own automatic thoughts. The therapist suggests alternative interpretations of a situation for consideration. Thus, problems that once seemed intractable are reduced to manageable proportions.

The system devised by Albert Ellis is similar in many ways to Beck's approach. Both theorists stress cognitions and thoughts as measurable behaviors, and challenging distortions in thinking is central to both systems. However, the approach of Ellis is more confrontational, didactic, and directive than that of Beck.

Another approach is Donald Meichenbaum's cognitive behavioral modification, which is also based on cognitive restructuring and in teaching of coping skills such as **Stress Inoculation Training,** whereby the client is gradually exposed to stress-inducing situations. It includes components such as direct instructions, behavioral rehearsals, relaxation training, and problem solving. The client learns to apply this method to deal with present and future difficulties.

S E E   A L S O :

Behavior Therapy
Stress Inoculation Training
Stress Management Methods

BIBLIOGRAPHY

Beck, A. T. (1993). Cognitive approaches to stress. In Paul M. Lehner & Robert L. Woolfolk (Eds.). *Principles and practice of stress management* (2nd ed., pp. 333–372). New York: Guilford Press.

Corey, G. (1991). *Theory and practice of counseling and psychotherapy* (4th ed.). Pacific Grove, CA: Brooks/Cole.

Ellis, A. (1996). *Better, deeper and more enduring brief therapy: The rational emotive behavior therapy approach.* New York: Brunner/Mazel.

Meichenbaum, D. (1993). Stress inoculation training: A 20-year update. In P. M. Lehrer & R. L. Woolfolk (Eds.), *Principles and practice of stress management* (2nd ed., pp. 373–406). New York: Guilford Press.

Meichenbaum, D., & Jaremko, M. (Ed.). (1983). *Stress prevention and management: A cognitive behavioral approach.* New York: Plenum.

Colitis

Description

Colitis (inflammation of the colon) is one of the gastrointestinal tract disturbances that is among the most frequent stress-tension complaints. Signs of digestive disturbances include diarrhea, constipation, vomiting with heightened temperature, and hemorrhoids. Serious colon conditions include mucus colitis, spastic colon, Crohn's disease, and ulcerative colitis. The symptoms are painful, and flare-ups can hinder regular, daily activities. Abdominal pains, for instance, can develop suddenly, as when one has intestinal cramps in tense social situations. An inflamed bowel makes it difficult to absorb the nutrients in food, so the victim may experience nutritional deficiencies, possible weight loss, and even anemia.

Causes

The colon is designed for the absorption and orderly evacuation of concentrated waste products. Because it is composed of only smooth muscle, like most of the rest of the **Gastrointestinal** tract the colon cannot be directly controlled volitionally as can skeletal muscle. Rather, the smooth muscles of the colon are largely controlled indirectly by the skeletal muscles, especially the layers over the abdomen. As a result, the stressors that one encounters can produce excessive abdominal tension, which in turn can lead to various kinds of gastrointestinal distress.

Some of the gastrointestinal disorders may have an organic, nontension-related basis, but many are directly due to chronic muscular overtension.

Treatment

People often try in vain to solve such gastrointestinal problems with patented medicines or altered diet. Prescribed medication can effect some temporary relief, but medication does not permanently solve the problem.

Spastic (overtensed) colon and other tension maladies of the gastrointestinal tract as yet can be permanently relieved only through the sensitive application of clinical relaxation principles. The typical case of overtension always has some degree of spasticity of the digestive tract that can be relaxed away. The extreme instance of a spastic colon, in which the colon has assumed an extensively malformed shape, can through diligence be restored to a normal condition. Accompanying symptoms of constipation and diarrhea can similarly be relieved, as can hemorrhoids.

Treatment cannot be effective if the condition has become so advanced that it is irreversible. Ulcerative colitis, for instance, may well require surgical intervention.

SEE ALSO:

Gastrointestinal Disorders
Progressive Relaxation

BIBLIOGRAPHY

Jacobson, E. (1938). *Progressive relaxation.* Chicago: University of Chicago Press.
Magalini, S. I., Magalini, S. C., & Francisci, G. (1990). *Dictionary of medical syndromes* (3rd ed.). Philadelphia: J. B. Lippincott.
McGuigan, F. J. (1992). *Calm down: A guide for stress and tension control.* Dubuque, IA: Kendall/Hunt.
Thompson, W. G. (1993). *The angry gut.* New York: Plenum.

Commuting Stress, Automobile

Description

Commuting in urban and even some suburban areas is one of life's daily hassles and is likely to have some type of negative consequences—immediate, intermediate, or long-term. Commuting is replete with stressors: noise, crowding, heat or cold, noxious fumes, wasted time, and aggressive or reckless drivers. Overreaction to such commuting stressors for some individuals affects job performance, relationships, and their psychological and physiological health.

Some direct effects of commuting stress on individuals are hours lost from work or leisure activities, vehicle wear and tear, excessive gasoline consumption, air and noise pollution, and traffic accidents. Indirect effects of commuting stress include personal strain, which may lead to personality or behavioral withdrawal, attitude changes, or lowered performance levels.

Causes

A long and difficult commute to work may cause increased secretions of body fluids (including gastric acid, which can cause **Gastrointestinal Disorders,** hormones, and other **Chemicals** that contribute to "fight or flight" reactions); it may also result in **Fatigue,** increased blood pressure or heart rate, and other physiological symptoms of stress.

Long-term causes of commuting stress may be more difficult to recognize but are just as harmful. Changes in the workforce, increased accessibility to automobiles, and the shift of employers to suburban areas have all increased the number of people commuting by private vehicles. Traffic congestion is often exacerbated by poor regional planning, as was especially true following the suburban building boom of the 1980s in the United States.

Treatment

Treatment of commuting stress includes avoidance of, as well as adaptations to, relevant stressors. And it also involves the individual as well as the organization. The individual can plan ahead in order to prevent the build-up of this stress. For instance, one could arrange for carpooling to alleviate stress on nondriving days, avoid last-minute bustling about by laying out clothing the night before, have all necessary papers and other items arranged and together ready to go, select nutritious meals, and get adequate restful sleep. Such measures can contribute to both physiological and psychological well-being.

Individuals can also learn how to control responses to stressors. These adaptations include various **Stress Management Methods** such as **Progressive Relaxation** and **Time Management.** Stress management techniques can be practiced before the experience and used in the midst of the stress experience.

With commuting stress becoming ever more prominent a factor in worker effectiveness, organizations are beginning to realize that they can provide interventions for preventing and for dealing with commuting stress. Companies might consider relocating to other, more easily accessible sites. Employers can reduce trip length or frequency through the use of flextime and telecommuting.

Long-range organizational solutions could be to focus on altering the make-up and relationship of cities, suburbs, and rural areas. Governments might also structure mass transit to promote its use by a greater percentage of the population via careful demographic studies aimed specifically at the commuting process, and then implementing improved public transit and road conditions involving access, toll costs, and even signs.

SEE ALSO:

Chemicals of the Body and Stress
Driving (Automobile) Stress
Fatigue, Chronic
Gastroinstinal Disorders
Progressive Relaxation
Road Rage
Stress Management Methods
Time Management

BIBLIOGRAPHY

Koslowsky, M., Kluger, A. N., and Reich, M. (1995). *Commuting stress: causes, effects, and methods of coping.* New York: Plenum.
Spilner, M. (1995, March). Destress your commute. *Prevention, 47,* 60–64.

Compulsive Behavior

Compulsions are ritualistically repeated responses. The usual diagnostic criteria for "compulsive personality disorder" include perfectionism, workaholism, indecisiveness, rigidity, stubbornness, strict compliance with rules, and excessive organization. In trying for impossible perfection, the individual is necessarily unhappy. Indecisive behavior may result from the fear of failing to make correct choices in difficult situations.

Many kinds of compulsive behaviors may seriously disrupt an individual's life. They are identified with the suffix *mania*. For instance, common stealing is kleptomania (*klepto* means steal; *mania* means mad or insane). Some other compulsive behaviors that have widespread significance for society include gambling, drug and alcohol abuse, and some eating disorders.

For elaboration, causes, and treatments see **Obsessive-Compulsive Behavior.**

SEE ALSO:

Addictive Behaviors
Anxiety
Emotional Behavior, Destructive

Gambling
Obsessive-Compulsive Behavior

BIBLIOGRAPHY

Cooper, A. M., Frances, A. J., & Sacks, M. H. (1986). *The personality disorders and neuroses.* Psychiatric Series (Vol. 1). Philadelphia: J. B. Lippincott.

Fals-Stewart, W., Marks, A. P., & Schaefer, J. (1993). A comparison of behavioral group therapy and individual behavior therapy in treating obsessive-compulsive disorder. *The Journal of Nervous and Mental Disease, 181,* 189–193.

Jenike, M. A. (1983). Obsessive compulsive disorder. *Comprehensive Psychiatry, 24,* 99–115.

Knox, L. S., Albano, A. M., & Barlow, D. H. (1996). Parental involvement in the treatment of childhood compulsive disorder: A multiple baseline examination incorporating parents. *Behavior Therapy, 27,* 93–114.

Marks, I. M. (1981). *Cure and care of neuroses: Theory and practice of behavioral psychotherapy.* New York: Wiley.

Rindfleisch, A., Burroughs, J. E., & Denton, F. (1997). Family structure, materialism and compulsive consumption. *Journal of Consumer Research, 23,* 312–325.

Schwartz, J. (1996). *Brain lock.* New York: ReganBooks.

Conditioning, Classical and Instrumental (Operant)

Classical conditioning is sometimes erroneously referred to as "Pavlovian conditioning"—erroneously, because Pavlov actually researched both kinds of conditioning. Classical conditioning occurs when a neutral stimulus (such as a tone) is presented just prior to the presentation of an unconditional stimulus (such as a bit of meat powder placed into the mouth of Pavlov's dogs). The unconditional stimulus evokes an unconditional response such as when the dog salivates to the meat powder. After a sufficient number of associations of the neutral stimulus (a tone, light, etc.) and the unconditional stimulus, the neutral stimulus comes to evoke the unconditional response (such as salivation)—at this time the neutral stimulus is referred to as a conditional stimulus and the unconditional response as a conditional response.

Much of animal and human learning can be accounted for according to these and other classical conditioning principles, for example, when we see lightning, we have been conditioned to expect the sound of thunder to follow within seconds, indicating the nearness of the storm. Many of our **Fears** and **Phobias** are classically conditioned in these ways.

More of our behavior can be understood, however, in terms of principles of instrumental (operant) conditioning. The basic principle is that when a reinforcement follows (is contingent on) a specified response, the response gains in strength. For instance, if you want to teach your dog to sit on command, you can say "sit" sometime when the dog sits on its own, and immediately give it a dog treat. By doing this several times, the dog can learn to sit when you tell it to. The word "sit" becomes a stimulus that can evoke the sitting response. These principles are widely applicable to human behavior, especially for child-rearing practices.

Unfortunately, many of our inappropriate behaviors in stressful situations have been learned according to principles of both classical and instrumental conditioning. The reader is encouraged to follow up on this brief introduction to the extensive literature on learning and to pursue the numerous variations of these principles and applications of them.

SEE ALSO:

Fear
Phobic Disorders
Systematic Desensitization

BIBLIOGRAPHY

Mazur, J. E. (1990). *Learning and behavior* (2nd ed.). Englewood Cliffs, NJ: Prentice-Hall.
McGuigan, F. J. (1994). *Biological psychology: A cybernetic science*. Englewood Cliffs, NJ: Prentice-Hall.

Constipation

Description

Constipation is the term describing difficulty in excreting fecal matter from the bowels. Symptoms often associated with constipation include fatigue, headaches, and abdominal pain.

Causes

Inadequate coping with stressors is a major contributing factor to constipation. Overtension of the striated muscles can cause excessive contraction of the intestines, which ultimately slows the movement of fecal matter through the intestinal tract. As this occurs, excess amounts of water are absorbed from waste products passing through the large intestine, thereby hardening the stool and rendering it more difficult to be removed as waste. The excess loss of water is exacerbated by the slow movement of fecal matter, which may also be attributed to insufficient bulk in the diet, lack of exercise, and so forth. Allergies, especially to milk, can also contribute to constipation.

Treatment

There are many ways in which constipation can be prevented. One way of avoiding it is to include sufficient fiber and liquid in your diet. Fiber can come from foods such as whole grains, and fresh fruits and vegetables (skins included). Exercising regularly also helps, as well as establishing a regular time each day for eliminating waste. It is important to note that relying on laxatives to remove waste actually does more harm in the long run because they inhibit the defecation reflexes.

Tension maladies of the gastrointestinal tract can be permanently relieved only through the sensitive application of clinical relaxation principles. People often try in vain to solve such gastrointestinal problems with patented medicines or altered diet. Prescribed medication can effect some temporary relief but, once again, medication does not permanently solve the problem. The typical case of overtension always has some degree of spasticity of the digestive tract which can be relaxed away. The extreme instance of constipation with a **Spastic Colon,** in which the colon has assumed an extensively malformed shape, can through diligence be restored to a normal condition (Jacobson, 1938). Similarly, elimination of symptoms of constipation and diarrhea should be conducted in a relaxed fashion rather than being forced.

SEE ALSO:

Gastrointestinal Disorders
Spastic Colon

BIBLIOGRAPHY

Everhart, J. E., Go, V. L. W., Johannes, R. S., Fitzsimmons, S. C., Roth, H. P., & White, L. R. (1989). A longtitudinal survey of self-reported bowel habits in the United States. *Digestive Diseases and Sciences, 34*, 1143–1162.

Jacobson, E. (1938). *Progressive relaxation* (Rev. ed.). Chicago: University of Chicago Press.

McGuigan, F. J. (1992). *Calm down: A guide for stress and tension control* (2nd ed.). Dubuque, IA: Kendall/Hunt.

Thiroloix, J. (1976). *Constipation: Its causes and cures.* New York: St. Martin's Press.

Whitehead, W. E. (1998). Gastrointestinal syndromes and disorders. In E. A. Blechman & K. D. Brownell (Eds.), *Behavioral medicine & women: A comprehensive handbook* (pp. 646–653). New York: Guilford Press.

Crying—A Stress Management Method?

Researchers have asked why people cry and how crying might help with stress. Although the eyes of all mammals are moisturized and soothed by tears, only human beings shed tears in response to emotional stress; yet we know little about this uniquely human behavior. One theory suggests that tears help to relieve stress by ridding the body of potentially harmful stress-induced chemicals. One finding is that emotionally induced tears have a higher protein content than tears produced in response to eye irritation, such as those caused by an onion.

Other provocative evidence includes a report that people with stress-related illnesses cry less than their healthy counterparts. Anecdotal reports are that people feel better "after a good cry." It has been documented that men cry less frequently than women. In America, frequent triggers of crying episodes involve interpersonal relations—such as arguments—and movie or television scenes. Thus, a primary crying time in this country is between seven and ten in the evening, when people are likely to be with others and/or watching television. So, when one is feeling stressed, crying is thought by some to be beneficial.

SEE ALSO:

Stress Management Methods

BIBLIOGRAPHY

Bloona, R. (1996). *Coping with stress in a changing world* (pp. 325–378). New York: Mosby.

De-Fruyt, F. (1997). Gender and individual differences in adult crying. *Personality and Individual Differences, 22*, 937–940.

McGrath, J. E. (1988). Behavioral psychology in medicine. In M. D. Dunnette (Ed.), *Handbook of industrial and organizational psychology.* Skokie, IL: Rand McNally.

D

Depression–Dwarfism

Depression

Description

Depression is a condition marked by such feelings as sadness, dejection, guilt, worthlessness, and self-blame. In severe depressions, psychomotor retardation (e.g., inactivity of the body) can lead to near stupor. Depressions are often accompanied by complaints of loss of appetite, insomnia, inertia, and the like. Withdrawal from social situations and distorted perceptions of reality are commonly present.

Causes

Depression as a clinical disorder usually builds over time as a result of prolonged, unrelieved, inadequate coping with traumatic life events, including environmental and social problems and chronic illness. The resulting chronic overtension helps to perpetuate the disorder. Genetic, psychological, and biochemical elements have all been implicated in various cases of depression.

A predisposition based on heredity seems to operate in some cases of depression, but it is more likely a factor in major depression rather than in the more moderate forms. Pathophysiology can induce depression, as in the case of hypothyroidism and by diminished activity in the noradrenaline system.

An insufficiency of two classes of brain chemicals—neurotransmitters and endorphins—has been related to a number of cases of depression. Neurotransmitters such as norepinephrine and serotonin function in the transmission of neural messages among brain cells. Norepinephrine functions in the activation of reward centers in the brain. Endorphins serve as pain killers and mood elevators. Stresosors may trigger depression by lowering the production of norepinephrine or endorphins; threats to one's well-being or frustration of strong needs increases the production of these biochemicals. If stress is chronic, then severe depletion of these "happiness chemicals" may result from tissue fatigue. When tissues producing norepinephrine and endorphins are fatigued, reward centers are understimulated and the person can be thrust into depression while the brain is recovering. Thus, severe depletion of either of these classes of chemicals can render a person incapable of fully experiencing rewarding sensations and can produce anhedonia, which is an incapacity of experiencing pleasure. Consequently, depressed persons may conclude that life holds little interest for them.

Treatment

Treatment for depression can take many forms. Pharmacology may be used especially in those instances when the patient may be a danger to himself or herself, or when the patient lacks the ability for self-help. Psychological means for the resolution of symptoms may be applied in the form of supportive and educational therapies, and psychotherapy.

As an adjunct to such psychotherapy, exercise, which also may stimulate endorphin production in the brain, and social interaction have been used to raise the patient from self-absorption and to increase the sense of well-being. Increasing social contacts and support systems, and improving communication skills are specific steps that are often taken, with positive results, to assist the depressed individual.

Progressive Relaxation, an empirically validated method of calming systems of the body, among other systems can be an important treatment for depression. A function of progressive relaxation is to place the individual back in control and counteract feelings of inadequacy. The patient can learn to describe especially the visual imagery that is a primary focus of the depressive experience—a depressed individual visualizes his or her difficulties in imagination. Then, the patient can alleviate the depression with the elimination of skeletal muscle tensions, especially of the eyes, which function in the generation of the visual imagery.

SEE ALSO:

Progressive Relaxation

BIBLIOGRAPHY

American Psychiatric Association (1994). *Diagnostic and statistical manual of mental disorders* (4th ed.). Washington, DC: Author.

Badal, D. (1988). *Treatment of depression and related moods: A manual for psychotherapists.* Northvale, NJ: Aronson.

McGuigan, F. J. (1993). *Calm down: A guide for stress and tension control.* Dubuque, IA: Kendall/Hunt.

Rehm, L. P., & Tayndall, C. I. (1993). Mood Disorders. In H. E. Adams & P. B. Sutker (Eds.), *Comprehensive handbook of psychopathology* (2nd ed., pp. 235–261). New York: Plenum.

Diabetes Mellitus

Description

In this disorder, the pancreas fails to produce sufficient insulin to achieve a proper blood sugar level. Insulin is the hormone secreted by the pancreas that is necessary for the absorption of glucose (sugar) from the bloodstream into the cells for energy production. It is estimated that 2 percent of the American population suffers from diabetes.

Symptoms include excessive urination throughout the day and night, resulting in enhanced thirst. There is an increased susceptibility for bladder infections since sugar in the urine attracts microorganisms. **Fatigue** also occurs because there is a lack of glucose available for metabolism of cells throughout the body. Consequently, weight loss may result from the body's burning fat and muscle for energy instead of glucose. Tingling hands and feet, reduced resistance to infections, blurred vision, impotence in men, and the loss of menstruation in women may occur. Complications after the onset of the disorder include those affecting the eyes, nerves, and kidneys. Diabetic persons are at increased risk for **Cardiovascular Disease,** including circulatory problems in the legs and feet.

Causes

Organic. Diabetes can be brought on by other diseases such as pancreatitis, Cushing's syndrome, and hyperthyroidism. Heredity is also an important factor in the onset of diabetes, with almost 33 percent of all cases having a family history of the disease. Advanced age is a factor due to decreasing efficiency of the pancreas in secreting insulin.

Stress. Stressful situations can cause an increase in the amount of glucose so that a shortage of insulin can cause bodily destruction. Excessively high blood levels of glucose lead to the body's using fat and protein for energy at a very high rate; this can cause kidney damage, even a diabetic coma. Ineffective stress management by a diabetic can thus inhibit efficient metabolism and exacerbate symptoms of diabetes because of excessive glucose in the blood. During stressful situations, a person may also not adhere to the diet prescribed for managing his or her disorder.

Treatment

In addition to medical treatment (insulin injections, etc.) and psychological programs for weight maintenance and dietary control, specific stress control methods are important; for example, relaxation training can have positive effects on the metabolism of diabetics.

SEE ALSO:

Cardiovascular Disease
Fatigue, Chronic
Stress Management Methods

BIBLIOGRAPHY

Garrison, W. T. (1996). Coping with chronic medical illness: Lessons from working with children and adolescents with diabetes mellitus. In C. R. Pfeffer (Ed.), *Severe stress and mental disturbance in children* (pp. 307–323). Washington, DC: American Psychiatric Association.

Goetsch, V. L., & Wiebe, D. J. (1995). Diabetes mellitus: Considerations of the influence of stress. In A. J. Goreczny (Ed.), *Handbook of health and rehabilitation psychology* (pp. 513–533). New York: Plenum.

Kunz, J. R. M., & Finkel, A. J. (1987). *The American Medical Association family medical guide.* New York: Random House.

Diarrhea

Description

Diarrhea is characterized by watery stools, generally accompanied by frequent defecation. In addition to the inconvenience associated with an increased frequency of eliminating waste, diarrhea can result in weakness and dehydration as a result of the accompanying loss of fluids containing essential minerals like potassium. In worst-case situations, prolonged diarrhea (i.e., greater than one week's duration) can have deleterious effects on the general health of the body.

Causes

A major cause of diarrhea is chronic overtension of the striated muscles of the body, especially those in the abdominal region. Such overtension is due to habitual, inappropriate tensing of the muscles in the face of the stresses of life. Those who are able to relax successfully in the face of these stressors are not likely to develop diarrhea for psychological causes.

Organically, diarrhea can be due to either an increased secretion of fluid into, or a decreased absorption of fluid from, the gastrointestinal tract. A major cause of diarrhea is food contamination or allergy, in which case the bowel tends to react to certain foods as though they were laxatives. Some typical allergenic foods include milk, fruit, and sugar.

Treatment

Pepto Bismol and similar medications can provide short-term relief. One should take special steps to avoid consuming contaminated foods or foods to which one is allergic.

The overtension that contributes to diarrhea can be controlled through **Progressive Relaxation,** which involves practicing a specific set of techniques to achieve a relaxed state of body, including mind.

SEE ALSO:

Gastrointestinal Disorders
Progressive Relaxation

BIBLIOGRAPHY

McGuigan, F. J. (1992). *Calm down: A guide for stress and tension control* (2nd ed.). Dubuque, IA: Kendall/Hunt.
Taylor, C. B., Ironson, G., & Burnett, K. (1990). Adult medical disorders. In A. S. Bellack, M. Hersen, & A. E. Kazdin (Eds), *International handbook of behavior modification and therapy* (2nd ed.), pp. 371–397. New York: Plenum.

Differential Relaxation

Differential relaxation is the optimal contraction of only those muscles required to successfully accomplish the task at hand. Those specific muscles should contract only to the extent required for the immediate purpose. All other muscles of the body should be relaxed.

Some of the common, everyday activities during which this principle should be applied include driving, eating, sleeping, sports, and airline traveling. Differential relaxation should especially be applied during stressful situations, such as dealing with aggression, temper, and tension control as a form of **Self-Operations Control.**

SEE ALSO:

Self-Operations Control
Progressive Relaxation

BIBLIOGRAPHY

McGuigan, F. J. (1992). *Calm down: A guide for stress and tension control* (2nd ed.). Dubuque, IA: Kendall/Hunt.

Disease and Stress

Description

Virtually all diseases seem to be affected by inadequate coping with stressors of life.

Causes

Susceptibility to infection is presumed to be primarily mediated by **Immune System** function. Stress may influence immunity through direct enervation of the central nervous system (CNS), or through neuroendocrine-immune pathways. A number of direct neural pathways linking the CNS to the immune system have been identified. Also, a wide range of hormones released under stressful conditions have been implicated in immune modulation. Behavioral changes occurring as coping responses to stressors may also influence immunity. For example, persons repeatedly experiencing stressors tend to engage in poor health practices. They tend to smoke more, drink more alcohol, eat poorly, and sleep less, all of which may influence the immune system.

Pathways proposed as responsible for influencing immune system function and predisposing persons to disease onset are also involved in modeling stress effects on duration and severity of disease. The course of an illness may be influenced by direct effects—not involving the immune system—on disease-involved tissues. For example, stress-triggered hormones such as cortisol and epinephrine may increase mucous secretion and vasodilation. Stress may also influence disease-involved tissue through changes in health practices. For example, increased smoking in reaction to stressors could irritate nasal and lung tissue. Failure to comply with medical regimens while experiencing stress could result in more severe and longer-lasting illness, either because undesirable behaviors aggravate existing problems or because failure to perform desirable behaviors results in disease progression. These actions may occur through influences on immune function or through influences of disease-involved tissue.

Treatment

While standard medical treatment is prescribed for specific diseases, special attention should also be given to the immune system. **Stress Management Methods** have been shown to beneficially affect the immune system.

SEE ALSO:

Cancer
Immune System Disorders
Stress Management Methods

BIBLIOGRAPHY

Bloona, R. (1996). *Coping with stress in a changing world.* New York: Mosby.
Blumenthal, S. J., Matthews, K., & Weiss, S. M. (Eds.). (1994). *New research frontiers in behavioral medicine: Proceedings of the national conference* (Publication No. 94-3772). Washington, DC: National Institute of Health.

Hall, N. R. S., Altman, F., & Blumenthal, S. J. (Eds.). (1996). *Mind-body interactions and disease and psychoneuroimmunology aspects of health and disease.* Orlando, FL: Health Dateline.

Kobasa, S. C. (1979). Stressful life events, personality and health: An inquiry into hardiness. *Journal of Personality and Social Psychology, 37,* 1–11.

Monjan, A. A., & Collector, M. I. (1977, April). Stress-induced modulation of the immune response. *Science, 196,* 307–308.

Stein, M., Miller, A. H., & Trestman, R. L. (1991). Depression, the immune system and health and illness. *Archives of General Psychiatry, 117,* 854–856.

Zautra, A. J., Okun, M. A., Robinson, S. E., Lee, D., Roth, S. H. & Emmanual, J. (1989). Life stress and lymphocyte alterations among patients with rheumatoid arthritis. *Health Psychology, 8,* 1–14.

Distress (Negative Stress)

Hans Selye (1978/1956) first distinguished between distress and **Eustress** (positive stress). "Distress" has been used to refer to negative aspects of the body's reactions to stress, such as depression, anxiety, anger, and exhaustion. There is a common notion that a stressor is an effect that is perceived as stressful by an individual, so that what is distressful for one person may not be so for another.

When one perceives negative stressful events, a number of complex internal processes follow. First, the entire body is activated in the startle reaction wherein neural impulses reverberate between the striated muscles and the brain; later the autonomic system becomes involved. The pituitary gland releases hormones, principally adrenocorticotropic hormone (ACTH), which acts on the cortex of the adrenal glands to release corticosteroids. The corticosteroids depress the immune system by inhibiting both the action of scavenger cells and various types of lymphocytes (cells from the lymph nodes) as well as their abilities to reproduce. When distress situations are chronic, there is atrophy of lymph node tissue and enlargement of adrenal glands. Distress has been linked with coronary heart disease, the speeding up of aging through hormonal imbalance, nervous conditions, and the development of degenerative diseases.

SEE ALSO:

Eustress (Positive Stress)
Selye, Hans (1907–1982), and the
    General Adaptation Syndrome (GAS)
Stress Defined

BIBLIOGRAPHY

Edwards J. R., Baglioni A. J., & Cooper C. L. (1990). Stress, Type A, coping, and psychological and physical symptoms: A multi-sample test of alternative models. *Human Relations, 43* (10), 910–956.

Selye, H. (1978/1956). *The Stress of life.* New York: McGraw-Hill.

Downsizing, Stress of

Description

The trend of downsizing and reorganization of corporations that began in the late 1980s and continues into the present time has resulted in the loss of jobs by thousands upon thousands of U.S. workers in professional and managerial positions. Many of these individuals had worked with the same corporation since they left college and had come to regard their employment status as secure. Displaced workers reported intense feelings of shame, anger, and hostility as a result of being laid off. They also found it difficult to secure new employment. One of the by-products of this intense reshaping of industry was a decrease in the number of positions that matched the qualifications of downsized workers, at the same time that the pool of applicants increased.

Symptoms of distress were not confined just to those who lost their jobs. Workers who remained also experienced physical and psychological symptoms. These employees were expected to take on an increased workload, thus making them susceptible to **Burnout.** The additional demands, combined with the sense of insecurity engendered by the layoffs, left many feeling apprehensive and resentful. Workers in businesses that have undergone reorganization have reported feelings of **Depression** and **Anxiety.** Moreover, the workplace has become less safe, and the incidence of accidents and **Workplace Violence** has increased. The overall effect of these added stressors places employees at risk for physical ailments such as **Cardiovascular Disease** and **Hypertension.**

Causes

Becasue labor represents a large portion of business costs, workers are particularly vulnerable to downsizing. Cost-conscious employers tend to focus on reducing their workforce when they want to make business savings. Such a trend has been fueled by the response of the stock market and by the short-term performance of downsized companies. An announcement to downsize is usually accompanied by a rise in the value of the company's shares. However, over the long term, companies that rely on downsizing alone to improve performance do not usually do as well as those that add to their workforce (Cascio, 1995). While the human cost of downsizing is seldom a consideration when such decisions are made, it nevertheless seems to negatively impact the company over time (Clay, 1998).

Treatment

One way to reduce the level of stress among workers and management during reorganization is through open and honest communication. Failure to do this lowers worker morale by allowing feelings of fear, distrust, and hostility to go unaddressed. Such inattention also feeds the rumor mill and, thus, amplifies the prevailing climate of suspicion and uncertainty.

Workers in a corporation undergoing reorganization can benefit from help in working through their feelings about their changing employment situations. They also profit from proactive techniques that equip them to map out their own career advancement plans. Such techniques, when practiced, improve their ability to increase earnings and decrease vulnerability to current and future job loss. Stress management techniques not only help workers cope with immediate stressors but they enable them to develop skills that enhance their professional effectiveness.

SEE ALSO:

Anxiety

Cardiovascular Disease

Depression

Executive Stress

Hypertension, Essential (High
   Blood Pressure)

Stress Management Methods

Violence, Workplace

Workplace Stress

BIBLIOGRAPHY

Cascio, W. F. (1995). *A guide to responsible restructuring.* Washington, DC: Government Printing Office.

Clay, R. A. (1998, January). Downsizing backfires on corporate America. *Monitor,* American Psychological Association.

Gowing, M. K., Kraft, J. D., & Quick, J. C. (1997). *The new organizational reality: Downsizing, restructuring and revitalization.* Washington, DC: American Psychological Association.

Kets de Vries, M. F. R. & Balazs, K. (1997). The downside of downsizing. *Human Relations, 50,* 11–50.

Quick, J. C. (1997). *Preventative stress management in organizations* (2nd ed.). Washington, DC: American Psychological Association.

Driving (Automobile) Stress

Description

It is common for people to feel rushed in all aspects of life, and their stressful behavior becomes particularly apparent in driving. The stresses of life often result in aggressive driving or risk-taking driving, both of which cause anxiety and possible danger to others on the highway. Aggressive driving is defined as such hostile actions as forcing another motorist off the road, shouting obscenities, or shooting at another car. Risk-taking driving includes speeding, tailgating, weaving dangerously, and ignoring stop signs. Risk taking is far more dangerous in terms of frequencies of injuries and deaths than is aggressive driving. Research has failed to find commonality in habits that define a bad driver. Driving stress is regarded by some specialists as resulting in social ills such as family discord, job dissatisfaction, and physical illness.

Causes

The primary cause of unsafe driving is the overtension that results from inadequate coping with life's stressors. Research has indicated that the longer and the farther people drive to work, the more stress they report. For instance, those who have long commutes to work have higher blood pressure than those who commute shorter distances, and those who have more roads to travel to get to their jobs call in sick more often than those who drive on fewer roads. Studies also indicate that traffic jams and other traffic stressors affect mood, health, work attendance, job stability, and life satisfaction.

Treatment

Adverse traffic conditions do not increase aggressive driving but do increase risk-taking behavior. Research has shown that people typically blame others rather than themselves for bad driving; therefore, merely asking people to drive safely is apparently ineffective. A graduated licensing system, taking into account variables conducive to safe driving (such as has been adopted in New Zealand), reduces traffic injuries.

However, the main solution to driving stress is for people to learn how to cope in general with stressors of life, concentrating on the highway. Individuals can most successfully accomplish this by practicing **Differential Relaxation** when driving an automobile.

One result of developing a good perspective is learning to drive defensively—as if everyone else on the highway is trying to kill you. Another good perspective to develop is to "drive ahead," anticipating what lies in front of you: It's really not terribly important if another driver beats you to the next stoplight.

SEE ALSO:

Commuting Stress, Automobile
Differential Relaxation
Road Rage

BIBLIOGRAPHY

Matthews, G., & Desmond, P. A. (1995). Stress as a factor in the design of in-car driving enhancement systems. *Travail-Humain, 58,* 109–129.
McGuigan. F. J. (1992). *Calm down: A guide for stress and tension control.* Dubuque, IA: Kendall/Hunt.

Drug Abuse in the Workplace

Description

As long as a significant portion of the American population takes drugs, many people will continue to bring their drugs with them to work. According to some experts, cocaine, and crack cocaine use is relatively greater than other forms of drug abuse. At least three widespread myths have contributed to cocaine's increasing popularity. Myth 1 is that cocaine is harmless. Myth 2 is that primitive people have used it for years to ward off cold and exhaustion (in reality, the coca leaves chewed by Bolivian Indians are not remotely comparable in potency to the powder snorted by employees). Myth 3 is that cocaine is nonaddictive. In fact, cocaine is perhaps the most addictive drug that employees abuse.

Causes

One of the causes of drug abuse is stress stemming from the job. Stimulants and hallucinogens, narcotics, and sedative-hypnotics are taken by employees across all job categories to relieve boredom, excessive stress, and related work problems.

Some firms, admitting that drug abuse occurs at work, use a variety of means to combat the problem—for example, drug-sniffing dogs that can search work areas, blood tests that can be administered to anyone who has had an accident on the job, and urine tests that can be required of employees upon being hired or whose behavior is questionable.

Treatment

To combat drug abuse, companies can recognize that work-related stress can lead or contribute to drug abuse. Then management can examine ways of relieving or controlling such stress. Additionally, since workers who abuse drugs may be potentially dangerous, it may be appropriate or necessary for employers to urge participation in a drug treatment program.

SEE ALSO:

Addictive Behaviors   Obsessive-Compulsive Behavior
Alcohol Abuse in the Workplace   Workplace Stress

BIBLIOGRAPHY

Baker, T. L. (July, 1989). Preventing drug abuse at work. *Personnel Administrator, 34,* 56–59.
Maheu, M. M. (1998). Worksite nicotine treatment. In E. A. Blechman & K. D. Brownell (Eds.), *Behavioral medicine & women: A comprehensive handbook.* New York: Brunner/Mazel.
Nace, E. P. (1995). *Achievement and addiction: A guide to the treatment of professionals.* New York: Brunner/Mazel.

Dwarfism, Psychological Stress-Related

Description

Extreme stress, especially during the crucial development years, may negatively affect growth and function of just about every physiological and psychological element. In addition to stunted growth, characteristics of stress dwarfism may include extreme nervousness, gastrointestinal ailments, diminished cardiovascular function, and stunted emotional, intellectual, and social development. These disorders often remain permanently, even after the stressors have been removed.

Causes

Optimal growth and development is dependent on appropriate intake of calories, a proper diet, keeping warm, and so forth. However, there is also a psychological component. When such necessities are severely lacking in the developing child, this extremely rare syndrome of "stress dwarfism," also known as psychosocial or psychogenic dwarfism, may result. The children who suffer stress dwarfism are not the children who experience the more or less normal stress of frequent moves or parental divorce; but rather, they are children of the type found locked in a dark closet for months, having been ritualistically and sadistically tormented by a disturbed caretaker.

A possible example of stress dwarfism is offered in this story informally passed on about a British Victorian family: When her beloved adolescent son David was killed in an accident, a mother grieved actively for years, ignoring her younger son and sometimes briefly imagining he was the older one returning to her. Her only solace was her belief that, when David had died, he was still perfect, still just a boy, not ruined by growing up and away from her. In reaction to being ignored by his mother (and to a virtually nonexistent father), the younger boy came to believe that if he remained a boy, he'd have at least some chance of winning his mother's love. He, thereby, ceased growing; as an adult he was barely 5 feet in height, and his marriage was unconsummated.

Thus, grotesque family psychopathology can cause children who are incessantly harassed and psychologically terrorized to become victims of stress dwarfism. More specifically, the condition also appears as a result of a threefold combination of (1) reduced production of growth hormones, (2) target cells becoming insensitive to growth hormones, and (3) diminished gastrointestinal function, resulting in reduced nutrient absorption.

Treatment

Clearly, any child experiencing psychological torment must be removed immediately from the offending family structure. It is necessary that they be placed in a nurturing environment emphasizing love, affection, caring, and attachment. If the stressors are removed from the child before the child is far into puberty, that is, before the long bones fuse and growth ceases, there is potential for some degree of growth "catch-up" to take place. However, shortness of stature and some degree of intellectual stunting usually persists into adulthood.

SEE ALSO:

Stress Management Methods

BIBLIOGRAPHY

Green, W., Campbell, M., & David, R. (1984). Psychological dwarfism: A critical review of evidence. *Journal of American Academic Child Psychiatry, 23,* 1.

Green, W. H., Deutsch, S. I., & Campbell, M. (1987). Psychosocial dwarfism, infantile autism, and attention deficit disorder. In C. B. Nemeroff & P. T. Loosen (Eds.), *Handbook of clinical psychoneuroendocrinology.* New York: Guilford Press.

Money, J. (1992). *The Kasper Hauser syndrome of "psychosocial dwarfism": Deficient statural, intellectual, and social growth induced by child abuse.* Buffalo: Prometheus Books.

E Eating Disorders–Exercise

Eating Disorders

Description

The variety of behavioral eating disorders includes, especially, compulsive eating, **Anorexia Nervosa, Bulimia, Food Abuse,** and **Obesity.** An estimated 34 million adult Americans are sufficiently obese that therapy is appropriate for them. Not only do obese individuals tend to overeat, they also tend to underexercise. Moreover, many compulsive eaters diet frequently, which can harm their health. As has been said, one may well lose a hundred pounds through dieting, but it is usually the same ten pounds lost and regained over and over again.

The definition of excessive weight is somewhat arbitrary. However determined, though, obesity is usually definitive and tends to increase the risk of disease and shorten the life span. Research has shown that it can contribute to diabetes, high blood pressure, high levels of blood fats associated with heart disease, some cancers, and a number of other health-threatening conditions. Obese males have higher death rates from cancers of the colon, rectum, and prostate, while obese females have higher death rates from cancers of the gall bladder, breast, and sexual organs. It should be emphasized, also, that an obese or overweight individual can still be malnourished.

The location of excessive fat differs between men and women and is relevant to health complications. For men, fat is concentrated in the waist, abdomen, and upper body, which is more unhealthy than the concentration in the hips and thighs that is common for women. However, we do not know what accounts for these differences in fat distribution.

Causes

Compulsive eating behavior typically is learned in youth and is associated with eating for reasons other than satisfying hunger. Compulsive eaters thus often fail to distinguish between their need for food and learned wants. Consequently, they may eat even though they are not hungry. Some learn to eat to reduce stressful reactions, just as one learns to abuse chemicals.

On the other hand, some people are physiologically predisposed to overeat due to such conditions as hormonal malfunctioning. One theory of obesity is that the infant has a specific number of fat cells that can increase to a genetically prede-termined size as they absorb nutrients. If there is overeating after infancy, new fat cells form that can lead to obesity.

The Set Point Theory of Body Weight.   This, the dominant theory, holds that healthy people have an innate mechanism centered in the hypothalamus that fixes and monitors body weight. The mechanism "controls" the body at a stable weight by modifying appetite, activity, and metabolic rate. However, those with an exces-sively high set point tend to gain excessive weight. If they successfully diet, eating later may return their body weight to its set point. One reason may be that an enzyme called adipose tissue lipoprotein lipase (AT-LPL) helps fat cells to fill up with fat. The amount of this enzyme in the body increases when an obese person loses weight and it returns to its previous level if the weight is regained. In a sense, AT-LPL instructs the body to regain the lost weight and return to the set point of body fat.

Treatment

Following the set point theory, the solution to successfully losing weight is to lower the set point. This can be accomplished by drugs such as amphetamines and nicotine (nicotine increases metabolic rate and thus burns more calories). But if the drugs are discontinued, the set point returns to normal, which again leads to a gain in weight. Regular exercise can help keep the set point at a low setting by increasing metabolic rate. Vigorous exercise burns calories at a relatively high rate that can continue for perhaps 15 hours.

Obese people seem to think more about food than do slender people. This is similar to **Conditioning** of an anticipatory response that may arouse an intense appetite when obese people are exposed to food stimuli. More generally, we all have learned such conditional anticipatory responses that influence us to seek various substances. This is a major basis of much advertising: The appearance of a desirable food product on television often influences us to go to the refrigera-tor. Because this is a learned response, successful treatment has focused on con-trolling the overeating response through behavioral conditioning (therapeutic) techniques.

S E E   A L S O :

Anorexia Nervosa
Behavior Therapy
Bulimia
Conditioning, Classical and
     Instrumental (Operant)

Food Abuse
Nutrition
Obesity
Stress Management Methods

BIBLIOGRAPHY

Capaldi, E. D. (Ed.). (1996). *Why we eat what we eat: The psychology of eating.* Washington, DC: American Psychological Association.

Garner, D. M., & Garfinkel, P. L. (Eds.). (1997). *Handbook of treatment for eating disorders* (2nd ed.). New York: Guilford Press.

McGuigan, F. J. (1994). *Biological Psychology: A cybernetic science.* Englewood Cliffs, NJ: Prentice-Hall.

Thompson, K. (Ed.). (1996). *Body image, eating disorders and obesity: An integrative guide for assessment and treatment.* Washington, DC: American Psychological Association.

Emotional Behavior, Destructive

Description

Emotional behavior ("emotions") is considered to include feelings that are both positive (euphoria, love) and negative or destructive (**Anger, Fear**).

Causes

Destructive emotional behaviors have been attributed to lack of empathy with others, exaggerated sense of self-importance, preoccupation with successful performance, extreme fluctuations in weight, widely varying sleep patterns, **Frustration,** and the like. Some scientists theorize that emotional characteristics are inborn, that individuals have genetic predispositions toward a particular emotional personality, and so forth. Various societal causes for different emotional states have been identified, such as an unbalanced family structure, hypercompetitiveness, poor education, lack of love and acceptance by others, and stress and stress-related symptoms (headaches, nervousness, etc.).

Treatment

Professional treatment may help promote modulated emotional behavior. This can be in the form of psychotherapy, (e.g., **Self-Operations Control** can help prevent destructive emotional behavior), psychopharmacology, and the like. Professionals may help individuals learn about their own emotional behaviors in order to modulate them. Regular exercise and regular eating, sleeping, and working habits have also been found to help control destructive emotional behavior.

SEE ALSO:

Anger

Fear

Frustration

Progressive Relaxation

Self-Operations Control

BIBLIOGRAPHY

Bruno, F. J. (1993). *Psychological symptoms.* New York: Wiley.
Kassinove, H. (Ed.) (1995). *Anger disorders: Definition, diagnosis and treatment.* Bristol, PA: Taylor & Francis.
McGuigan, F. J. (1992). *Calm down: A guide for stress and tension control* (2nd ed). Dubuque, IA: Kendall/Hunt.
Pennebaker, J. W. (Ed.). (1995). *Emotions, disclosure and health.* Washington, DC: American Psychological Association.

Esophageal Spasm/Globus Hystericus

Description

Esophageal disorders include spastic esophagus, rumination, and esophageal reflux. Spastic esophagus has been described by patients as a choking sensation or feeling of tightness or pressure or distension, something like a ball, lump, or clutching in the throat region. This condition often interferes with the passage of food. Pain associated with this condition is usually intermittent. Rumination involves the return of food through the esophagus to the mouth, where it is then rechewed and reswallowed, or expelled. Esophageal reflux is the return of acid through the esophagus to the mouth, causing pain and inflammation.

Causes

Prolonged conditions of fearfulness produce chronic muscular spasm of the esophagus known as **Globus Hystericus.** In the case of a phobia-heightened anxiety, the esophagus is particularly, and chronically, constricted.

Treatment

Progressive Relaxation has been used successfully to effect the relaxation of a constricted esophagus (Jacobson, 1938).

SEE ALSO:

Gastrointestinal Disorders
Progressive Relaxation
Spastic Colon

BIBLIOGRAPHY

Clouse, R. E. (1992). Psychiatric interaction with the esophagus. *Psychiatric Annals, 22,* 598–605.
Jacobson, E. (1938). *Progressive relaxation* (Rev. ed.). Chicago: University of Chicago Press.
McGuigan, F. J. (1992). *Calm down: A guide for stress and tension control* (2nd ed.). Dubuque, IA: Kendall/Hunt.

Eustress (Positive Stress)

Hans Selye (1978/1956) referred to eustress as a pleasant experience of fulfillment, a kind of stress that has positive consequences, versus the negative consequences of **Distress**. It has been held that distress occurs when one feels helpless and out of control in facing a stressor. In contrast, when one is in control, there is a positive state of stress referred to as eustress. It has been held that eustress is the attainment of an optimal level of stimulation characterized by a sense of accomplishment, joy that can derive from accomplishment in work and in simply playing.

Research has indicated that the more often one is in a state of eustress the less often one is in a state of distress, and consequently, the less one is subject to bodily disturbances linked with distress. Consequently, there are positive health benefits from eustress that have been noted in a variety of researches. A major characteristic of eustress is that it promotes physical, emotional, and mental health. As he originated the concept of eustress, Selye held that its effects are not detrimental to the body. In fact, he emphasized that health may be promoted by eustress (Edwards and Cooper, 1988) and established that eustress increases the production of anabolic hormones, HDL ("good") cholesterol, and other beneficial biochemical changes. In particular, stresses related to what we call "hope," "love," and "happiness" may have beneficial effects on health. In his book, *Anatomy of an Illness*, Norman Cousins tells how he discharged himself from a hospital and went home to care for himself. His treatment included encouraging himself to laugh, as by watching old comedy movies. A similar finding is that some people have significantly put off dying until after an important event, such as Christmas or a birthday. Perhaps laughter, pleasant occasions, and other such factors release endorphins that have a beneficial physiological effect. One possibility is that when we are happy, the body releases beta endorphins (neuropeptides created in nerve cells from amino acids) that mimic drugs such as opium; specific opiate receptors in nerve cells that can be activated by beta endorphins just as they can be by opiate-like drugs such as morphine, codeine, and heroin.

SEE ALSO:

Distress (Negative Stress)
Selye, Hans (1907–1982) and the General
    Adaptation Syndrome (GAS)
Stress Defined

BIBLIOGRAPHY

Bloona, R. (1996). *Coping with stress in a changing world.* New York: Mosby.
Edwards, J. R., & Cooper, C. L. (1988). The impacts of positive psychological states on physical health: A review and theoretical framework. *Social Science magazine, 27* (12), 1447–1459.
Selye, H. (1978/1956). *The Stress of life.* New York: McGraw-Hill.

Executive Stress

Description

The stress experienced by executives in the workplace, executive stress, is certainly a major influence on their lives. And it is a fact of organizational life. In one study, the annual cost of executive stress in the United States was estimated at $20 billion.

There are many personal and organizational stressors to which contemporary managers and executives are subject, and they can have very serious consequences. **Anger, Anxiety, Cardiovascular Disease, Depression, Fatigue, Headaches, Insomnia,** and exacerbated **Ulcers** are some of the problems executives may experience if they do not manage their stress well.

Causes

While the sources of stress for executives are many, a study of 300 managers from 12 major companies by J. H. Howard, Ph.D., of the University of Western Ontario, pinpointed four factors in executive jobs that seem to produce the most stress:

1. *A feeling of helplessness.* When executives are prevented from acting out their proper roles, they may feel helpless, and this feeling can engender tremendous stress. For example, an executive may work hard to develop reasonable solutions to some tough problems, but be unable to apply what he or she knows because of constraints within the organization.

2. *Uncertainty.* When one is not sure of the facts (about company policy, the vagaries of a proposed budget, or what is expected of him or her) decision making is difficult and increases stress. Uncertainty about future promotions or recognition from top management also causes stress.

3. *Urgency and anxiety.* The executive's day is filled with tasks that demand great attention and effort. On average it has been found that managers do something different about every seven minutes. Their jobs may be characterized in large part by brevity and fragmentation. This, of course, is a major cause of stress if the managers do not know how to properly relax while carrying out their duties and tasks. In another context, physicians in clinical practice make life-and-death decisions on a regular basis, and this causes a lot of stress to them.

Concerns with success often generate anxiety. The intensity of this success ethic is strongest among middle managers. The quest for success through achievement and all of the symbols that go with it, such as money, power, and prestige, creates a conflict situation in which individuals compete against each other. Individuals who are especially oriented to upward mobility often suffer severe anxiety and depression.

4. *Overwork.* Executive jobs are often described as "much work at an unrelenting pace," causing executives to strain under a heavy workload. As a result of overwork, they may not be able to take time off to relax; they are under pressure to complete one project after the other.

These four stress producers can appear in all kinds of on-the-job situations. They can generally be attributed to poor management, lack of authority, blurred organizational structure, company politics, personnel problems, and so forth. It is important to manage stress effectively in the workplace to ensure appropriate productivity.

Treatment

Effective control of executive stress should result in numerous benefits for the organization: increased productivity, good health of personnel, and the like. One obvious strategy for coping with stress is to eliminate or change the conditions that cause the stress. But since one cannot always avoid or change the environment, executives can build up their "stress resistance" by changing their approaches to and perceptions of stressful situations. In a study of executives involved in the 1983 Bell System breakup, it was found that there were big differences between executives who withstood the stresses of organizational change and those who knuckled under. Executives bothered the least by stressful circumstances had fewer illnesses than executives who had trouble coping with the same circumstances.

A first step in the process of stress control is discovering what is truly stressful to the individual and why: It is thought that understanding one's stress lessens it and gives one some control over it. Next, it helps to reconstruct a previous stressful situation. This approach has been held to "disarm stress" by putting a stressful situation in proper perspective, helping one to work out different options for handling it.

Some "anti-stress" strategies that can help executives cope with stress include **Stress Management Methods.** Relaxation techniques are especially important for controlling stress levels among executives; for example, **Differential Relaxation** (the optimal contraction of only those muscles required to successfully accomplish a given purpose, which can be practiced any time twenty-four hours a day) achieves many of those purposes.

S E E   A L S O :

Anger

Anxiety

Depression

Differential Relaxation

Fatigue, Chronic

Headaches, Migraine and Tension

Insomnia

Management-Induced Stress

Stress Management Methods

Success, Excessive Drive for

Workplace Stress

BIBLIOGRAPHY

Alisau, P. (Oct. 2, 1992). Executives and stress. *Business Mexico, 2,* 44–45.
Matteson. M. T., & Ivancevich, J. M. (1987). *Controlling work stress: Effective human resource and management strategies.* San Francisco: Jossey-Bass.
Maturi, R. (1992, July 20). Stress can be beaten. *Industry Week, 241,* 22–26.
McGuigan, F. J. (1992). *Calm down: A guide for stress and tension control.* Dubuque, IA: Kendall/Hunt.

Exercise, Benefits of

Exercise can serve many purposes. It can enhance skills, improve flexibility, build muscle strength and tone, relieve tension, help in weight loss and maintenance, and improve the body's general physiological condition, especially the ease with which the heart can supply oxygen to body tissues. Particular types of exercise may serve some of these goals but not others. For example, bowling and golf can help one become more skillful at these games, strengthen certain muscles, and expend energy (burn calories), but these are anaerobic exercises that rarely involve enough continuous activity to condition the cardiovascular system. Similarly, isometric exercises (such as weight lifting, waterskiing, and arm wrestling) can promote strong muscles but are not cardiovascular conditioners and may actually be harmful to persons with heart disease.

Aerobic exercises in which there is continuous activity for many minutes or even hours, such as running or walking, can help improve cardiovascular efficiency and metabolism, perhaps strengthening the body's resistance to the debilitating effects of stress. The heart is strengthened, blood vessels become more elastic, oxygen use becomes more efficient, resting pulse rate is lowered, and blood fats such as triglycerides and cholesterol will likely be lowered. The result is a decreased likelihood of **Cardiovascular Diseases.** The simplest, most readily available forms of aerobic exercise are brisk walking, jogging, and sustained running. (However, sprinting is not an aerobic activity.) Other effective aerobic activities include swimming, bicycling, cross-country skiing, rowing, and jumping rope.

Aerobic exercises should be performed at least three times a week for 20 minutes at a time, during which the heart rate is within the individual's "target zone." The target zone falls between 70 and 85 percent of the maximum rate the heart can achieve. The maximum heart rate (or pulse rate, counted as beats per minute) can be estimated for the average healthy person as 220 minus one's age in years. Take 70 to 85 percent of that number for the pulse rate range that is your target zone. A conditioning exercise should be done regularly, or the benefits will be lost rapidly. If you stop for a week or more, resume at a lower-level workout and gradually build up again.

Some research suggests that exercise may be effective in reducing the stress-related ailments of anxiety and depression. Fifteen to 20 minutes of vigorous exercise appears to stimulate the secretion of both catecholamines and endorphins. Depressive people are often deficient in catecholamines, and endorphins are natural pain killers and mood elevators.

In choosing an exercise, it is important to know what you hope to get out of it and whether that choice will help you achieve your goals. Most people start exercising because they want to look better and feel better. Often, however, the chosen activity spurs a change or expansion of goals. For example, those who take up tennis to reduce stress or flab may find themselves huffing and puffing on the court. Realizing that they are "out of condition," they may start running or cycling to improve their bodies' ability to deliver oxygen to their muscles.

Any type of exercise, from hanging laundry and scrubbing floors to badminton, skating, football, or long-distance running, can help you control your weight. Weight gain represents an excess number of calories consumed over the number of calories your body burns up for energy.

Any kind of motion involves the expenditure of more calories than your body uses at rest. The more you move, the more calories you burn. And the heavier you are to start with, the more calories it takes to move yourself a given distance. As an added benefit, moderate exercise improves the accuracy of your body's **Weight Control** mechanism and more frequently decreases rather than increases appetite. In addition to the calories burned while exercising, your body continues to burn calories at a higher than normal rate for up to four hours after you stop exercising. Some activities are intense energy guzzlers, using eight or more times the amount of calories your body burns at rest. These include sustained running at more than 5.5 miles an hour, cycling 13 or more miles an hour, playing squash or handball, and skipping rope. But you can burn as many calories playing Ping-Pong or volleyball for an hour as you would running for half an hour.

Studies by Dr. James Rippe, head of the Center for Clinical and Lifestyle Research at Tufts University, provides good news for those who are not die-hard athletic exercisers but are still concerned about getting enough exercise. The traditional recommendation has been to exercise at least 20 minutes at least three times per week, at 60 to 90 percent of maximum heart rate. However, Dr. Rippe found that even small amounts of exercise, such as 10 minutes of gardening or 15 minutes walking the dog, helped prevent heart attacks. Dr. Rippe proposed that accumulating 30 minutes of any activity most days as a lifelong habit substantially decreases your risk of heart disease.

When choosing an exercise regime, it would be wise to consider these factors:

■ *Time availability:* Running and indoor stationary cycling can be conveniently done. Organized sports tend to be more time-consuming and restrictive. For those short of time and who can take the rigor of the activity, jumping rope for 10 minutes can provide a conditioning effect equivalent to 30 minutes of jogging.

■ *Cost and convenience:* Tennis, for example, may involve driving miles to a court, paying high fees, searching for a partner, and arranging schedules, all of which may discourage regular participation. The cost of a bicycle (indoor or out) may be prohibitive for some, but a jump rope is inexpensive. Sex may be convenient, inexpensive, and burn calories, but to achieve a conditioning effect, the pre-orgasmic level of activity would have to be maintained for at least 20 minutes.

■ *The body's capabilities.* If you are not well-coordinated, ball games, jumping rope, and the like may prove frustrating. If you are tight-jointed, you may need flexibility-enhancing exercises (calisthenics) before you try running or tennis.

■ *Age, health status, and physical condition:* The older the person, the less rigorous the activity he or she needs to bring the heart rate into the target zone. The older one is, the more important it is to check with a physician before starting a rigorous exercise program. The physician may give you an exercise stress test to see what level of activity your cardiovascular system can tolerate.

Beyond about age 50, you should condition yourself first through a walking program before beginning more strenuous exercises. Beyond age about 60, most people should be cautious about beginning the more taxing exercises, such as jogging and competitive sports; perhaps walking, swimming, and cycling should be considered. At any age, if you have been sedentary for years or are out of condition, start slowly and work up to more demanding activities. Anyone with a chronic illness or muscle or joint problems should consult a physician before starting to exercise.

■ *Personal taste:* You are more likely to stick with an exercise that you enjoy, but you should give a new activity a real trial before deciding to stop it. There is no one best exercise for everyone. In fact, varying your exercise activities will help to exercise different parts of your body, diminishing the chances of injury that can result when some muscles are developed at the expense of others.

SEE ALSO:

Cardiovascular Disease
Running, Relaxed

Sports Performance, Bodily
Conditioning and Injuries

BIBLIOGRAPHY

Davis, S. A. (1983). *How to stay healthy in an unhealthy world.* New York: William Morrow.
Dubbert, P. M. (1992). Exercise in behavioral medicine. *Journal of Consulting and Clinical Psychology, 60,* 613–618.
Dubbert, P. M. (1998). Exercise. In E. A. Blechman & K. D. Brownell (Eds.), *Behavioral medicine & women: A comprehensive handbook.* New York: Guilford Press.
Laitner, W. (1994, June 28). *Exercise accumulated during day also counts.* Detroit, MI: Detroit Free Press.
Marcus, B., Dubbert, P. M., King, A. C., & Pinto, B. M. (1995). Physical activity in women: Current status and future directions. In A. Stanton & S. Gallant (Eds.), *The psychology of women's health* (pp. 349–379). Washington, DC: American Psychological Association.
Zohman, L. R. (1974). *Beyond diet: Exercise your way to fitness and heart health.* Englewood Cliffs, NJ: CPC International.

F

Family Stress–Frustration

Family Stress

Description

A family that functions well is one that draws upon its resources to meet stressors and becomes stronger by conquering problems. A family that does not bring forth enough resources to cope with stressors allows the strain to fragment the group. The healthy family, in contrast to the unhealthy family, develops creative techniques, flexible rules, and mutual support.

Family stress uniquely involves intimate interrelationships such that, if one member is under stress, it affects the whole family.

The toll on individuals in these highly stressed situations is extremely high. Some research indicates that people who are divorced have higher rates of suicide, homicide, and cancer and are three times more likely to get into car accidents than nondivorced people.

Causes

Serious family stressors include major illnesses, death of a loved one, change or loss of job, change of home location, separation, and divorce. Divorce has become one of the most common and most damaging of these stressors to the American family. Children and parents are often hurt emotionally and develop scars that hinder effective family functioning. The most frequent stressor reported in families is in the area of economics: the financing and budgeting of family life. Other stressors, in order of priority after the first, are children's behavior/discipline/sibling fighting; insufficient time for couples; lack of shared responsibility in the family; and insufficient time for the individuals.

Surveys of individuals indicate that 34 percent of women reported poor self-image and self-esteem as well as feelings of unattractiveness as significant stressors, while only 1 percent of men so reported this category. Men cited as a source of top stress that they want to spend more time viewing television, particularly sports, naming it as their number one "me time" activity.

Treatment

An important step for becoming resilient to these stressors is to create stable family relationships. The more emotional support one has from friends and family, the more options there are for support in stressful situations. Activities that include healthy interactions are essential for building a social support system. Reaching out to extended family can also strengthen support options.

Healthy families view stressors as a normal part of life and do not seek "perfection"; they anticipate stressors and develop ways of coping that are both traditional and unique. The healthy family shares ideas and feelings, makes use of supports, and is adaptable.

A family's ability in dealing effectively with stressors has been related to how much prior experience they have had in coping with them. The more stressors they had faced, the more skills they developed. Stress-effective families also distinguish between stressors they can and cannot control. They focus their energies on controllable stresses and tolerate the others.

SEE ALSO:

Addictive Behaviors   Grief
Alcoholism   Money (Financial) Stress

BIBLIOGRAPHY

Curran, D. (1987). *Stress and the healthy family.* San Francisco: Harper & Row.
Figley, C. R. (1997). *Burnout in families: The systematic costs of caring.* Boca Raton, FL: St. Lucie Press.
Hetherington, M. E., & Blechman, E. A. (Eds.). (1996). *Stress, coping and resiliency in children and families.* Mahwah, NJ: Erlbaum.
Kaslow, F. W., & Ridenour, R. I. (1984). *The military family.* New York: Guilford Press.

Fatigue, Chronic

Description

Chronic fatigue (the so called "yuppie flu"), also referred to as chronic fatigue syndrome, is a debilitating fatigue for which other medical diagnoses have been excluded. It manifests itself as an inability to concentrate or to perform, as muscular soreness, and as difficulty in relaxing fully. This "syndrome" is typically described by patients as a feeling of being "completely worn out." Other symptoms may include ocular disorders, weakness, sore throat and lymph nodes, confusion, **Headaches, Gastrointestinal Disorders** and **Bruxism. Depression** may also occur when the fatigue is so long-standing that the individual sees no way out and feels hopelessness and extreme unhappiness.

Causes

Chronic fatigue may be caused by long-term, unrelieved overtension in the muscles used in the fight-or-flight pattern, produced by inadequate coping with stressors. Overtension in the muscles used to "fight" leads to muscular fatigue and spasm in the arms, shoulders, neck, and chest. Muscles involved in "fleeing" include those of the hips, back, and legs. Muscle fatigue occurs due to a buildup of metabolic waste products such as lactic acid, resulting in the reduced capacity of muscle tissue to contract and relax. Emotional fatigue occurs as a general debilitated state resulting from excessive conflicts, frustrations, and anxieties. Mental fatigue occurs as cognitive weariness stemming from either long-term mental concentration or boredom.

Treatment

Fatigue can be prevented or alleviated by conserving energy of the body. This can be accomplished by first making a moment-by-moment subjective observation of one's energy expenditure. As individuals monitor themselves, they identify unwanted muscular tensions and then relax them. In the early stages of monitoring tensions and relaxing them away, the process is a conscious one. However, with continued practice, individuals can reach a state of unconsciously performing the act. In time, individuals can be able to automatically and optimally tense only those muscles that are required to perform the act at hand; they can thus conserve energy 24 hours a day to allow for vigorous activity directed to primary goals. This process is referred to as **Differential Relaxation.**

When other physiological symptoms are involved, medical attention (including medication) may also be necessary.

S E E   A L S O :

Bruxism
Depression
Differential Relaxation

Fatigue, "Nervous"
Gastrointestinal Disorders
Headaches, Migraine and Tension

B I B L I O G R A P H Y

Demitrack, M. A., & Abbey, S. E. (Eds.). (1996). *Chronic fatigue syndrome: An integrative approach to evaluation and treatment*. New York: Guilford Press.
McGuigan, F. J. (1992). *Calm Down: A guide for stress and tension control* (2nd ed.). Dubuque, IA: Kendall/Hunt.
Solomon, N., & Lipton, M. (1989). *Chronic fatigue and other ailments*. New York: Wynwood.

Fatigue, "Nervous"

Description

Fatigue is one of the most common complaints or symptoms in the field of medicine. It may be accompanied by nervousness or an unhealthy way in which one "looks" to others. Fatigue may be a contributing cause of organic disorders within the body, and may affect a person's personality and relationships with others. The pathophysiology of "nervous" fatigue is a common concern among many health professionals.

A person who suffers from neuromuscular hypertension and therefore possible fatigue as well may look relatively calm. The accepted way to detect the high rate of such overtension (excess neuromuscular activity) is through laboratory testing with an electromyograph. This system well reveals a person's failure to relax.

Causes

Possible causes of fatigue are numerous but primarily include failure to cope with various environmental stressors. Fatigue occurs when skeletal and other muscles surpass the ordinary state of **Tension.** Therefore, increased skeletal and visceral muscle tension plays an important role in causing and understanding nervous fatigue. Other factors include poor nutrition, poor sleep habits, and insufficient exercise.

Treatment

As always for problems that concern overtension ("stress"), the best treatment for decreasing or controlling nervous fatigue is, through the practice of **Relaxation,** to acquire the desired neuromuscular control of the body. One can then optimally use only the muscles needed to perform the task at hand, saving energy and preventing the nervousness that causes fatigue.

Change of diet, medication, hobbies, vacations, and other such things are not effective methods of treatment. Not only will these fail to work in controlling nervous fatigue, they could possibly contribute to further nervousness and stress.

SEE ALSO:

Fatigue, Chronic
Progressive Relaxation

BIBLIOGRAPHY

Gottlieb, B. H. (Ed.). (1997). *Coping with chronic stress.* New York: Plenum.
Gutwirth, S. W. (1957, May). *Elimination of nervous fatigue.* Chicago: Dental Survey.
Solomon, N., & Lipton, M. (1989). *Chronic fatigue and other ailments.* New York: Wynwood.
Teitelbaum, J. (1995). *From fatigued to fantastic.* Annapolis, MD: Deva.

Fear

Description

Fear is a natural inborn avoidance response pattern with a propensity to flee or hide; it is characterized by unpleasant, often intense, feelings. Fear is accompanied by heightened activity of the sympathetic nervous system, the nervous system that functions to shift blood flow and make other bodily adjustments for energy needed for fight or flight. Common bodily reactions accompanying fear include pounding heart, rapid pulse, heightened muscle tension ("stress"), irritability, dry throat, nervous perspiration, increased respiration, and "butterflies" in the stomach. The esophagus, containing a combination of smooth and striated muscles, responds to threat by contracting into a mild spasm that can last for hours, days, or even months. In a prolonged condition of anxiety and fear, chronic muscle spasm can feel like a "lump" in the throat (**Esophageal Spasm/Globus Hystericus**). In fact, the term "anxiety" was introduced into the English language from the thirteenth-century French word *anguisse,* which meant a "painful sensation in the throat," as when a fishbone was stuck there.

When recurring fear is intense and unreasonable, it may be classified as a **Phobia.** Phobias may be fears that are out of proportion to real dangers (such as refusing to go into an elevator) or to a stimulus that poses no threat (such as a fear of the color yellow).

Causes

Noxious stimuli can lead to the motivated behaviors referred to as fear and anxiety that energize us for fight or flight. The tensing of muscles is a natural reaction, part of the primitive startle response pattern that prepares us for fight or flight. We learn to fear certain objects or events because they are associated with pain or prospect of pain. Representations of a feared stimulus are carried in those muscles.

Fear has survival value: When we learn to fear a painful stimulus, we can anticipate it in order to avoid it. If we have too little fear, we might not behave effectively to avoid a painful or harmful stimulus. There is an optimal amount of fear for efficient behavior.

However, excessive and inappropriate learned fears can generate behaviors that interfere with effectiveness. If we are fearful to the pathological point of anxiety or phobia, we can expect ineffective behavior for life's tasks.

A stressful situation may set off a first anxiety attack, then the fear of the anxiety attack itself can take on a life of its own. An initial fear experience is often an unforgettable anxiety attack, which may occur when the person is under unusual physical or psychological stress. Typical prephobic stresses include getting married or divorced, the birth of a child, the serious illness of a loved one, moving away from home, a personal illness, a serious accident, or a surgical operation. Any major life change can be stressful and may, in a vulnerable person, precipitate fear and an anxiety attack.

Treatment

Since a learned fear is represented in the striated muscles, relaxation of those muscles can relax the fear away. **Progressive Relaxation** can significantly program one to control fear evoked by stressors and can teach one to face situations with calm confidence. Another form of treatment is desensitization, exposing yourself little by little to the situation and saying to yourself that as bad as it feels, it will pass; and it can work.

Certain antianxiety medications such as Xanax, Ativan, Librium, and Serax can reduce feelings of panic. However, addiction is a risk factor with these drugs.

Cutting down on alcohol and caffeine may be effective because they can trigger the release of adrenaline, which has been linked to **Panic Attacks.**

SEE ALSO:

Agoraphobia
Anxiety
Esophageal Spasm/Globus
    Hystericus
Panic Attacks

Phobic Disorders
Progressive Relaxation
Social Phobia
Systematic Desensitization

BIBLIOGRAPHY

Amacon, R. T. (1993). *The psychology of fear and stress.* New York: McGraw-Hill.
Ryan, K. (1991). *Driving fear out of the workplace.* San Francisco: Jossey-Bass.

Female Stress

Description

"Female Stress Syndrome" is a label for what a woman experiences when chronic or excessive social or psychological demands are placed upon her by others or by herself. Early symptoms include **Fatigue,** loss of concentration, **Headaches,** and **Depression.** Extreme cases of female stress can lead to premenstrual tension, loss of menstruation, **Sexual Dysfunction** (frigidity, vaginismus, etc.), infertility, postpartum depression, and menopausal melancholia, as well as **Anorexia, Bulimia,** and **Anxiety.**

Causes

The major causes for the stresses and tensions faced by many women today stem from the socialization process and role expectations placed upon them at an early age. A common idea that women should be less assertive, less logical, more emotional, and more nurturing than men often conflicts with the demands placed upon them, especially in the workplace. Furthermore, because women are traditionally viewed as being homemakers as well, the energy requirements to fulfill both career and homemaking can be stress-inducing.

It has also been held that an important cause of the "Female Stress Syndrome" is women's fear of failure and fear of success. Fear of failure may be the result of years of being shamed or teased by boys, brothers, fathers, mothers, or teachers when a public performance of athletic, mechanical, or combative prowess was attempted. Fear of success may result from years of being warned against being "too smart" or "too strong" or "too independent." Consequently, all of these factors may cause and contribute to women's stresses in today's society.

Treatment

Women experiencing such stress can themselves first recognize when symptoms occur. Then they should support themselves with a healthy diet, regular exercise, time for their own enjoyments, and adequate rest. Working women could strive to assure more assertiveness over their careers and lifestyles; this includes setting challenging goals, focusing on achievement rather than seeking praise, basing decision-making on solid facts rather than mere opinions, and avoiding self-blame.

SEE ALSO:

Anorexia	Headache, Migraine and Tension
Anxiety	Infertility
Bulimia	Menopause
Depression	Menstruation
Fatigue, Chronic	Sexual Dysfunction in Women

BIBLIOGRAPHY

Murphy, P. A. (1993). *A career and life planning guide for women survivors: Making the connections workbook.* Boca Raton, FL: St. Lucie Press.

Murphy, P. A. (1993). *Making the connections: Women, work, and abuse.* Boca Raton, FL: St. Lucie Press.

Stanton, A. L., & Gallant, S. J. (1995). *The psychology of women's health: Progress and challenges in research and application.* Washington, DC: American Psychological Association.

Witkin-Lanoil, G. (1984). *The Female stress syndrome: How to recognize and live with it.* New York: Newmarket.

Food Abuse

Description

An estimate is that about 23 percent of the people in the Western world suffer from a food abuse disorder. Food abuse exists when an individual responds to food in pathological and self-defeating ways. Some characteristics associated with the psychological disorder of food abuse include obsessively thinking about food, inability to exercise voluntary control over eating, going on and off diets, and being extremely dissatisfied with one's body image.

Causes

One of the principal reasons that people abuse food is that they connect it with satisfying certain emotional needs. The wish to eat often arises in many people in the face of almost any emotional lack. Depression, anxiety, anger, boredom, and stress are common causal factors in food abuse. Thus, excessive eating may possibly take the place of sexual satisfaction, be a reaction to excessive anxiety, be an attempt to control stressful reactions, be a way to attempt to cope with boredom, be possible substitutes for love and attention, be an expression of anger, and so forth.

SEE ALSO (AND FOR TREATMENT):

Behavior Therapy   Obesity
Eating Disorders   Stress Management Methods

BIBLIOGRAPHY

Capaldi, E. D. (Ed.). (1996). *Why we eat what we eat: The psychology of eating.* Washington, DC: American Psychological Association.

Christensen, L. (1996). *Diet-behavior relationship: Focus on depression.* Washington, DC: American Psychological Association.

Garner, D. M., & Garfinkel, P. L. (Eds.). (1997). *Handbook of treatment for eating disorders* (2nd ed.). New York: Guilford Press.

Kaplan, A. S., & Garfinkel, P. (1993). *Medical issues and the eating disorders.* New York: Brunner/Mazel.

Frustration

Description

Frustration has been described as a subjective feeling that an individual experiences when meeting an obstacle that prevents the achievement of a desired goal or outcome. Frustration may lead to **Anger,** then often to Aggression. The chronically frustrated person may suffer from such ailments as high blood pressure, gastrointestinal disorder, and depression. The aggression that an individual expresses may not always be outward (overt) but may also be directed within (covert). Frustration may, in these ways, cause emotional upset that interferes with attention, planning, and other important mental processes.

Causes

Any situation that blocks the achievement of a desired outcome may cause frustration. These barriers may be, for example, a lack of skill to perform a particular task, or bad weather that prevents a picnic.

Treatment

One way to overcome frustration is to eliminate the barrier to progress. This process of dealing with the barrier and seeking readjustment has been called a "coping sequence." For example, when a motivated individual pursuing a goal encounters a barrier that prevents further progress, that person may search for a way to overcome the obstacle by varying the responses to the barrier; or he or she may choose to settle for a less effective adjustment such as withdrawing from the situation, pursuing a substitute goal, or, unfortunately, retreating into a world of his or her own creation.

The seminal work on frustration was done by Dollard and his colleagues (Dollard et al., 1969).

SEE ALSO:

Anger
Emotional Behavior, Destructive

Hypertenstion, Essential (High
Blood Pressure)
Role Conflict

BIBLIOGRAPHY

Janis, I. L. (1971). *Stress and frustration.* New York: Harcourt Brace Jovanovich.
Dollard, J., Doob, L., Miller, N., & Sears, R. (1969). *Frustration and aggression.* New Haven, CT: Yale University Press.
Humphry, J. H. (1998). *Job stress.* Boston: Allyn & Bacon.
Yates, A. (1962). *Frustration and conflict.* New York: Wiley.

G

Gambling–Grief

Gambling

Description

Compulsive—or addictive—behavior often fits a positive feedback model wherein there is repeated uncontrolled acting out of the behavior pattern until the abuser's system goes out of control. For example, a cocaine addict may ingest a substance until death, an alcoholic may similarly experience blackout, and a gambler may run out of money or collateral.

Compulsive gamblers usually continue gambling regardless of whether they are winning or losing. However, lack of control is more serious when they are losing, perhaps because they are obsessed with the notion that a big win is just one bet away. Some gamblers typically believe that the laws of probability, which are certain to lead to losses, do not apply to them. But even if they understand that they will eventually lose, their control is less than that of noncompulsive gamblers.

Compulsive gamblers often destroy their families as they ignore family needs and lose money to gambling. The compulsion to make up for their losses frequently leads them to run up large debts and then even to steal. Further, the compulsive gambler is often self-destructive. For example, one-third of the compulsive gamblers sampled in one study had serious weight problems, 42 percent were drug abusers, 38 percent had cardiovascular problems, and 50 percent had violated laws.

Destructive gambling often extends beyond racetrack betting and the like to include actions by financially successful business entrepreneurs. Why someone who has millions or billions of dollars breaks laws to amass even more constitutes a really serious behavioral control problem for society; for example, the citizens of the United States lost upwards of $500 billion in a series of savings and loan facility failures in the late 1980s. Perhaps some of that loss could be accounted for by executives who gambled with other people's money.

Causes

Compulsive gambling is typically learned by age 20, but there are gender differences—women generally prefer lotteries, bingo, and slot machines, while men prefer sports betting. Like other behaviors, gambling is maintained through reinforcement. Because the reinforcements are intermittent (not given on each and every bet), the conditioning is very powerful (i.e., those who receive only occasional, intermittent reinforcements for a response take longer to extinguish the response than those who are continuously reinforced for each response). Reinforcements include not only money, but also the excitement of placing bets and anticipating winning.

Treatment

A general therapeutic principle is that control of both normal and aberrant behavior can be achieved by behavioral methods. If learned, gambling behavior can be controlled through conditioning. For example, mild electric shocks administered to the fingers as gamblers played slot machines, read racing forms, and so on have been moderately successful in correcting gambling behavior. **Relaxation** therapy has also been somewhat successful—the individuals visualize themselves approaching the gambling situation, then relax their muscles. Through such relaxation therapy, they may gain control of the muscles they use to engage in gambling behavior.

SEE ALSO:

Addictive Behaviors
Alcoholism
Alcohol Abuse in the Workplace
Compulsive Behavior

Drug Abuse in the Workplace
Obsessive-Compulsive Behavior
Progressive Relaxation
Tobacco Use

BIBLIOGRAPHY

Gottheil, E., Druley, K., Pashko, S., & Weinstein, S. P. (1987). *Stress and addiction*. New York: Brunner/Mazel.
Legg-England, S., & Gotestam, K. S. (1991). The nature and treatment of excessive gambling. *Acta Psychiatrica Scandinavica, 84,* 113–120.
McCarthy, J. (1995). Addictive behaviors: Relationship factors and their perceived influence on change. *Genetic, Social and General Psychology Monographs, 121,* 39–64

Gastrointestinal Disorders

Description

The gastrointestinal tract is a long tube consisting almost exclusively of smooth muscles; it extends from the mouth through the stomach, intestines, and anus. Gastrointestinal tract conditions can also affect the pancreas and liver. Estimates are that about 18 percent of Americans have some form of gastrointestinal tract disorder, including **Colitis, Constipation, Diarrhea, Hemorrhoids, Irritable Bowel Syndrome, Pain, Spastic Colon,** ulcerative colitis, and **Ulcers.** Some common characteristics are breakdown of the mucus lining of stomach and intestine walls, vomiting, bleeding, cramping, weight loss, and fecal urgency.

Causes

Chronic muscular overtension is a primary contributor to many gastrointestinal disorders. In turn, high levels of gastric acid secretion with pathologic consequences may be increased by such conditions as anger or resentment and extreme compulsive traits.

Helicobacter pylori bacteria play a primary causative role in peptic **Ulcers;** since antibiotics help to alleviate ulcers, infection is almost always a causal agent, though ulcers can be exacerbated by inadequate coping with stressors. There is some suggestion that a genetic component, in terms of a predisposition, is involved in ulcers. Stress, bad food, and diet do not cause ulcers, though they can exacerbate them.

Treatment

Barium contrast X rays have allowed indirect visualization of the gastrointestinal tract for many years; modern fiber optics and video endoscopy have revolutionized diagnosis and treatment of gastrointestinal disorders. Direct visualization of the upper gastrointestinal tract with an endoscope allows detection of ulcers, tumors, and inflammatory lesions. The various gastrointestinal disorders have been treated with medication and surgery. **Progressive Relaxation** is very effective treatment for many of these stress-related gastrointestinal tract disorders.

Therapeutic applications of upper endoscopy include detection of scars, removal of polyps, and treatment of bleeding sites. Endoscopic visualization of the colon allows direct visualization of colonic polyps, cancers, and inflammation.

SEE ALSO:

Colitis

Constipation

Diarrhea

Esophageal Spasm/Globus Hystericus

Hemorrhoids

Irritable Bowel Syndrome

Pain

Progressive Relaxation

Spastic Colon

Ulcers, Peptic, Gastric and Duodenal

BIBLIOGRAPHY

Brandt, Lawrence. J. (1991). *Gastrointestinal disorders.* Glasgow, England: Collins Fount.

Magalini, S. I., Magalini, S. C., & Francisci, G. (1990). *Dictionary of medical syndromes* (3rd ed.). Philadelphia: Lippincott.

Sapolsky, R. M. (1994). *Why zebras don't get ulcers: A guide to stress, stress-related diseases, and coping.* New York: Freeman.

Thompson, W. G. (1993). *The angry gut.* New York: Plenum.

Grief

Description

Grief is a common initial reaction to the stress of serious loss. It is a stressful behavior in which, among other reactions, there is excessive muscular **Tension** that exacerbates emotional behavior. The loss of one who is dearly loved brings great subjective emotional pain and grief. One may feel "numb," restless, guilty, and disorganized, and one may cry. Often the sufferer thinks he or she could have done more for the one who died—perhaps, though, not knowing how. **Anger** may occur against the world in general because the person died. Loneliness is one of the most serious results of grief.

Causes

Grief is considered a major form of stress. On **Stressful Life Events** scales, loss of a principal attachment figure is perceived as the most significant stressor. This loss creates a crisis wherein the person may be thrown into a state of helplessness, coping mechanisms may no longer be successful in mastering problems, defenses are weakened, and the person is dependent on the help of others. This crisis state can last for many weeks, with intermittent feelings of strong and weaker grief.

A woman, for instance, who loses her husband may have much cause for alarm. Perhaps she lost a confidant with whom she discussed matters. She is likely to be exposed to novel situations that create problems in her new role as widow. For people in this situation, the world can seem a treacherous place in which grief is typical.

Treatment

There are a number of assumptions that are maintained about how to respond to serious loss, such as death of a loved one. Some expect that there will be a period of intense distress and that failure to experience such distress indicates a psychological problem. Some assume that successful adjustment to loss requires that people "work through" their feelings of grief and not deny them. By such grieving, it is anticipated that within a reasonable period of time people recover from their loss and return to their typical level of functioning.

In contrast to such common beliefs, Grecco (1992) reports that: (1) intense distress does not invariably follow a major loss or a severe disabling injury; (2) those who fail to experience distress do not necessarily have difficulties later: actually, to the contrary, those most depressed following a loss also are most depressed one or two years later; (3) a substantial minority of individuals continue to exhibit distress for a much longer period than is normally assumed; and (4) individuals are not always able to achieve resolution of the loss.

Thus, some persons do not show distress initially or even after a period of time, others continue to remain in a state of high distress, yet others follow a course from high to low stress, and so forth. Just how a person reacts to a particular stressor depends on many factors: the characteristics of the stressor; the individual's repertoire of coping techniques; how he or she perceives the situation in the light of previous experiences; his or her capacity to tolerate anxiety, and so forth.

Therapy or bereavement groups are often prescribed as treatment, depending upon the characteristics of the person. It is quite normal not to recommend a group until some of the initial "numbness" has worn off and the person has begun to understand the reality of the situation. Individuals, sometimes, have a tendency to isolate themselves, which usually has not proven to be a healthy or successful bereavement strategy—typically one requires support of a group, family, and friends. Such support assists in relieving the feelings of "loss of control" that many individuals experience and the dependence one initially has on others. Eventually the person can get back in charge, promote dependence on self, and relieve health damaging stress. After the initial shock diminishes, relaxation therapy can help.

SEE ALSO:

Stressful Life Events
Stress Management Methods
Tension Awareness

BIBLIOGRAPHY

Dershimer, R. A. (1990). *Counseling the bereaved.* New York: Pergamon Press.
Grecco, M. (1992). *Emotion and stress.* Washington, DC: American Psychiatric Press.
Kubler-Ross, E. (1986). *Death: The final stage of growth.* New York: Simon & Schuster.
Parkes, C. M. (1974). *Bereavement.* New York: International Universities Press.
Rando, T. A. (1993). *Treatment of complicated mourning.* Champaign, IL: Research Press.
Raphael, B. (1983). *The anatomy of bereavement.* New York: Basic Books.
Sprang, G., & McNeil, J. (1995). *The many faces of bereavement: The nature and treatment of natural, traumatic and stigmatized grief.* New York: Brunner/Mazel.

H | Headache–Hypochondriasis

Headache, Migraine and Tension

Description

Pain that occurs over various parts of the head constitutes headaches—one of humankind's most common afflictions. In the United States alone, up to 50 million persons seek medical help for this problem every year, and about half a billion dollars is spent on headache remedies annually.

Headaches are characterized by tension and muscle cramping through the head, neck, and shoulders. Individuals suffering from headaches may lose concentration and/or be unable to work. Additionally, migraine headaches are often accompanied by nausea, vomiting, and visual disturbances. Tension headaches have been described by victims in such graphic terms as having a rawhide band wound tightly around the forehead, or a hammer beating inside the skull.

A migraine headache is usually concentrated on one side of the head (*migraine* from the Greek meaning "pain in one side of the head"). These headaches are often preceded by such warning symptoms as fatigue, nausea, vomiting, blurred vision, and sensitivity to light and sound. Approximately a third of migraine sufferers also experience the sensation of flashing light in the eyes (an aurora), numbness in the arms and legs, slurred speech, dizziness, ringing in the ears, difficulty in expressing themselves, and the feeling of pins and needles spreading around the mouth. When the migraine headache actually starts, the warning symptoms tend to dissipate but are replaced by intense, gripping pain that often spreads across the forehead. A throbbing pain follows, which usually develops in the entire head but may be centered between the nose and eyes. The duration varies considerably. In extremely rare occurrences, the visual disturbances and numbness have been known to become permanent.

There is a very high incidence of depression and analgesic abuse in patients with chronic daily headache.

Causes

The mechanism of all tension headaches is a contraction of the muscles, especially over the eyes, at the back of the head, in the neck, and above the shoulders. The tensed muscles impinge upon various nerves, and the contractions also constrict blood vessels. Such constriction of blood vessels and irritation of the nerves lead to the eruption of the headache. Headaches vary accordingly in location, frequency, intensity, and duration.

The term "tension headache" implies to some that emotional tension is a precipitating mechanism. Patients with this condition typically have headaches as responses to the stresses of every day life.

Age, heredity, gender, and diet appear to be factors in migraine headaches. Children rarely have migraine headaches prior to reaching puberty; however, those who have unexplained abdominal pain have a tendency to develop migraines later in life. If one has not experienced a migraine before age 40, it is rare for migraines to begin, and some victims experience relief during middle age. Migraines may run in families and are slightly more common in women. Some migraine sufferers are affected by diet. Such foods as cheese, chocolate, red wine or coffee may trigger attacks. Certain medications such as birth control pills may also contribute to the onset of migraines.

Stressors that can trigger a migraine include sudden changes in weather, barometric pressure, sleep habits, and emotional pressures, as well as missing meals. Those who react intensely to stressful situations and criticism, or who are prone to taking on guilt for not meeting the expectations of self or others, are also at an increased risk for migraines.

Treatment

Headaches have been treated in numerous ways throughout history. As long ago as 5000 B.C., the Chinese used acupuncture. The Greek physician Galen wrote about headaches in his treatise *Maintaining Good Health;* following his lead, Roman and medieval physicians used cathartics and bloodletting for treatment.

Tension headaches typically do not respond effectively to simple analgesics. Chronic tension headaches are sometimes related to depression and are often treated with antidepressant drugs.

Biofeedback has been used to teach tension headache patients how to prevent the muscle spasms that bring on their pain. Biofeedback treatment of migraine headaches has been used on the presumed vascular mechanism associated with the condition. Treatment has often focused upon skin temperature feedback, since complaints of cold hands and feet are common among migraine sufferers. There is good evidence that patients who suffer from migraine attacks can be helped by means of biofeedback and relaxation training.

Relaxation techniques, by definition, help tension headache sufferers, if effectively applied. The most effective method is **Progressive Relaxation,** where the primary muscle controls are typically those of the brow and eyes. Consequently, special attention is paid to the practice of controlling tension in the eye region. This concentration starts at the neck muscles, which, as physiologists have long known, are extensions of the eyes. After relaxing the neck muscles, the patient practices wrinkling the forehead, frowning, and then systematically tensing and relaxing the eye muscles themselves. Eventually, with diligent practice, the patient can differentially relax the eye musculature in all of its components, thereby eliminating the pains of tension headaches. While progressive relaxation can successfully treat tension headaches, it has also been effective in controlling migraine headaches.

SEE ALSO:

Biofeedback
Headaches in Children
Progressive Relaxation

BIBLIOGRAPHY

Holroyd, K. A., & Andrasik, F. (1980). Self-control of tension headache. In F. J. McGuigan, W. E. Sime, & J. M. Wallace (Eds.), *Stress and tension control: Vol. 1.* New York: Plenum.
Madders, J. (1980). Group relaxation in the treatment of migraine: A multifactorial approach. In F. J. McGuigan, W. E. Sime, & J. M. Wallace (Eds.), *Stress and tension control: Vol. 1.* New York: Plenum.
McGuigan, F. J. (1992). *Calm down: A guide for stress and tension control* (2nd ed.). Dubuque, IA: Kendall/Hunt.
Murphy, W. (1982). *Dealing with headaches.* Alexandria, VA: Time-Life Books.
Wycoff, B. (1991). *Overcoming migraine.* Barrytown, NY: Station Hill.

Headaches in Children

Description

About 1.5 percent of children experience headaches by the age of seven, 5 percent by the age of 15. Muscle contraction (**Tension**) and migraine headaches are believed to occur in them with about equal frequency. In addition, children have mixed headache disorders, vascular headaches, and so forth.

Causes

Muscular contraction headaches are caused by excessive muscle tension due to inadequate coping with stressors. Migraines and others are more complex, as developed under **Headache, Migraine and Tension.**

Treatment

A number of studies have evaluated the effectiveness of relaxation training for people experiencing chronic pain, especially headaches, and found it effective; for example, Engel (1992) supported the use of **Progressive Relaxation** treatment for recurrent nonmalignant headaches in children. The children were given training for six weeks, which included integrating relaxation skills into routine activities of daily living. None of the subjects had satisfactory responses to conventional medications. During weekly sessions, which were attended by a parent of the child, progressive relaxation techniques were used. Tapes were given to children to facilitate daily home practice. The children were instructed to keep a log of their daily relaxation and pain responses.

Upon completion of the program, 80 percent of the children had an average of 15 percent increase in headache-free days. All of the subjects reported decreases in daily headache duration. Eighty percent of the subjects reported decreases in the peak severity of their headaches during treatment. There were also average reductions in necessary rest times for headaches as well as decreased medication intake.

SEE ALSO:

Headache, Migraine and Tension
Progressive Relaxation
Tension Awareness

BIBLIOGRAPHY

Engel, J. M. (1992). Relaxation training: A self help approach for children with headaches. *The American Journal of Occupational Therapy, 46*, 591–596.
Holroyd, K. A., & Andrasik, F. (1980). Self-control of tension headache. In F. J. McGuigan, W. E. Sime, & J. M. Wallace (Eds.), *Stress and tension control: Vol. 1.* New York: Plenum.
McGuigan, F. J. (1992). *Calm down: A guide for stress and tension control* (2nd ed.). Dubuque, IA: Kendall/Hunt.
Murphy, W. (1982). *Dealing with headaches.* Alexandria, VA: Time-Life Books.
Wycoff, B. (1991). *Overcoming migraine.* Barrytown, New York: Station Hill.

Hemorrhoids

Description

Hemorrhoids are protrusions inside and from the anus, usually with a mucus discharge; bleeding often occurs. There are three primary internal hemorrhoidal masses with three to five secondary hemorrhoids. A history of protrusion, anal pain, or bleeding, confirmed by proctologic examination, provides a sound diagnosis.

Usually the symptoms of hemorrhoids are mild and intermittent, but severe cases can develop.

Causes

A primary cause of hemorrhoids is chronic overtension of the striated muscles, which can be exacerbated locally by straining at the stool; by constipation; and by prolonged sitting, as at a desk job. Sometimes cancer of the colon or rectum can aggravate hemorrhoids or produce similar complaints. Consequently, a sigmoido-scopy, preceded by a barium enema should be employed for serious medical treatment of hemorrhoids.

The hemorrhoids that often develop during pregnancy tend to subside afterwards without further treatment.

Treatment

Hemorrhoids are one of the first complaints that are alleviated in a patient undergoing **Progressive Relaxation** treatment (just as the condition of spastic esophagus is among the last gastrointestinal disorders to respond).

Conservative treatment that otherwise may help is adopting a low-roughage diet, using laxatives to produce soft stools, employing warm sitz baths, and the insertion of an appropriate anal suppository.

Surgery is a treatment of last resort.

SEE ALSO:

Gastrointestinal Disorders
Progressive Relaxation

BIBLIOGRAPHY

Kunz, J. R. M., & Finkel, A. J. (Eds.). (1987). *The American Medical Association family medical guide.* New York: Random House.
Janicke, D. M. (1996). Anorectal disorders. *Emergency Medicine Clinics of North America, 14,* 757–758.
MacRae, H. M., & McLeod, R. S. (1997). Comparison of hemorrhoidal treatments: A meta-analysis. *Canadian Journal of Surgery, 40,* 14–17.

Humor (Gelatology) as a Stress Management Method

Description

Humor and laughter have been found to reduce stress. Different types of humor include "productive humor," that which a person creates; "reactive humor," one's reaction to another's humor; and "coping humor," which is used as a method of dealing with stress.

Stress has been cited as a contributing cause of depression, anxiety, and several other psychological problems. Humor is one means that has been used for reducing stress disorders. Several studies indicate that, with a sense of humor, there is an easier acceptance of the stresses of life, it mitigates depression, and that laughter can overcome the fear of death itself. Laughter has been likened to "stationary jogging": It relieves tension physiologically while exercising heart, lungs, and muscles. Laughter increases heart rate and blood pressure. Circulation of blood is thus enhanced, increasing the amount of oxygen and other metabolic and nutritional components that are carried to various parts of the body. It can help relieve pain through the release of endorphins into the bloodstream. Laughter's most profound effects may occur on the immune system. Natural killer cells that destroy viruses and tumors apparently increase during a state of mirth.

Gelatology, the science of laughter, is recognized as a legitimate field of study. Studies of therapies for treating various problems due to stress indicate that humor can be therapeutic. It can be incorporated into groups as a learned interaction.

SEE ALSO:

Stress Management Methods

BIBLIOGRAPHY

Anderson, C. A., & Arnoult, L. H. (1989). An examination of perceived control, humor, irrational beliefs, and positive stress as moderators of the relation between negative stress and health. *Basic and Applied Social Psychology, 10,* 100–117.
Bizi, S., Keinan, G., & Beit-Hallahmi, B. (1988). Humor and coping with stress: A test under real-life conditions. *Personality and Individual Differences, 9,* 951–956.
Porterfield, A. L. (1987). Does sense of humor moderate the impact of life stress on psychological and physical well-being? *Journal of Research in Personality, 21,* 306–317.
Richman, J. (1995). The lifesaving function of humor with the depressed and suicidal elderly. *The Gerontologist, 35,* 271–273.

Hypertension, Essential (High Blood Pressure)

Description

Hypertension refers to chronic or recurring, excessively high blood pressure. Hypertension occurs when the blood is pumped through the arteries at a pressure that is much greater than necessary to maintain an even flow.

Blood Pressure is measured as systolic and diastolic in terms of millimeters of mercury (mm/Hg). Systolic pressure is measured at the peak of when the heart muscle pumps out blood. Diastolic pressure is measured when the heart is at rest, permitting the inflow of blood. Systolic pressure is higher than diastolic. Systolic pressure is indicated by the numerator of a ratio in which a "normal" value is less than 140 mm, and diastolic is the denominator with a "normal" value of less than 90 mm. Thus, a ratio of 140/90 is "borderline" hypertension.

An especially prevalent condition of the Western World, hypertension is present in about one of every four North American adults. The incidence rate is about twice as high among black Americans, while women are only one-half to three-fourths as likely as men to have hypertension.

Hypertension is associated with stroke and heart disease, which are leading causes of death for adults. Consequences of long-term hypertension include Atherosclerosis, kidney problems, and cerebral hemorrhage.

Symptoms of hypertension are not usually obvious unless the blood pressure is dangerously high, in which case headaches, palpitations, and a general feeling of ill health may be reported. A corresponding sign that is indicative of serious hypertension is excessive muscle **Tension.**

Causes

Arterial blood pressure is influenced by excessive contraction of the smooth muscles in the arterioles (small blood vessels); when the arterioles contract, they decrease the diameter of those vessels, driving up the pressure. The four classifications of hypertension are essential, secondary, malignant, and borderline. Essential hypertension is most common and occurs without any readily apparent reason. Secondary hypertension may occur as the result of a disorder of the kidneys, hormonal system, and the like, or with the use of oral contraceptives and during pregnancy. Malignant hypertension is characterized by a sudden, excessive, and dangerous rise in blood pressure and can be either essential or secondary. Borderline hypertension occurs frequently among smokers.

Hypertension often occurs due to aging (because of reduced elasticity of the blood vessels), hereditary factors, lifestyle, body weight, poor kidney function, and improper diet (especially excessive salt intake).

Stressors apparently can interact with a genetic predisposition to create hypertension. Children of parents with high blood pressure have an increased risk of hypertension and excessive heart reactions when experiencing stressful life events (stressors).

Anxiety can increase the risk of developing hypertension, and **Destructive Emotions** such as anger may be contributing factors. Stress may cause blood pressure to elevate to the extent of causing a cardiovascular accident (CVA), such as a stroke or an aneurysm (a permanent swelling of an artery at a weak area in the wall), which can burst or contribute to blood clotting.

Stressful life events can result in the retention, rather than the excretion, of salt and fluid. This interferes with the normal blood pressure corrective process by the kidneys, especially in people who are high heart rate reactors to stress. Blood pressure tends to fluctuate in response to a variety of external and internal factors, with sustained elevation more prevalent for those in a stressful occupation.

In some people, stressful life events result in "additional" cardiac activity, which is in excess of the amount required on the basis of physical energy demands. This leads to surplus blood in the muscles, for which adjustments to the circulatory system are made. These autoregulatory adjustments include increased arterial resistance, leading to elevated blood pressure, which can remain (even when the cardiac increase subsides) and leads to a new, higher level of blood pressure.

Treatment

If the cause of the hypertension is organic, the treatment is medical or surgical, though a stress management method may help. Dietary changes should include control of salt intake and, if one uses alcohol, it should be taken in moderate amounts. In addition to the above-mentioned concepts, prescribed medication may be necessary with careful attention to dosage and side effects.

If the cause of hypertension is nonorganic, the treatment is usually stress management in which the patient learns to alter his or her response to stress. Since a major cause of the contraction of blood vessels is that the skeletal muscles are excessively tense due to inadequate coping with stressors, relaxation of those muscles can relieve the smooth muscle contraction of the blood vessels (see the figure in the Introduction on p. xiii). **Progressive Relaxation** has been found to decrease often high blood pressure. **Exercise, Biofeedback, Breathing (Deep),** and **Systematic Desensitization** may also be beneficial. The ability to express and release anger and resentment may help.

Other treatment includes the cessation of smoking, since both tobacco and hypertension are linked to coronary heart disease. Weight reduction for those who are overweight can be especially beneficial since thin people are less likely to have hypertension and diseases linked with it.

Hypertension treatment measures are often long-term, since permanently lowered blood pressure is not rapidly achieved. Damage caused to the circulation system is irreversible. Bringing hypertension under control would allow the heart to work under less strain and prolong life expectancy.

SEE ALSO:

Biofeedback
Blood Pressure, Proper
    Measurement of
Breathing Techniques
Cardiovascular Disease

Cardiovascular Reactivity
Emotions, Destructive
Progressive Relaxation
Systematic Desensitization

BIBLIOGRAPHY

Kunz, J. R. M., & Finkel, A. J. (Eds.). (1987). *The American Medical Association family medical guide.* New York: Random House.
McGuigan, F. J. (1992). *Calm down: A guide for stress and tension control* (2nd ed.). Dubuque, IA: Kendall/Hunt.
Turner, J. R. (1994). *Cardiovascular reactivity and stress, patterns of physiological response.* New York: Plenum.
Wassertheil-Smoller, S. (1998). Hypertension. In E. A. Blechman & K. D. Brownell (Eds.), *Behavioral medicine & women: A comprehensive handbook* (pp. 667–672). New York: Guilford Press.

Hyperventilation

Description

Hyperventilation (an excessive breathing phenomenon) may occur when a person experiences a sense of suffocation, then becomes more anxious. There may be constant pressure in the chest, dizziness, giddiness, numbness of the limbs, muscle spasms, blurred vision, heart pounding, stomach discomfort, and fainting. This sudden respiratory change excessively eliminates carbon dioxide from the body, overexcites nerve cells, and alters the ph of the blood so that the body becomes excessively alkaline. Symptoms can recur several times per day, lasting for a few minutes to over half an hour. The person often is unaware of the hyperventilation and panic, which can add to the severity of the attack. Fried (1987) has mentioned symptoms common to those of the hyperventilation syndrome: Tension, irritability, anxiety, dyspnea (choking sensation, lump in throat, sighing), fatigue, insomnia, heart palpitations, depression, dizzy spells, coldness in extremities, inability to concentrate, and bloating.

Causes

Hyperventilation may initially be brought on by anxious thoughts wherein there is excessive muscular tension, especially in the chest muscles, which triggers over-breathing: for example, a false fear of heart or stomach ailments may be compensated for by taking many deep breaths.

Treatment

One common remedy is to breathe into a paper bag, which may quickly reduce symptoms. This procedure allows the person to retain more carbon dioxide and return the body's ph to normal. Once the person realizes what has happened and knows what to do, the onset of symptoms can usually be self-controlled.

Recurring or prolonged anxiety affecting this condition should be addressed through therapy, such as learning self-operations control. A goal of such therapy is to relieve the person from excessive tension by modifying the body's reactions to stressors. Fried (1993) describes as therapy "the rapid alert relaxation exercises" (p. 318), which combine modified progressive relaxation, deep abdominal breathing, and mental imagery as a successful treatment.

SEE ALSO:

Anxiety
Breathing Techniques
Fear

Hypochondriasis
Self-Operations Control
Tension Awareness

BIBLIOGRAPHY

Bloch, G. J. (1985). *Body and self: Elements of human biology, behavior, and health.* Los Altos, CA: Wm. Kaufmann.

Fried, R. (1987). *The hyperventilation syndrome.* Baltimore, MD: Johns Hopkins University Press.

Fried, R. (1993). The role of respiration in stress and stress control: Toward a theory of stress as a hypoxic phenomenon. In P. M. Lehrer & R. L. Woolfolk (Eds), *Principles and practice of stress management* (2nd ed., pp. 301–331). New York: Guilford Press.

Hypnosis

Artificial somnambulism, also called magnetic somnambulism, was a major discovery made by de Puysegur in 1782. In 1841, James Braid first witnessed two demonstrations of de Puysegur's artificial somnambulism, and somewhat later Braid renamed the phenomenon "hypnotism" or "nervous sleep." Among Braid's conceptions of hypnotism were that it (1) is a state of concentrated attention, (2) can be established within about five minutes, (3) *is an all-or-none condition without degrees,* (4) appears like sleep, and (5) is always accompanied by spontaneous amnesia for all events transpiring during its presence. *Suggestion was minimally used by Braid!*

The process by which de Puysegur's and Braid's concepts of hypnotism eroded is a complex one. To a large extent it was transformed through the work of A. A. Liebeault and H. Bernheim from an all-or-none state to a graded one, and suggestion increasingly became a major tool for the production of hypnotic phenomena. De Puysegur's phenomenon is thought to occur in less than 1 percent of individuals. What we now frequently encounter in the laboratory and clinic is not hypnotism at all in the original sense.

Many authorities would now agree that hypnosis occurs (1) within the context of a special hypnotist/subject relationship, during which (2) suggestions of distortions of cognition, perception, memory, and affect can be responded to by (3) some individuals. Many of the arguments about the nature of hypnosis depend on which of these three aspects is the focus of theory and research. Thus hypnosis appears to be characterized by the subject's ability to temporarily accept as reality the suggested distortion of perception, cognition, and affect.

Some researchers today disavow a unique state known as hypnosis; some assert that it is merely role playing. Hypnosis is not generally held to be just a state of concentration. Nor is it a state of relaxation, since the hypnotized person is mentally very active, as electromyographic records of the muscular condition attest. Two centuries after the discovery of artificial somnambulism, the only consensus seems to be that if there is a unique state of hypnosis, it is *not* sleep. Yet hypnotic "experts" abound. Many just read a book and assume they are competent hypnotists. Lay hypnotists hold no bonafide degrees but use such titles as "clinical hypnotist." Records show that some lay hypnotists arrive in a city, simultaneously hypnotize 50 or so persons in a one-session smoking clinic, and then leave. They advertise that people can control such habits as smoking, dieting, and drinking and also can be psychotherapeutically treated. But horror stories abound; for example, a man with emphysema attended a one-session hypnosis clinic and required emergency medical attention because the suggestion that he relax his breathing deprived him of sufficient oxygen; a woman who was hypnotized by a stage entertainer was admitted to a hospital in a catatonic state and required intravenous feeding.

The use of hypnosis as an adjunctive treatment modality has been increasing rapidly as it becomes more accepted and training facilities improve. Hypnosis is a technique that may be integrated into the specialized skills of the professional in his or her own area of competence. Like any adjunctive method, it is the skill of the therapist—what to treat, when not to treat, possible side effects and complications—that defines the safety and efficacy of the technique. So-called hypnotechnicians and other groups are quite active in many areas, in the mistaken belief that mere hypnotic suggestion helps with stress or can cure a variety of disorders. Referring patients to such nonprofessionals must be considered unethical.

Hypnosis has been glamorized in our search for medical cures. Scientific study has been limited, and its therapeutic use is poorly regulated. A scientific strategy for leading us out of the chaos would be to psychophysiologically or physiologically explicate the phenomenon. Some model research has studied alpha and beta brain waves and p300 amplitudes of evoked potentials. Through electromyographic study, neuromuscular changes often result from a specific state of hypnosis. Sustained psychophysiological research using sound experimental methodology could eventually lead to an understanding of what hypnosis is, because clearly we don't know now.

One who seeks its use as a stress management method should tread lightly.

S E E   A L S O :

Stress Management Methods

B I B L I O G R A P H Y

Corsini, R. J. (Ed.). (1987). *Concise encyclopedia of psychology.* New York: Wiley.

Greenberg, J. S. (1993). *Comprehensive stress management,* Dubuque IA: Brown & Benchmark.

Lehrner, P. M., & Woolfolk, R. L. (Eds.). (1993). *Principles and practice of stress management* (2nd ed.). New York: Guilford Press.

McGuigan, F. J. (1994). *Biological psychology: A cybernetic science.* Englewood Cliffs, NJ: Prentice-Hall.

Rhue, J. W., Lynn, S. J., & Hilgard, E. R. (1993). *Handbook of clinical hypnosis.* Washington, DC: American Psychological Association.

Waxman, D., Misra, P. C., Gibson, M., & Basker, A. (Eds.). (1985). *Modern trends in hypnosis.* New York: Plenum.

Hypochondriasis

Description

Commonly called hypochondria, this disorder affects people who are pathologically obsessed about symptoms and overly sensitive to disease; they may behave as if they are seriously ill when they are not. Their inaccurate interpretation of various physical conditions is thought to document their illnesses. Hypochondriacs frequently visit physicians to discuss their "symptoms" and fears. They often use nonprescription and invalidated medicines, and they read health or medical literature excessively. This disorder usually occurs as a complication of a condition such as **Anxiety.**

Causes

Hypochondriasis is usually related to a condition of excessive anxiety that leads the individual to misperceptions of his or her health condition, difficulty in concentrating, and unrealistic fears. The threat of potential pain and illness is represented in tensed striated muscles to cause further symptoms and signs such as breathing difficulty, heart palpitations, fatigue, dizziness, and increased fear.

Treatment

When physicians fail to substantiate reasons for the complaints, psychotherapy might be prescribed. Relaxation methods are often very helpful for discovery and interpretation of the relevant muscular tensions and thereby relieving the difficulties.

S E E A L S O :

Anxiety

B I B L I O G R A P H Y

Barsky, A. J. (1993). The diagnosis and management of hypochondriacal concerns in the elderly. *Journal of Geriatric Psychiatry, 26,* 129–141.

Kunz, J. R. M., & Finkel, A. J., (1987). *The American Medical Association family medical guide.* New York: Random House.

Rogers, M. P., Weinshenker, N. J., Warshaw, M. S., & Goisman, R. (1996). Prevalence of somatoform disorders in a large sample of patients with anxiety disorders. *Psychosomatics, 37,* 17–22.

I Immune System Disorders–Irritable Bowel Syndrome

Immune System Disorders

Description

The immune system is one of the most complex aspects of the human body, with a variety of components functioning together to defend against infection and disease. The potential effects of immune system disorders are far-reaching, ranging from simply increased susceptibility to the common cold virus to **Cancer,** rheumatoid **Arthritis,** thyroid disorders, and **AIDS.** Two main types of immune system disorders are (1) antibody production deficiency and (2) insufficient or unhealthy lymphocytes. Antibodies function to protect the body from infectious disease, but a deficiency can be inherited. Lymphocytes—white blood cells produced by bone marrow and the lymph glands—surround and kill organisms foreign to the body. Antibodies come from a variety of lymphocytes, including T-cells that derive from the thymus gland and function to protect the body from infectious disease.

Causes

The immune system can be impaired by diseases such as leukemia, lymphoma, Hodgkin's disease, cancer, diabetes, and uremia. Steroids, anticancer drugs, and radiation therapy can also be detrimental to the immune system.

Those who are chronically exposed to stressors without adequate coping skills have less efficient immune systems and lowered defense against infections and cancer. Damage to the immune system is determined more by the duration of the stress experienced and the perceived lack of control over it than by its intensity. Significant weakening of the immune system takes place if one is experiencing prolonged stressors. For example, marital disruption due to death or divorce is a powerful sociodemographic predictor of physical and emotional illness. A person's "state of mind" is known to produce important biochemicals that influence the health of the rest of the body.

Treatment

Stress management may be helpful. If an antibody production deficiency is inherited, antibodies can be collected from others and injected into the body on a frequent basis.

SEE ALSO:

AIDS and Stress   Disease and Stress
Arthritis, Rheumatoid   Psychoimmunology
Cancer

BIBLIOGRAPHY

McGuigan, F. J. (1994). *Biological psychology: A cybernetic science.* Englewood Cliffs, NJ: Prentice-Hall.
Namir, S., Wolcott, D. L., Fawzy, F. I., & Alumbaugh, M. J. (1987). Coping with AIDS: Psychological and health implications. *Journal of Applied Social Psychology, 17,* 309–328.
Nichols, S. E. (1985). Psychosocial reactions of persons with the acquired immune deficiency syndrome. *Annals of Internal Medicine, 103,* 765–767.

Impotence

Description

Impotence is the loss of a man's ability to acquire and maintain an erection. An erection is immediately produced by nerve stimulation that has more distant controls in the spinal cord and brain. During an erection, blood vessels enlarge and dilate to allow an increased flow of blood so that the penis becomes engorged.

Causes

The causes of impotence can be psychological or physical. Psychological factors include a loss of sexual interest. Temporary situations such as marital conflict, stress, fatigue, or anxiety can lead to impotence. Some who cannot perform sexually may still have a strong sexual drive. Physical causes include side effects of drugs such as tranquilizers and antidepressants and drugs that treat hypertension, including diuretics or fluid pills. Chronic alcohol abuse can affect the liver, which then can lower the amount of testosterone circulating in the blood stream. Testosterone, the primary male sex hormone, affects male characteristics including stimulating the sex drive and sperm production. Physical diseases such as arteriosclerosis, Atherosclerosis, **Diabetes, Hypertension,** and kidney failure may contribute to impotence.

Treatment

When one consistently is unable to achieve or maintain an erection, the physician needs to determine whether the causes are psychological or physical. The physician can measure the amount of testosterone in the blood system and, if the patient is on medications, they may be removed systematically to determine if one of them is the cause.

If psychological problems are relevant, one can consult a psychiatrist, a psychologist, or a sex therapist who can prescribe relaxation techniques and the like.

Injections of drugs into the penis may produce erections, as can the surgical insertion of a prosthetic device. Drugs such as Viagra and Vasomax, which enhance blood flow to the penis, are pharmacological treatments for impotency. These drugs are expensive and need to be taken under close supervision of one's physician.

SEE ALSO:

Diabetes Mellitus
Hypertension
Sexual Dysfunction in Men

BIBLIOGRAPHY

Rosen, R. C., & Leiblum, S. R. (1995). Treatment of sexual disorders in the 1990's: An integrated approach. *Journal of Consulting and Clinical Psychology, 63,* 877–890.
Slosarz, W. (1992). Psychological aspects of erectile and ejaculatory dysfunction. *Sexual and Marital Therapy, 7,* 267–273.
Zorgniotti, A., & Lizza, E. F. (1991). *Diagnosis and management of impotence.* Philadelphia: B.C. Decker.

Infertility

Description

Infertility has been defined as the inability of a person to conceive a child after having made attempts for one year. Estimates are that approximately 15 percent of married couples are unable to conceive.

Causes

The causes of infertility are many: defective functioning of the reproductive organs, impaired functioning of the pituitary gland, abnormal functioning of the hypothalamus, inadequate sexual behavior, and stress referred to as "emotional, mental, or physical."

Emotional factors have been implicated in about 12 percent of the cases of infertility. For example, anxiety or fear may underlie changes in such physiological functions, especially those occurring in organs and tissues affected by secretions of the adrenal glands, the activity of the autonomic nervous system, and relevant regions of the brain including the hypothalamus, limbic system, and frontal cortex. Patients suffering from **Anorexia Nervosa** are almost always infertile, and even less severe states of undernutrition can alter the activity of the pituitary gland—possibly the hypothalamus as well—thereby lowering the levels of sex hormones in the bloodstream.

Anxiety and **Depression** are commonly responsible for inhibition, which often triggers a vicious circle: Inadequate sexual excitement leads to further anxiety caused by fear of failure, a perceived need to please the partner, or a sense of not meeting some fantasied standard of sexual performance—all of which lead to decreased sexual excitement. As a whole, the reproductive system is very sensitive to these changes. Within the brain, any condition that alters the ability of the hypothalamus to produce and secrete various hormonal releasing factors can cause infertility. A number of findings indicate that stress and depression can alter the activity of hypothalamic neurons that regulate the production and secretion of releasing factors.

Treatment

In treating infertility, clearly organic causes can be addressed through medical or surgical means. If anxiety or stress appear to be major causes, behavior modification, teaching the couple relaxation techniques, encouraging an open sexual dialogue between them, and decreasing stressful life events such as occupational pressure are often successful.

SEE ALSO:

Anorexia Nervosa	Impotence
Anxiety	Sexual Dysfunction in Men
Depression	Sexual Dysfunction in Women

BIBLIOGRAPHY

Leiblum, S. R. (1993). The impact of infertility on sexual and marital satisfaction. *Annual Review of Sex Research, 4,* 99–120.
Morokoff, P., & Calderone, K. L. (1994). Sexuality and infertility. In V. J. Adesso, D. M. Reddy, & R. Fleming (Eds.), *Psychological perspectives on women's health* (pp. 251–284). Philadelphia: Taylor & Francis.
Wasser, S. K. (1994). Psychosocial stress and infertility—cause or effect? *Human Nature, 5,* 293–306.

Insomnia (Sleep Difficulties)

Description

Insomnia is one of several sleep disorders recognized by the American Sleep Association. The term "insomnia" typically means "sleeplessness" or "inability to sleep." More precisely, common patterns are (1) resistance to falling asleep, (2) difficulty in remaining asleep, (3) poor sleep quality, and (4) awakening too early.

Common complaints related to chronic insomnia are **Fatigue,** irritability, inability to concentrate, interference with short-term **Memory,** drowsiness, and abuse of stimulants. Transient insomnia occurs in most people who are under great distress or emotional upheaval. Women tend to be more affected than men, and the frequency of both increases with age. Chronic insomnia can begin at any age, but the majority of such patients experience persistent difficulty prior to age 40.

Causes

Physiological factors that may interfere with sleep include heart disease, high blood pressure, "heartburn" associated with a hernia, and chronic breathing problems. However, the majority of cases of insomnia lack any obvious physiological basis. Stressful experiences that create unresolved excess **Tension** are primary causal factors in insomnia. Psychological factors such as **Anxiety** and anger can keep a person "on alert" if he or she goes to bed in a nervous state or angry at someone. And a highly active imagination and the reviewing of the day's activities creates tension that interferes with one's capacity to fall asleep.

Treatment

The most frequently used drug-free treatment has been some type of relaxation training that can reduce the excess tension and resulting cognitive intrusions. Increasing self-control by conditioning behaviors incompatible with pre-sleep intrusive cognitions has been used in combination with relaxation. Cognitive therapies and medication are also used. Other strategies aim at modifying negative self-statements and expectations. Improvements with sound methods seem to be fairly robust over time, with 70 to 80 percent of dedicated participants making and maintaining positive results.

Some concern has been raised with regard to the long-term use of medications to initiate sleep because the drugs appear to interfere with REM sleep, and thus the quality of the sleep is compromised.

SEE ALSO:

Fatigue, "Nervous"   Sleep, Healthy and Unhealthy
Memory, Poor Recall   Tension Awareness

BIBLIOGRAPHY

McGuigan, F. J. (1992). *Calm down: A guide for stress and tension control* (2nd ed.). Dubuque, IA: Kendall/Hunt.

Ogilvie, R., & Harsh, J. (Eds.). (1994). *Sleep onset: Normal and abnormal processes.* Washington, DC: American Psychological Association.

Pressman, M. R., & Orr, W. C. (Eds.). (1997). *Understanding sleep: The evaluation and treatment of sleep disorders.* Washington, DC: American Psychological Association.

Sanavio, E., Vidotto, G., Bettinardi, O., Rolletto, T., & Zorzi, M. (1990). Behavior therapy for DIMS: comparison of three treatment procedures with follow-up. *Behavioral psychotherapy, 18,* 151–167.

Irritable Bowel Syndrome (IBS)

Description

Irritable bowel syndrome may also be referred to as **Spastic Colon,** and irritable colon. IBS is a benign, chronic gastrointestinal (GI) disorder that affects at some time more than one-half the general population. This syndrome, the most common GI disorder, is characterized by altered bowel habits, which impacts lifestyle. IBS can affect emotional well-being and social life due to the sudden and frequent need to relieve oneself. It is most likely to appear before age 60. Three major symptoms include pain from intestinal spasms, **Diarrhea,** and **Constipation,** without any diagnosable physical cause. Other symptoms include attacks of nausea, cramping abdominal pain, abdominal distention, excess gas, and a sensation that the rectum is never completely emptied.

It is important to note that IBS is *not* characterized by rectal bleeding, significant weight loss, or anorexia, which may indicate more serious diseases. It differs from **Colitis** in that inflammation, tissue damage, and disease are not typically present.

There is generally no diagnosable physical cause for IBS.

Causes

There does not appear to be a clear personality profile for IBS sufferers. However, a high incidence of panic or anxiety is often associated with these individuals. IBS may be influenced by a hereditary disorder of smooth muscle movement of the colon. IBS may be the result of hormonal, emotional, or neurological factors targeting the colon, which responds to these stimuli; IBS is a psychophysiological response to emotional and environmental stress due, at various times, to stresses of travel, changes in occupation, and diet. During emotional excitement or anxiety, the colon contracts. When these contractions are excessive, more water is extracted from the colon. This makes the process of body waste through the colon difficult, stools become hard and dry, and constipation may occur. If the contractions are too few, the movement too fast, and not enough water is absorbed, the result may be diarrhea.

Treatment

Recommended treatment is aimed at restoring to normal the muscular contractions of the intestines. Treatment of IBS through psychological interventions has had encouraging results. For general relaxation and control of intestinal mobility, **Progressive Relaxation,** thermal **Biofeedback,** and other **Stress Management Methods** have been valuable behavioral strategies. If feces have been hard and irregular, a drug to soften them or a bulk laxative may be prescribed; if, however, the main symptom is diarrhea or abdominal pain, the physician may prescribe antispasmodic drugs, or mild sedatives or tranquilizers.

Information and awareness, together with emotional support and short-term counseling, can be beneficial to the IBS sufferer.

SEE ALSO:

Biofeedback	Gastrointestinal Disorders
Colitis	Progressive Relaxation
Constipation	Spastic Colon
Diarrhea	Stress Management Methods

BIBLIOGRAPHY

Blanchard, E. B., Schwarz, S. P., & Neff, D. F. (1988). Two-year follow-up of behavioral treatment of Irritable Bowel Syndrome. *Behavior Therapy, 19,* 67–73.

Magalini, S. I., Magalini, S. C., & Francisci, G. (1990). *Dictionary of medical syndromes* (3rd ed.). Philadelphia: J. B. Lippincott.

Moser, R. S. (1986). Irritable Bowel Syndrome: A misunderstood psychophysiological affliction. *Journal of Counseling and Development, 65,* 108–109.

Thompson, W. G. (1993). *The angry gut.* New York: Plenum.

J

Jacobson–Jet Lag

Jacobson, Edmund (1888–1983)

Edmund Jacobson received his Ph.D. in psychology at Harvard University, having started his studies in 1908. His major professors were William James, Josiah Royce, and Hugo Münsterberg. He next joined Edward Bradford Titchener at Cornell University before going to Chicago, where he received his M.D. degree. After a brief period at the University of Chicago, he opened his own office and laboratory in downtown Chicago where he conducted research and practiced for the rest of his life.

Jacobson first began his research on the startle reflex at Harvard, which led to his development of the classic method of **Progressive Relaxation.** His extensive clinical work in applying progressive relaxation for a variety of psychiatric and psychosomatic disorders was quite compatible with his major interest in the nature of the human mind. He conducted classical studies implicating covert muscular events in mental activities, establishing himself as the father of quantitative electromyography. He summarized one aspect of his research on the mind by stating that it might be naive to say that we think with our muscles, but it would be inaccurate to say that we think without them.

SEE ALSO:

Mind and Mental Events   Self-Operations Control
Progressive Relaxation   Tension Awareness

BIBLIOGRAPHY

Jacobson, E. (1938). *Progressive relaxation* (Rev. ed.) Chicago: University of Chicago Press.

Jealousy

Description

Jealousy has been described as an emotional state experienced when a person is threatened by the loss of an important relationship with another person, in which case the threat involves the loss of the relationship to a rival. The relationship need not involve love, and the rival need not be a person. For example, a man may be jealous of his wife's love of law school, another woman, or her car. Because there is a positive correlation between the level of jealousy and the level of **Anxiety** that an individual experiences, jealousy can indirectly contribute to stressors in one's immediate environment. Jealousy is a state of **Tension,** unresolved and torment-ing. Jealousy is a universal emotional experience, although cultures do differ in the frequency and forms of their jealousy. It may be experienced in a number of ways, but typically these are thought to include fear of loss, **Anger** over betrayal, and insecurity.

Causes

Many causal conditions of jealousy may occur. Jealousy can spring from self-doubt, a lack of self-confidence, and feelings of inadequacy. Aspects of jealousy may be related to biological disposition, cultural influence, personality character-istics, and the like. Causal conditions that affect jealousy have been derived from learning, social learning, and trait theories of psychology.

One view follows from the conception that stress occurs when the pressure of the environment is perceived to exceed the person's capacity to adapt to it. Thus a threat of a rival relationship, change in social status, or romantic relationship, may be perceived to exceed the person's ability to master the threat. Anxious inse-curity expressed in the form of anger, hurt, and depression usually follows from the perception of threat to a relationship, although hostility is the most primitive and common reaction of the jealous individual.

Treatment

To cope with the stress induced by the feelings of jealousy, one obviously needs to improve the primary relationship, to make it more attractive to the partner than is the secondary relationship. For this, one should judiciously increase the rewards of not being jealous. Those rewards depend on the specific nature of the relation-ship. They can derive from new sources of mutual confidence, enjoyable interper-sonal experiences, seeking new individuals of mutual interest, communicating with friends, finding new meaningful activities, and the like. A jealous person may be encouraged to realize that there is poor communication about the jealousy as well as about other aspects of life together—so that communication can be improved. Any activity or condition that enhances one's self-confidence may also mitigate the jealousy.

S E E   A L S O :

Anxiety   Frustration
Emotional Behavior, Destructive   Tension Awareness

BIBLIOGRAPHY

Clanton, G. C., & Smith, L. (Eds.). (1986). *Jealousy.* New York: United Press of America.
Salovey, P. (Ed.). (1991). *The psychology of jealousy and envy.* New York: Guilford Press.
Tov-Ruach, L. (1980). Jealousy, attention, and loss. In A. O. Rorty (Ed.), *Explaining emotions* (pp. 465–488). Berkeley, CA: University of California Press.
White, G. L., & Mullen, P. E. (1989). *Jealousy: theory, research, and clinical strategies.* New York: Guilford Press.

Jet Lag

Description

Jet lag is the disruption of the body's normal circadian rhythms (those rhythms that follow a 24-hour cycle, like sleep–awake) brought on by rapid travel around the Earth. It occurs when you move into a new time zone and the body continues functioning according to how circadian rhythms were set in the previous time zone. The jet lag created by the disruption of the normal functioning of circadian rhythms can pose a threat to our ability to perform effectively.

Causes

Virtually every internal physiological and external environmental cue we use changes in the new part of the world, causing our rhythms also to change. Body temperature, which normally drops at night in sleep and is at its lowest early in the morning, follows that sequence, even though it may be in the middle of the day in the new time zone. Similarly, urine output, heart rate, and blood pressure all normally decrease at night, though they would do so inappropriately in the new time zone. Hormone and other chemical secretions, blood circulation, and so forth also become desynchronized. As a result, sleep can be severely disturbed, and alertness and performance levels decrease. A vicious cycle can result such that, without adequate sleep, effectiveness of the immune system is lowered; subsequently, resistance decreases, whereupon we may become fatigued or even ill, which in turn disturbs sleep.

Treatment

Jet lag is self-correcting, given enough time (perhaps a day for each time zone). One problem is that by the time one has adjusted, then it is time to return home—wherein jet lag sets in anew.

There are a number of efforts that have been made to correct or prevent the problems created by jet lag. For instance, one can adjust performance of tasks to the new time zone as Henry Kissinger, when he was secretary of state, was said to have done. To prevent ill effects of jet lag, Kissinger scheduled foreign meetings according to Washington, D.C., time.

One suggestion is to consume a lot of fluids such as water, herbal tea, or decaffeinated coffee. However, alcohol is detrimental when one is suffering from jet lag.

High-carbohydrate foods such as pasta, salad, fruits, and rich desserts provide energy for about an hour or so and then lead to the feeling of being drowsy and all set to sleep. On the other hand, high-protein foods such as fish, fowl, meat, eggs, dairy products, and beans provide up to five hours of long-lasting energy, which can be counterproductive for jet lag.

Melatonin, a hormone released by the pineal gland, acts on a small region in the posterior of the hypothalamus in the brain, which apparently contains receptors for it. Melatonin production is controlled as follows: Light activates the retina to send information through the hypothalamus to the pineal gland to inhibit the production of melatonin. On the other hand, lack of light increases the secretion of melatonin. Consequently, large amounts of the hormone melatonin are released at night and small amounts are released in the daytime. A conclusion is that melatonin is a chemical stimulus that induces sleep. It plays a role in fatigue, the immune system, sleep disorders, and memory. Administering melatonin may thus reset the biological clock to produce better sleep. In fact, research has indicated that melatonin treatment does relieve the symptoms of jet lag. More specifically, people who were administered the hormone had a better quality of sleep and were more alert than comparison travelers who did not receive the treatment. Melatonin apparently is not toxic and is well tolerated by humans. It may be useful for treating other biological disorders too. For instance, some data suggest that depressed people who are exposed to a comination of bright light and sleep scheduling have benefited therapeutically.

Some use melatonin now in the form of pills, but one must be careful of the dosage and also of the purity of the product.

S E E   A L S O :

Chemicals of the Body and Stress
Insomnia, Sleep Difficulties
Sleep, Healthy and Unhealthy

B I B L I O G R A P H Y

McGuigan, F. J. (1994). *Biological psychology: A cybernetic science.* Englewood Cliffs, NJ: Prentice-Hall.
Sweeney, D. (1989). *Overcoming insomnia: A medical program for problem sleepers.* New York: Putnam.

L Locus of Control

Locus of Control, Internal Versus External

In considering the topic of self-control it may be advantageous to refer to this concept. Locus of control refers to a set of beliefs about how one behaves and the relationship of that behavior to how one is rewarded or punished. In his seminal work, Julian Rotter (1966) measured, through a psychometric instrument—a "paper and pencil test"—the degree to which a person believes that control of reinforcement is internal versus the degree to which it is external. If one believes that rewards are the results of their own behavior, this would be an internal locus of control. On the other hand, if one believes that rewards occur as a result of intervention by others, for instance, one believes in an external locus of control.

With regard to stress, one's belief in the locus of control can affect how one behaves in the face of stressors. Thus, one who believes in an internal locus of control would be better prepared to take stress management steps to control any stressor. On the other hand an individual oriented toward believing in an external locus of control would be less prepared to rely on his or her behavior to control stressors.

SEE ALSO:

Self-Operations Control

BIBLIOGRAPHY

Rotter, J. B. (1966). Generalized expectancies for internal versus external control of reinforcement. *Psychological Monographs, 80,* 1–28.

Rotter, J. B. (1990). Internal versus external control of reinforcement: A case history of a variable. *American Psychologist, 45,* 489–493.

Seaward, B. L. (1994). *Managing stress: Principles and strategies for health and well being.* Boston: Jones and Bartlett.

Strickland, B. (1989). Internal-external control expectancies: From contingency to creativity. *American Psychologist, 44,* 1–12.

M Management-Induced Stress–Muscular System Discomfort

Management-Induced Stress

Description

Many managers may unknowingly contribute to the stress disorders afflicting their employees. They may do this by inefficiently directing their employees' energies. As a result, the concentration and judgment of the employees can be impaired. The organization's productivity also can suffer, along with the individual employee. Sometimes managerial-induced stress can increase the likelihood of accidents in the workplace.

Common signs of stress among employees are groaning, continual complaining, frequent shifting of the eyes, an unnaturally high-pitched voice, jumping with alarm at sudden noises, and being highly emotional or anxious. Clenched fists, a tight jaw, and tension in the neck and shoulder area are signs that a person may be trying to suppress an outburst.

Resulting chronic, excessive muscular tension constitutes a serious health problem. It has been linked with high blood pressure, insomnia, gastrointestinal disorders including colitis, gout, headaches, backaches, asthma, and the like. Further, when one is under stress, the immune system weakens.

Causes

There are many different management behaviors that can contribute to employee tension. These are some:

- Piling excessive amounts of work on employees with little direction as to priorities
- Calling frequent, lengthy meetings, and then criticizing employees for not spending enough time at their desks getting work out
- Setting impossibly high goals in the mistaken belief that it will make employees try harder
- putting employees on the spot, especially in front of others, rather than giving them time to research answers to your questions
- repeatedly taking employees off one project to work on others, requiring them to juggle many projects simultaneously

- involving the entire staff in every problem or crisis even though some of the individuals can do nothing to help alleviate the difficulty
- bringing up employees' past mistakes when you are correcting them for current errors

Treatment

There are many ways that management can help employees feel less stressed and thereby be more productive:

- put themselves in their employees' shoes to recognize what is causing the subordinates' stress
- keep emergency projects to a minimum
- sharpen communication skills so that employees really understand directives
- be quick to praise and reinforce good work
- give reprimands in a calm manner and in private
- allow room for interaction; don't use ultimatums
- help employees prioritize assignments
- learn for self and encourage employees to learn the stress-reducing techniques of **Progressive Relaxation**

SEE ALSO:

Executive Stress
Progressive Relaxation
Workplace Stress

BIBLIOGRAPHY

Humphrey, J. H. (1998). *Job Stress.* Boston: Allyn & Bacon.
Keita, G. P., & Hurrell, J. J., Jr. (Eds.). (1994). *Job stress in a changing workforce.* Washington, DC: American Psychological Association.
McGuigan, F. J. (1986, April). Alleviating stress in the workplace. *Production, 97,* 33–34.
Nelton, S. (1986, September). Getting over giving ulcers. *Nation's Business, 74,* 42.
Sauter, S. L., & Murphy, L. R. (Eds.). (1995). *Organizational risk factors for job stress.* Washington, DC: American Psychological Association.

Medical School Stress

Description

In general, academic achievement is negatively affected by distress in school, which also has a deleterious impact on physical (including psychological) health. Almost one quarter of medical school students experience clinical levels of depression. In a study by Mosley et al. (1994), somatic distress was reported by 59 percent of the medical students, and undesirable stress levels reached upwards of 50 percent.

Causes

Medical school is recognized as a significantly stressful situation due to the intensity of study and long hours required of students. One's ability to tolerate high stress levels plays a large role in the manifestation of depression and somatic distress.

Treatment

Students who used coping strategies characterized as "Engagement Strategies" (those strategies that involve a proactive coping style versus an avoidant style) suffered from fewer depressive symptoms. Such proactive coping strategies are discussed in **Stress Management Methods.**

SEE ALSO:

Nursing Stress in Students
School/College Stress
Stress Management Methods

BIBLIOGRAPHY

Mosley, T. H., Perrin, S. G., & Neral, S. M. (1994). Stress, coping and well-being among third-year medical students. *Academic Medicine, 69,* 765–767.

Meditation

There has been widespread use of various meditation techniques for a number of purposes. These techniques typically originated in Eastern religions but have spread in the Western world. Despite their variety, a common goal of meditation techniques is to reduce somatic (and "mental") arousal. In one technique, the meditator silently repeats a particular term (a mantra) to help induce a state of calm. However, some techniques are designed to increase arousal (e.g., Maulavi, a dancing practice of the whirling dervishes, involves considerable body activity).

The word *meditate* derives from the Latin *meditari,* which means to actively think about, to reflect, or to consider. Consequently, the term *meditation* indicates that some bodily activity is occurring, for example, speech muscles are covertly active during silent meditation. Other research using brain wave criteria indicates that meditators often go to sleep.

Meditation has been clinically applied to treat psychiatric disorders, **Hypertension, Asthma,** inflammation of the gums, drug abuse, alcohol abuse, **Insomnia,** and **Stuttering,** among other disorders. Meditation is sometimes used as a psychotherapeutic technique because it is believed that it will facilitate the control of arousal in threatening situations. However, in an insightful review of the experimental evidence, Holmes (1984) reached the following conclusions:

When the somatic arousal of meditating subjects was compared to the somatic arousal of resting subjects [there were no] consistent differences between meditation and resting subjects on measures of heart rate, electrodermal activity, respiration rate, systolic blood pressure, diastolic blood pressure, skin temperature, oxygen consumption, EMG activity, blood flow, or various biochemical factors. Similarly, a review of the research on the effects of meditation in controlling arousal in threatening situations did not reveal any consistent differences between meditating and non-meditating subjects. (p. 1)

On the other hand, positive effects of procedures like meditation and yoga are sometimes reported by people. The extent to which such techniques have been thought to be therapeutically beneficial is probably due to several causes. For one, merely taking time out of the day's activities and resting may help to restore the body, although as Jacobson (1938) showed, instructions to rest were quite ineffective compared to applying progressive relaxation. Other reasons may be suggestive placebo variables and unsound methodology.

S E E   A L S O :

Alcoholism

Asthma and Stress

Hypertension, Essential (High Blood
  Pressure)

Insomnia (Sleep Difficulties)

Stress Management Methods

Stuttering

B I B L I O G R A P H Y

Carrington, P. (1993). Modern forms of meditation. In P. M. Lehrer & R. L. Woolfolk (Eds.), *Principles and practice of stress management* (2nd ed., pp. 139–168). New York: Guilford Press.

Frew, D. R. (1977). *Management of stress: Using TM at work.* Chicago: Nelson-Hall.

Holmes, D. S. (1984). Meditation and somatic arousal reduction: A review of experimental evidence. *American Psychologist, 39,* 1–10.

Jacobson, E. (1938). *Progressive relaxation* (Rev. ed.). Chicago: University of Chicago Press.

McGuigan, F. J. (1994). *Biological psychology: A cybernetic science.* Englewood Cliffs, NJ: Prentice-Hall.

Seaward, B. L. (1994). *Managing stress: Principles and strategies for health and well being.* Boston: Jones and Bartlett.

Memory, Poor Recall

Description

The inability to recall certain events is typical and normal. There are some events, however, that exacerbate memory loss.

Causes

Psychologists well understand why normal forgetting occurs—the interference theory of forgetting accounts for most memory loss in everyday life. According to that well-substantiated theory, we fail to remember some events because other events interfere with them; and the more similar the interfering events are to the ones desired to be recalled, the greater is the inability to remember or recall them.

The presence of stressful events seems to retard the ability to remember some situations. For instance, researchers, including Michael Meaney, at McGill University, have found that the stress hormone, cortisol, which is secreted when faced with stressors, correlates with subtle memory and attention abilities. That is, the higher the level of cortisol, the more difficult it is to remember subtle events and to pay attention to present situations.

Anterograde amnesia occurs when an individual cannot remember events occurring soon after a trauma. For example, an accident that causes brain injury can produce unconsciousness and coma; the person awakens later and is disoriented, confused, and unable to remember events happening after the trauma.

Retrograde amnesia occurs when one is unable to recall events immediately before a trauma, such as with a traumatizing accident—this type of amnesia of events acts backward in time from the precipitating incident. There may be amnesia concerning events that preceded the trauma for hours, days, or months.

In addition, taking certain drugs, both legal and illegal ones, may cause forgetfulness. In advancing age, some types of memory become relatively ineffective.

Treatment

The appropriate treatment for stress-related forgetting is to adopt an effective **Stress Management Method.**

SEE ALSO:

Alzheimer's Disease
Stress Management Methods

BIBLIOGRAPHY

Pennist, E. (1993, December 4). Memory loss tied to stress. *Science News, 144,* 322.
Loftus, E. F. (1980). *Memory.* Reading, MA: Addison-Wesley.

Menopause

Description

This is the medical term for the normal ending of menstrual cycles, including both ovulation and menstrual periods. Menopause generally occurs between the ages of 40 and 50 and is often preceded by months or years of disrupted and irregular periods.

Symptoms of this natural life stage range from few, if any, changes, to inconvenient or distressing symptoms such as hot flashes, sweat, dizziness, numbness, nausea, heart palpitations, vaginal dryness, **Headaches,** and **Backaches.**

The hot flashes frequently experienced by women during menopause have been described as a sudden rush of warmth that lasts from a few seconds to an hour. The normal duration is from several seconds to a minute, occurring perhaps five times a day on the average, mostly at night, and they may disturb sleep. They are especially apparent in the upper chest through the neck, back, and face.

Many women may develop osteoporosis which, in severe cases, may lead to increased susceptibility to bone fractures and to compression of the spine. Psychiatric disorders often associated with menopause are **Depression, Anxiety,** irritability, difficulty concentrating, lack of confidence, and **Insomnia.** These characteristics may last from only a few weeks to years.

Causes

Menopause is due to complex hormonal changes that occur as a natural part of the aging process. It is not known what precisely sets the flashes off or what makes them go away. Some notions are that consuming hot food or liquids, alcohol, or certain medications can bring them on. They seem to be caused by an upset in the intricate hormonal balance of the body and the body's attempt to correct the disturbance of the balance. One notion, though, as to their cause is that the change in hormones affects the hypothalamus in the brain, which has been described as the "brain's thermostat"—it functions in the regulation of body temperature. The hypothalamus responds to the difference between the events in the hypothalamus and the body's temperature; the heat flash occurs because blood vessels underneath the skin dilate, which causes sweating. As the body sweats, it cools, and the difference between hormone levels and the "thermostat" in the hypothalamus is resolved, bringing the body back to normal.

Treatment

Women should keep track of their menstrual cycles and especially any changes that occur. They should also continue regular medical examinations and consultations with their physicians, keeping apprised of significant changes. Symptoms may be associated only with menopause, or they may be indicative of other disorders or diseases.

Treatment for hot flashes has been low doses of oral estrogen (1 mg. of DES) a day or with progestoral drugs such as Provera or Megace. Clonidine, a blood pressure drug, has been thought also to reduce the number and duration of hot flashes. Behavioral treatment has been somewhat effective. For instance, by relaxing the striated muscles through **Progressive Relaxation,** the smooth muscles surrounding the blood vessels also become relaxed; thus, body temperature is lowered and some hot flashes during the waking hours are controlled.

Robert R. Freedman, in the department of psychiatry at Wayne State University, has conducted experimental research with post-menopausal women, who were given respiration training, in which hot flash frequency significantly declined relative to a control group.

Regular physical **Exercise** and diet rich in calcium will give good protection against osteoporosis. Exercise has also shown to be helpful in combating depression.

Women at this stage are often advised by their physicians to take hormones (estrogen, progesterone) to balance their changing hormone levels. The doses and combinations of these hormones need to be worked out with the individual over several months to ensure proper treatment. This hormone replacement therapy has some risk factors, so the individual should discuss with the physician the advantages and disadvantages of this treatment.

SEE ALSO:

Anxiety

Backache

Depression

Female Stress

Headache, Migraine and Tension

Insomnia (Sleep Difficulties)

Menstruation and Pre-Menstrual
  Syndrome

Progressive Relaxation

BIBLIOGRAPHY

Bromberger. J. T., & Matthews, K. A. (1996). A longitudinal study of the effects of pessimism, trait anxiety, and life stress on depressive symptoms in middle-aged women. *Psychology and Aging, 11,* 207–213.

Dennerstein, L., Smith, A. M. A., & Morse, C. (1994). Psychological well-being, mid-life and the menopause. *Maturitas, 20,* 1–11.

Griffin, M. (1995). The sexual health of women after menopause. *Sexual and Marital Therapy, 10,* 277–291.

Kurt, S. S. (1994). *The realities of aging.* Boston: Allyn & Bacon.

O'Hanlan, K. A. (1998). Menopause. In E. A. Blechman & K. D. Brownell (Eds.), *Behavioral medicine & women: A comprehensive handbook* (pp. 520–527). New York: Guilford Press.

Robinson, G. (1996). Cross-cultural perspectives on menopause. *Journal of Nervous and Mental Disease, 184,* 453–458.

Menstruation and Pre-Menstrual Syndrome (PMS)

Description

About 82 percent of menstruating women become aware of at least one behavioral change in the week or so prior to menstruation. About 12 percent experience positive symptoms, such as increased energy and heightened desire for sex. On the other hand, about 70 percent have negative symptoms that include blemishes on the face, tenderness and swelling of the breasts, bloated abdomen, irritability, depression, and fatigue.

What is referred to by some as premenstrual syndrome (PMS) is perhaps experienced by 3 to 10 percent of women who have undesirable symptoms such as painful and sensitive breasts, some characteristics of asthma, diabetes, arthritis, ovarian cysts, mood swings, and feelings of depression that can disrupt their lives for a week or two each month and strain social relations.

Many women who seek treatment for menstrual disorders report wide mood changes throughout the month. When women charted their mood changes daily, moods were not cyclic. Typically, the women who sought treatment, and they are a small minority of women in general, reported that they were depressed and anxious most of the time during the premenstrual period. Some researchers thus disagree that there is PMS at all, although there may be a premenstrual magnification (PMM) of ongoing moods. Those who do not refer to PMS use such terms as *premenstrual tension, menstrual disorder,* or *menstrual distress.*

Causes

There are many biological changes prior to menstruation, so that it is difficult to isolate any particular changes that could produce menstrual symptoms. Unpleasant and disruptive symptoms often appear when a woman is in her thirties. Frequently they follow an interruption of the menstrual cycle that may occur through pregnancy, hysterectomy, or the use of birth control pills.

Perhaps PMS (or PMM) results from an excess of endorphins in the brain that are then acutely withdrawn. According to this notion, just as estrogen and progesterone levels are cyclic, levels of the brain opiates (endorphins) also rise and fall; they peak about a week before menstruation and then fall off abruptly, producing distress.

Treatment

Research directed at treatment found that placebo treatments have been as effective as progesterone. Although there is no effective treatment that is validated, almost any treatment seems to provide some temporary relief (e.g., the mere suggestion of treatment may release natural brain opiates—endorphins—that temporarily relieve pain and anxiety). Some women find that their symptoms are relieved by treatments that alter the activity of progesterone and/or estrogen, such as with the combined oral contraceptive pill. Other women find that monthly injections of progesterone, diuretics, or vitamin E supplements help.

Exercise may help ease some of the symptoms; drinking less and eliminating salt for a week or two prior to a period will prevent accumulation of fluids, which often contributes to physical stress. A physician can recommend medication for reduction of pain and inflammation.

SEE ALSO:

Chemicals of the Body and Stress   Menopause
Female Stress   Sexual Dysfunction in Women

BIBLIOGRAPHY

Fontana, A., & Pontari, B. (1994). Menstrual-related perceptual changes in women with premenstrual syndrome: Factors to consider in treatment. *Counselling Psychology Quarterly, 7,* 399–406.
Howard, R. C., Mason, P. A., & Taghavi, E. (1994). Impulsivity, mood and the contingent negative variation in women with and without premenstrual changes in impulsive behavior. *Personality and Individual Differences, 16,* 605–616.
Woods, N. F., Mitchell, E. S., & Lentz, M. J. (1995). Social pathways to premenstrual symptoms. *Research in Nursing and Health, 18,* 225–237.

Mental Health and Stress

Description

The association between mental health and stress has been a focus of mental health researchers; that relationship has been especially at the forefront within recent years. As Avison & Gotlib (1994) stated: "Investigators have become aware of the vast array of different experiences that constitute the universe of stressors. Similarly, they have recognized that stressors manifest themselves in a wide range of different mental health outcomes" (p. vii).

Research has considered stressful life events—especially those that are chronic, the vulnerability of individuals to these stressors, and how stressors influence the varieties of health disorders. In fact, the potential influences of chronic stressors on that great variety of mental health disorders are so numerous that we sample here but a few.

Mental health disorders are critical problems for untold millions of people in all countries. Perhaps up to one-third of all primary health care visits worldwide are accounted for by **Depression** and **Anxiety** disorders. **Suicide** consistently ranks as one of the most frequent causes of death; in particular, it is among the top two or three causes of death for young people.

Causes

The factors that affect mental health exert their influence in ways too numerous to enumerate here; but many are cited in the index. Some examples are as follows. Psychological trauma is inflicted on perhaps millions of children due to child prostitution; and industrial slavery involving in excess of 50 million children, subjects them to mental abuse, mental trauma, severe depression, withdrawal, and the like. Alcohol-related diseases affect as many as 10 percent of the world's population. Political violence has affected more than 40 million refugees and displaced persons, resulting in depression, anxiety disorders, and post-traumatic distress (Long, 1996).

Treatment

Effective political changes can help to eliminate numerous instances of mental health disorders due to stress by reducing the inhumane treatment of both adults (especially women) and children. Otherwise, the institution by governments, countries, companies, and other organizations of effective **Stress Management Methods,** including effective therapies, can help.

One barrier is that there is a strong stigma against admitting that one has a mental health problem, especially in some countries. Fortunately, in the United States, individuals are becoming more likely to admit that they have mental health problems, according to the Centers for Disease Control in Atlanta (CDC). In an extensive survey, the CDC found that some 31 percent of those sampled were willing to admit that on at least one day in the preceding month they had struggled with stress and depression. Disabled individuals reported only about 11 "good days," while those with high incomes, college graduates, and Asian-Pacific Islanders reported among the highest average number of good health days, approximately 26 per month. Thus, factors of a good education, some effect of geographical location, age, smoking, marital status, and employment status influence frequency of mental health problems.

SEE ALSO:

Anxiety   Stress Management Methods
Depression   Suicide

BIBLIOGRAPHY

Avison, W. R., Gotlib, I. H. (1994). *Stress and mental health.* New York: Plenum.
Long, B. B. (Nov., 1996). *World Federation for Mental Health Newsletter.* Alexandria, VA: World Federation for Mental Health.

Migraine Headaches

Description

Migraine headaches are a severe form of headache that occur in a varied frequency, intensity, and duration, and are often preceded by warning symptoms that can last for minutes to hours. Among these symptoms are fatigue, nausea, vomiting, blurred vision, and sensitivity to light and sound. Approximately 33 percent of migraine sufferers also experience the sensation of flashing light in the eyes, numbness in the arms and legs, slurred speech, dizziness, ringing in the ears, difficulty in expressing themselves, and the feeling of pins and needles spreading around the mouth. When the migraine actually starts, the warning symptoms tend to dissipate but are replaced by intense, gripping pain that often spreads across the forehead. A throbbing pain then usually develops in the entire head but may be centered between the nose and eyes. The duration is usually unpredictable. In extremely rare occurrences, the visual disturbances and numbness have been known to become permanent.

Causes

Organic: Age, heredity, gender, and diet appear to be factors. Children rarely have migraine headaches before reaching puberty; however, those who have unexplained abdominal pain may develop migraines later on. If one has not experienced a migraine before age 40, it is rare for them to begin, and some people experience relief during middle age. Migraines may run in families and are slightly more common in women. Some migraine sufferers are affected by certain foods—such as cheese, chocolate, red wine, or coffee—that may trigger attacks. Certain medications such as birth control pills may also contribute to the onset of migraines.

Stress: Stressors that can trigger a migraine include sudden changes in weather, barometric pressure, sleep habits, emotional pressures, and missing meals. Those who react intensely to stressful situations and criticism, or who are prone to taking on guilt for not meeting the expectations of self or others, are also at a greater risk for migraines.

Treatment

Consultation with a physician is important since migraines usually require special treatment. **Progressive Relaxation** can alleviate, and sometimes even eliminate, the migraine. Professional help can help to relieve symptoms, but a general cure remains unknown for this condition. Early treatment is most effective, with medication taken under close supervision, as well as adherence to a special diet.

S E E   A L S O :

Headaches, Migraine and Tension
Progressive Relaxation

B I B L I O G R A P H Y

Holroyd, K. A., & Andrasik, F. (1980). Self-control of tension headache. In F. J. McGuigan, W. E. Sime, & J. M. Wallace (Eds.), *Stress and tension control: Vol. 1.* New York: Plenum.
Madders, J. (1980). Group relaxation in the treatment of migraine: A multifactorial approach. In F. J. McGuigan, W. E. Sime, & J. M. Wallace (Eds.), *Stress and tension control: Vol. 1.* New York: Plenum.
McGuigan, F. J. (1992). *Calm down: A guide for stress and tension control* (2nd ed.). Dubuque, IA: Kendall/Hunt.
Murphy, W. (1982). *Dealing with headaches.* Alexandria, VA: Time-Life Books.
Wycoff, B. (1991). *Overcoming migraine.* Barrytown, NY: Station Hill.

Mind and Mental Events

A variety of mental functions are identified with such terms as ideas, images, thoughts, dreams, hallucinations, fears, depression, and anxiety. Regardless of the term, by a strict physicalistic model of mind, all such mental events occur when selective systems of the body interact in a highly integrated fashion. The principal systems involved are those of the receptors (eyes, ears, and so on), the brain, the skeletal muscles, and the autonomic system (the gastrointestinal tract, the cardiovascular system, the pupils of the eyes, the sweat glands, and so on). When these systems are activated and interact in a highly specialized and integrated fashion, mental processes can be generated. The principal mechanisms for generating mental activity are those of neuromuscular circuits activated when muscles contract to generate neural impulses that are conducted to and from the brain. Most mental processes are generated when muscles of the eyes and speech regions tense, whereupon specialized neuromuscular circuits to and from the brain are activated. Other pathways are activated also, as in those involving autonomic functions that add emotional tone to our mental processes.

According to this model of the mind, any interruption of these neuromuscular circuits will eliminate thoughts, preventing them from occurring. Some drugs can interrupt neuromuscular circuits but the simplest, most natural way to cause these circuits to be tranquil is by relaxing these muscles; that is, since muscles are intimately involved in thought processes, when we relax those muscles, undesired thoughts such as phobias and worries can be eliminated. Specifically, if you relax the muscles of your tongue, lips, jaws, throat, and cheeks, thought components having to do with linguistic (verbal) mental activity can be eliminated. By relaxing the complex set of muscles around the eyes, the visual components of your thoughts can be relaxed away. By relaxing all of the muscles of the body, all mental processes can be brought to zero. Relaxed muscles do not generate control signals. A totally relaxed person becomes unaware of any aspect of the body and thus unaware of anything. For instance, it is not unusual for a beginning practitioner of progressive relaxation to become unaware of the existence of his or her arms. Totally relaxed individuals report being unconscious while in this state, with no thoughts at all.

In short, we can use the skeletal muscles to control activities of the body, including mental processes. By systematically controlling our skeletal muscles and using only those muscles needed to perform the tasks at hand (**Differential Relaxation**), we can efficiently guide our thoughts and our emotions as well. This practice is especially valuable for complaints of "racing thoughts," "overactive mind," and the like.

In conclusion, by this definition the human mind is generated by the functioning of the systems of the body. As those systems selectively interact, they program both overt and covert behaviors to accomplish an individual's purposes. Principal programming is carried out by the circuits that include the eye and speech musculature as one visualizes and verbalizes self-instructions. As the circuits reverberate, the mental events on which we may behaviorally report are generated.

SEE ALSO:

Progressive Relaxation
Tension Awareness

BIBLIOGRAPHY

McGuigan, F. J. (1994). *Biological psychology: A cybernetic science.* Englewood Cliffs, NJ: Prentice-Hall.
McGuigan, F. J. (1997). A neuromuscular model of mind with clinical and educational applications. *The Journal of Mind and Behavior, 18,* 351–370.

Money (Financial) Stress

Description

Two conditions that are major stressors for people are (1) having too little money and a poor (or no) financial plan; and (2) having too much money with a bent toward greed. Although the latter is relatively uncommon, it does make our headlines sporadically when multimillionaires gamble huge fortunes and even commit illegal acts in order to further enhance their already sizable finances.

Focusing on the first condition, one problem is that many people overburdened with debt are not aware that they are headed for financial stress. To help people become aware of such stress, the Los Angeles Consumer Credit Counseling Services published the following signs:

- Pervasive worry about money
- Fighting with spouse about money (80% of divorces are linked to money problems)
- No savings
- Living from paycheck to paycheck (is the month longer than your money?)
- Debts add up to 20% or more of income (add up all monthly debt payments, excluding first mortgage, and divide into net income; the percentage should not exceed 20%)
- Using credit cards for basic living expenses, such as groceries
- Making only minimum payments on your debt (Markam, 1996, D6)

Causes

The most frequent cause of money stress, of course, occurs as a result of inadequate finances. Many people live way beyond their means such that the bills constantly come due and cannot be covered—constituting a continuous series of stressors.

One of the most obvious behaviors that leads to serious financial debts is paying interest that is not necessary. Paying 19 percent on credit card balances, for instance, is tantamount to throwing money down the sewer.

Treatment

Whatever the income level, if it is sufficiently above that of poverty, families and individuals need to rationally set their expenses at less than or, at worst, equal to that income. Spending at less than income level is far preferable in that it allows the family to invest, and their income can grow.

It can be emotionally draining for those in debt to develop a reasonable financial plan, but that is essentially the only way that they are going to eliminate financial stress. An alternative, bankruptcy, is certainly not a good choice because, for one, all essential assets, including a home, are thereby lost. Consulting with professionals, such as certified financial planners, can help through this replanning phase.

SEE ALSO:

Self-Operations Control
Stress Management Methods

BIBLIOGRAPHY

Chilman, C. S., Cox, F. M., & Nunnally, E. W. (1988). *Employment and economic problems. Families in trouble series* (Vol. 1). Newbury Park, CA: Sage.
Markam, J. D. (June 26, 1996). Make-over: Spending plan should help family avoid bankruptcy. *Los Angeles Times*, p. D-6.
McLoyd, V. C., & Wilson, L. (1991). The strain of living poor: Parenting, social support, and child mental health. In L. C. Huston (Ed.), *Children in poverty: Child development and public policy* (pp. 105–135). Cambridge, England: Cambridge University Press.

Multiple Personality

Description

The predominant feature of the extremely rare multiple personality is that of the existence of two or more apparently distinct (often independent) and separate personalities inside of one individual. Each of these personalities is associated with unique ways of thinking, behaving, and expressing emotion.

In some cases the multiple personalities are fully developed in the sense that they are associated with distinctly different types of identities and have different memories for past events.

In other cases, characteristics of the personalities overlap so that they share some traits and memories. Either way, a person with the disorder responds differently on psychological tests—and may even demonstrate different patterns of brain activity—for each personality.

The transition from one personality to another typically is abrupt and is precipitated by a stressful experience or environmental cue.

Patients with multiple personality disorder vary in the extent to which they are aware of their condition. Typically, the primary personality is unaware of the secondary personalities, while the secondary personalities are aware of both the primary and other secondary personalities. Switches from one personality to another are usually abrupt and dramatic, and are often precipitated by intense emotion. The extent of the functional impairment of these patients varies from mild to severe.

Causes

The major theories advanced in an attempt to describe the causes of multiple personality disorder are psychological. One theory states that multiple personality results at an early age from amnesia-like repression of severe emotional shock. The repressed emotions presumably then manifest themselves as secondary personalities.

Another psychological theory proposes autohypnosis as the cause of multiple personality; at an early age the subject unwittingly induces a self-trance in order to deal with intolerable **Stressful Life Events.** The trance state subsequently results in secondary personalities, as well as accounting for amnesia of the primary personality.

Most theorists agree that multiple personality results from severe psychosocial stress at an early age, leading to a vulnerability in later life to use dissociation in order to deal with emotional crisis.

Treatment

Multiple personality disorder is usually chronic. The treatment most often recommended is psychotherapy, with a twofold goal: (1) try to make the patient aware of his or her tendency to disassociate in response to painful events, and (2) help the patient understand his or her individual conflicts so that these conflicts may become integrated with the primary personality.

However, the limited success of this therapy has been attributed to patients' reverting to dissociation when under stress. Most therapists agree that techniques are necessary in order to lower patient **Anxiety,** thus preventing some need for the patient to dissociate. **Progressive Relaxation** therapy has been established as quite effective in controlling anxiety.

SEE ALSO:

Anxiety
Progressive Relaxation
Stressful Life Events

BIBLIOGRAPHY

Atchinson, M., & McFarlane, A. C. (1994). A review of dissociation and dissociative disorders. *Australian and New Zealand Journal of Psychiatry, 28,* 591–599.
Cooper, A. M., Frances, A. J., & Sacks, M. H. (1986). *The personality disorders and neuroses. Psychiatry Series,* Vol. 1. Philadelphia: J. B. Lippincott.

Spanos, N. P. (1996). *Multiple identities and false memories: A sociocognitive perspective.* Washington, DC: American Psychological Association.

Spiegel, D., Koopman, C., & Classen, C. (1994). Acute stress disorder and dissociation. *Australian Journal of Clinical and Experimental Hypnosis, 22,* 11–23.

Taylor, W. S., & Martin, M. F. (1944). Multiple personality. *Journal of Abnormal and Social Psychology, 39,* 281.

Winer, D. (1978). Anger and dissociation: A case study of multiple personality. *Journal of Abnormal Psychology, 87,* 368.

Muscular System Discomfort

Description

Chronic stressors can have lasting effects on all parts of our bodies if we do not adequately control them. Pain and soreness in the muscular system can be one of the most obvious consequences of inadequate coping with stressors. Though stressors also affect other systems of the body, the striated (skeletal, voluntary) muscular system consists of the only components of the body that we can volitionally move; we may distinctly notice pain and discomfort therein under certain conditions when we use them.

Causes

The main cause of chronic pain and soreness in the muscular system is the misuse of muscles and the unnecessary wasting of energy in the muscles. "Muscles contract when they are performing a job. But when the job is finished they must know how to relax" (McQuade and Aikman, 1974, p. 82). If people do not know how to relax their muscles when they are not using them, the result can be a chronic muscle spasm. This type of muscle spasm is a common cause of trouble and discomfort for people who suffer from recurrent backaches. To explain this phenomenon more clearly, "when a person feels like acting but does not allow himself to act, his or her muscles remain tensed in readiness, sometimes for months or years at a time, immobilized into a state of semi-contraction even during sleep...." This condition unfortunately causes the affected muscles to lose their elasticity, which in turn causes the previously mentioned "chronic muscle spasm" (McQuade and Aikman, 1974, p. 82).

Although much chronic muscle tension is felt in the back, pain and discomfort can be experienced all over the body; for example, excess tension in the jaws or mouth area can contribute to the experience of a toothache, or in the head area when one suffers from a tension headache. A toothache can result from habitually clenching the jaws (**Bruxism**), which is a muscular exertion that if left untreated can eventually lead to early tooth loss by way of problems in the jawbones and gums. Similarly, **Tension Headaches** are caused by overtensed, overstressed muscles, specifically those of the eyes, neck, and scalp. Regardless of the exact location of the pain or discomfort, all muscular tension or stress-related problems form a cyclical type pattern: The muscle tension can cause the discomfort (see physiological discussion of **Pain**), but then the resulting conditions creating discomfort can cause more tension so that the muscles continue to tense causing even further pain.

Treatment

Treating the slight symptoms of muscle discomfort "early on" is a key to eliminating more serious problems later. McQuade and Aikman (1974) offer many suggestions as to how to treat the ongoing problems of stress and overtension; they include treatments altering one's exercise and diet, participating in such activities as **Psychotherapy** and **Biofeedback,** and using prescribed drugs such as tranquilizers to relieve stress. However, though these approaches may be beneficial, the most effective method for controlling and managing tension is through learning and continually practicing **Progressive Relaxation.**

SEE ALSO:

Biofeedback
Bruxism
Pain

Progressive Relaxation
Tension Awareness

BIBLIOGRAPHY

Malow, R. M., & Olson, R. E. (1986). Behavioral assessment and treatment of facial pain. In P. A. Keller & L. G. Ritt (Eds), *Innovations in clinical practice: A source book* (Vol. 5, pp. 189–201). Sarasota, FL: Professional Resource Exchange.
McGuigan, F. J. (1991). Control of normal and pathologic cognitive functions through neuromuscular circuits: Applications of principles of progressive relaxation. In J. G. Carlson & A. R. Seifert (Eds.), *International perspectives on self-regulation and health. Plenum series in behavioral psychophysiology and medicine* (pp. 121–131). New York: Plenum.
McQuade, W., & Aikman, A. (1974). *Stress.* New York: Bantam Books.
Resnick, R. J., & Rozensky, R. H. (Eds.). (1996). *Health psychology through the life span: Practice and research opportunities.* Washington, DC: American Psychological Association.

N
Nervous Breakdown–
Nutrition and Stress

Nervous Breakdown

Description

This term refers to the loss of an individual's capacity to conduct business and social affairs due to emotional disturbance, in spite of the fact that the nervous system remains structurally intact.

There is evidence that more people are suffering from "nervous breakdowns" than ever before—apparently because the world's population is becoming excessively tense, which deleteriously affects their behavior. The rate of "mental" or "emotional" collapse has been estimated to be approximately one in ten, affecting about seventeen million people in the United States. Reflecting on this high-strung condition, the era in which we live is often called the age of anxiety or stress.

Causes

Excessive, chronic (muscular) **Tension** is evoked because of inadequate coping with the stresses of life, leading to the kind of aberrant behavior commonly referred to as "nervous breakdown."

Treatment

The person suffering a nervous breakdown needs increased effectiveness of self-management. Management is order, and excessive tension causes disorder. As the individual learns to relax, he or she tends to achieve a greater measure of internal order than is usually accomplished by the various verbal therapeutic treatments. When the learner has been trained in physiological methods to meet hardships and tragedy in life with due—but not undue—concern, he or she is much better adjusted. Such an individual progresses along a path of effective adjustment to stressors, preventing any need for tranquilizers and the like.

S E E   A L S O :

Anxiety
Tension Awareness

BIBLIOGRAPHY

Gutwirth, S. W. (1975). *The prevention and elimination of "nervous breakdown" through cultivated tension control methods.* In F. J. McGuigan (Ed.), *Tension Control: Proceedings of the First Meeting of the American Association for the Advancement of Tension Control.* Blacksburg, VA: University Publications.

McGuigan, F. J. (1992). *Calm down: A guide for stress and tension control* (2nd ed.). Dubuque, IA: Kendall/Hunt.

Noise Pollution

The concept of noise pollution has a relatively recent origin. Most people, especially those who live in urban areas, are surrounded by excessive noise. Noise pollution is a composite of sounds generated by activities with machines, including car engines, radios, lawn mowers, gardener blowers, factory machinery, office equipment, home appliances, televisions, and overhead jets. Noise is generally associated with industrialized societies, where heavy machinery, motor vehicles, and aircraft have become everyday items. Noise pollution is more intense in the work environment than in the general environment.

Psychologically, the definition of noise is any unwanted sound, in which case it qualifies as a stressor. That includes sounds that might be annoying in one situation and not in another. Any kind of music, for example, even if it is normally soothing, can be irritating ("stressful") if it interferes with what one is trying to do.

A readily measurable physiological effect of noise pollution is damage to hearing, which may be either temporary or permanent; either may cause disruption of normal activities or just general annoyance. The effect is variable, depending upon individual susceptibility and duration of exposure. The stressor of noise pollution can also contribute to such other physiological disorders as ulcers, high blood pressure, and headaches. A variety of factors play a part, including the pace of living in an urban environment and the stresses of cramped living quarters.

Psychological effects of high noise levels have been attributed to increased irritability, lower productivity, decreased tolerance levels, and increased severity of **Headaches, Fatigue,** and **Allergic** responses to continued exposures to high-level noise in the workplace and the general environment.

Whatever the origin, there are steps we can take to control our environment and cushion our ears from unwanted sounds that may create unnecessary stress in our lives. Many American businesses have recognized this and have taken measures to help alleviate noise pollution. Noise can be lowered in the workplace or the home by several methods, including the following:

- Carpeting floors or using area rugs to absorb sound
- Using wallpaper—fabric is better—and hanging paintings or other art objects to help break up the flat wall surface that tends to bounce back sound
- Placing plants and furniture in front of flat surfaces to help absorb noises and keep them from echoing

- Using sound-absorbing dividers in large office areas to create smaller work stations
- Placing padding under appliances that sit on counters to keep them from vibrating
- Designating a "quiet place" to allow people to take a break from unwanted noise and provide for a period of relaxation

SEE ALSO:

Stressful Life Events

BIBLIOGRAPHY

Bell, P. A. (1993). Noise, pollution, and psychopathology. In A. Missagh, A. Ghadirian, & H. E. Lehmann (Eds.), *Environment and psychopathology* (pp. 21–37). New York: Springer.

Krishna, A., & Rai, S. N. (1988). Post noise frustration tolerance as a function of controllability of noise and dependence proneness. *Indian Journal of Psychometry and Education, 19,* 85–89.

Nebel, B. J. (1996). *Environmental science* (5th ed.). Upper Saddle River, NJ: Prentice-Hall.

More quiet means less stress. (1990, Dec). *USA Today.*

Nursing Stress in Students

Description

Nursing is a profession perceived as quite stressful relative to many others. Trainees in nursing education commonly report stressors such as those involving professional relationships, medical procedures, handling the critically ill and dying, fear of failure with feelings of inadequacy, work overload, and observing the suffering of others. Similarly, common responses to stressors among nursing students are reported at levels considerably beyond those expected in the population at large. Examples are absenteeism due to sickness, depression, leaving nurse training, or psychosomatic (somatoform) events such as gastrointestinal disorders, asthma, palpitations, rashes, colds, backaches, neck pains and physical exhaustion (**Fatigue**).

Learning to be a nurse has long been described as a perilous enterprise because it requires learning how to cope with many stressful situations. There are those who would argue that experiencing stressors is necessary to motivate nursing students to learn and excel, yet too much exposure to stressors is clearly undesirable because resulting high anxiety not only disrupts physical and mental health, but also retards learning and performance.

The emotional responses most frequently reported by nursing students include anxieties and frustrations about work and feelings of guilt, misery, and anger when dealing with others. The most frequently reported acts that nursing students relate to stressors include attempts at and thoughts about resigning from their training and searching for alternate careers. In 1992 alone, 35 percent of nursing students in Hong Kong abandoned their training.

Causes

There have been anecdotal reports suggesting that much of the stress inherent in learning to become a nurse arises from the part of the curriculum that is based in the hospital environment. Hospital-based nursing training in some cities has recently introduced changes with the purported aim of rendering the discipline more holistic. However, such additions can result in an expansion of an already considerable curriculum and to new and further demands on nursing students who are training mostly in hospitals. Student nurses in hospital-based training may suffer excessively from unexamined procedures, and much of this may find expression in the above-cited stress symptoms and concurrent reductions in learning; there is the possibility that unwarrantedly stressful conditions imposed by the hospital-based training itself may be a principal cause of stress among student nurses.

Potent stressors to nursing students include problems with supervisory support, timely feedback, and unclear guidelines on performance—the latter being especially emphasized in circumstances where students are required to perform procedures for which they have not received adequate training. High stress ratings are related to the necessity of studying excessively long hours without sufficient free time. There is further conflict between expected and actual clinical practice. This is so probably because of the increasing knowledge and professional concern of the student nurses; that is, conflicts become more apparent and can be reinforced by an enhanced understanding of what is needed and what is actually provided by prevailing expedient practice. It is unreasonable to expect students to learn appropriately if they see an incongruence between instruction as to what should be done and what is actually done.

Students spend most of their time working alone or with other students. This may reinforce their feelings of frustration and stress because inadequate supervision can result in reduced or faulty feedback. If students are asked to perform nursing procedures for which they may not have received sufficient training and under conditions of inadequate guidance and supervision, the excessive fear of the consequences of any errors mounts as training progresses; it takes its toll on learning and on the ability to benefit from training.

Treatment

A more caring and supportive approach to those learning the nursing profession should often be implemented. Practical changes toward this end could include the following:

- Provide the students with more and better information about what to expect through appropriate and accurate orientation programs as well as ward–learning objectives with goal statements during the course of their training.

- Build a realistic bridge between the classroom and the ward. Clinical instructors could facilitate this transition to soften the often demoralizing shock at the discrepancy between theory and the harsh reality of expedient practice.
- Design curriculum to reflect a reasonable concern for students' basic needs.
- Ensure that nurse educators and administrators have special relevant skills to qualify them as such; these should be analogous to those of other professions. Simple seniority or the obtaining of higher degrees should not by themselves be sufficient conditions to teach.

Some degree of experiencing stressors is inseparable from most professional endeavors, and so it is in nursing study and practice. However, every effort should be made to optimize the existing levels and amounts of stressors.

SEE ALSO:

Fatigue, "Nervous"   School/College Stress
Medical School Stress   Student Control

BIBLIOGRAPHY

Bigger, T., Zimmerman, R., & Alpert, G. (1988). Nursing, nursing education and anxiety. *Journal of Nursing Education, 27,* 411–417.
Kelly, B. (1993). The "Real World" of hospital nursing practice as perceived by nursing undergraduates. *Journal of Professional Nursing, 9,* 27–33.
Lindtop, E. (1989). Individual stress and its relationship to termination of nurse training. *Nurse Education Today, 9,* 172–179.
Lindtop, E. (1991). Individual stress among nurses in training: Why some leave while others stay. *Nurse Education Today, 11,* 110–120.
Parkes, K. (1980). Occupational stress among student nurses. *Nursing Times, 76,* 113–116.
Parkes, K. (1985). Stressful episodes reported by first year nursing students: A descriptive account. *Social Science Medicine, 20,* 945–953.
Sellek, T. (1982). Satisfying and anxiety creating incidents for nursing students. *Nursing Times, 78,* 137–140.

Nutrition and Stress

Description

Estimates are that the human body needs between 40 and 60 nutrients to maintain proper functioning. When under stress the body's needs increase, and a nutrient-poor diet increases vulnerability to stress. Thus a cycle can occur wherein stress leads to poor eating habits and illness, which in turn increases stress. Nutrition and stress are especially linked in the aged because older people in particular change their eating habits as they become stressed. An example of how poor nutrition exacerbates stress occurs when a calcium-deficient diet deprives the body of the calcium needed to counteract the higher levels of lactic acid produced by tense muscles. The result is greater fatigue, anxiety, and irritability than if one ate a more balanced diet.

A sound diet can help control or prevent many stress-influenced disorders such as high blood pressure, indigestion, ulcers, constipation, obesity, and diabetes. Proper nutrition may also aid in the reduction of depression, irritability, anxiety, headaches, fatigue, and insomnia.

Causes

Some nutritionists contend that dietary deficiency is often rooted in the fact that modern foods do not adequately meet our nutritional needs: Today's supermarket foods are often so nutritionally inadequate that there are estimates that the average American would have to eat approximately three times the quantity of food his or her grandparents ate in order to obtain an equivelant nutritional value. Dietary deficiency can also arise from the fact that the stressed individual is more likely to engage in unhealthy eating practices, thereby increasing the possibility that nutritional needs are not met, which in turn increases the effects of stress.

Treatment

Arguably, vitamin and mineral supplements are important adjuncts to the treatment of stress and related disorders. B vitamins function synergistically with each other and are necessary for the proper functioning of the nervous system; they also can be beneficial by counteracting the increased levels of lactic acid caused by excessive muscle tension.

A well-nourished person is always better able to cope with the nutritional demands caused by stress than a person who doesn't maintain a "well-balanced" diet. This is because during prolonged stress, there is an alteration in the body's metabolism of vitamins and minerals and a depletion of amino acids from skeletal muscle. Therefore, individuals who are under chronic or severe stress may need to increase their intake of proteins and other nutrients more so than will nonstressed or moderately stressed individuals.

SEE ALSO:

Eating Disorders

BIBLIOGRAPHY

Capaldi, E. D. (Ed.). (1996). *Why we eat what we eat: The psychology of eating.* Washington, DC: American Psychological Association.

Garner, D. M., & Garfinkel, P. L. (Eds.). (1997). *Handbook of treatment for eating disorders* (2nd ed.). New York: Guilford Press.

Girdano, D., & Everly, G. (1979). *Controlling stress and tension: A holistic approach.* Englewood Cliffs, NJ: Prentice-Hall.

Goliszek, A. G. (1988). *Breaking the stress habit: A modern guide to one minute stress management.* Winston-Salem, NC: Carolina Press.

McGuigan, F. J. (1994). *Biological Psychology: A cybernetic science.* Englewood Cliffs, NJ: Prentice-Hall.

Thompson, K. (Ed.). (1996). *Body image, eating disorders and obesity: An integrative guide for assessment and treatment.* Washington, DC: American Psychological Association.

O
Obesity–Obsessive-Compulsive Behavior

Obesity

Description

A common description of obesity is being overweight by about 30 percent more than the norm, as given in standard tables of ranges for optimal weights, based on gender, body type, and age. Body fat testing is also used to determine the degree of obesity. Guidelines of a fat-to-muscle ratio of 20 to 35 percent for women, and of 15 to 25 percent for men are considered satisfactory.

Obesity can contribute to or is associated with a wide range of serious disorders. It is known to contribute to increased illness and death from diabetes, coronary artery disease, stroke, and kidney and gallbladder disorders. The higher the amount of excess weight, the greater the chances for serious problems. For example, a person who is 40 percent overweight is twice as likely to die from coronary heart disease as the person who is not overweight. A person with diabetes who is 20 to 30 percent overweight is three times as likely to die from diabetes as the normal-weighted diabetic. The loss of excess weight has been known to resolve problems such as hypertension and diabetes in some cases.

Causes

Two general causes of obesity are: (1) Endogenous obesity, which is due to physiological conditions involving the pituitary, adrenal, or thyroid glands, and is relatively rare. Genetic/heredity factors are also involved in certain cases of obesity. (2) Exogenous obesity, which is very common, especially in the United States where an estimated one of every five men and almost one of every three women are obese. Exogenous obesity is caused by overeating. As an excess number of calories are consumed relative to the amount of energy expended by the body for normal growth and repair of tissues, the body stores these excess calories as fat. An unbalanced diet with excessive levels of sugars, fats, and starches and the consumption of large amounts of food in general contribute to the process.

During times of increased exposure to stressors, certain people become compulsive eaters and may not be fully aware of how much and how often they eat. Psychological variables may also be involved, such as low life satisfaction, **Frustration,** and **Anger.**

Exogenous overeating often is a learned behavior. Compulsive eaters often fail to distinguish between their need for food and learned wants. The behavior of ingestion involves an amazing number of brain and body regions, neurotransmitters, specialized neurons, and receptors. They combine with external stressors to make obesity a complex disorder that generally requires extended treatment.

Treatment

Several kinds of treatment are often used (sometimes in conjugation). They include **Psychotherapies,** cognitive restructuring, diet and lifestyle changes, **Behavior Therapy, Exercise, Progressive Relaxation,** and medication. Balanced diet and caloric reduction, combined with moderate regular exercise, are good self-help measures. Massive weight loss in a short period of time is not healthy, and loss of only 1 to 2 pounds of weight per week is recommended. What is eaten as well as when it is eaten is important. Self-control techniques for the treatment of obesity include the removal of undesirable foods from the house (such as high fat and high sugar content foods), and the consumption of at least three balanced meals per day.

Appetite suppressant drugs are available, but many physicians are reluctant to prescribe them due to possible side effects. Appetite suppressants may not be effective, especially if the user eats compulsively, whether or not hunger is a factor.

SEE ALSO:

Anger

Behavioral Therapy

Eating Disorders

Exercise, Benefits of

Progressive Relaxation

Psychotherapies

Stress Management Methods

BIBLIOGRAPHY

Beech, H. R., Burns, L. E., & Sheffield, B. F. (1982). *A behavioral approach to the management of stress: A practical guide to techniques.* New York: Wiley.

Garner, D. M., & Garfinkel, P. L. (Eds.). (1997). *Handbook of treating eating disorders* (2nd ed.). New York: Guilford Press.

McGuigan, F. J. (1994). *Biological psychology: A cybernetic science.* Englewood Cliffs, NJ: Prentice-Hall.

Peeke, P. M., & Chrousos, G. P. (1995). Hypercortisolism and obesity. In G. P. Chrousos, R. McCarthy, K. Pacak, G. Cizza, E. Sternberg, P. W. Gold, & R. Kvetnansky (Eds.), *Stress: Basic mechanisms and clinical implications. Annals of the New York Academy of Sciences,* (Vol. 771, pp. 665–676). New York: New York Academy of Sciences.

Thompson, J. K. (1996). *Body image, eating disorders, and obesity: An integrative guide for assessment and treatment.* Washington, DC: American Psychological Association.

Wadden, T. A., & Van Itallie (Eds.). (1992). *Treatment of the seriously obese patient.* New York: Guilford Press.

Obsessive-Compulsive Behavior

Description

Obsessive-compulsive behavior can be a psychiatric disorder with roots in **Stress** and **Anxiety.** Sufferers who exhibit obsessive-compulsive behavior usually experience intrusive thoughts that interfere with concentration; they may also perform ritualized behaviors that consume long periods of the day and interfere significantly with daily life. The resulting mood disturbances can be as painful as those experienced in affective disorders (depression, etc.). Attempts to resist a compulsion produce mounting tension and anxiety, which are revealed immediately by the individual's giving in to it. Obsessive thoughts and compulsive behaviors are often performed in attempts to "ward off harm" from the individual or a loved one. Approximately 2 to 3 percent of the general population suffers from this disorder.

Obsessions are unwanted, repetitive, irresistible thoughts or urges. These thoughts or urges are based on irrational ideas that the person consciously both believes and disbelieves. Compulsions are apparently meaningless acts that one must engage in repeatedly: continuously counting numbers, washing hands over and over, or performing some ritualistic act such as checking doors *exactly five times* before retiring for the night. Typically, obsession and compulsion are tied together. For example, a person might be obsessed with an irrational fear of hurting a loved one, and to ward off this fear, may act out by checking a child's room 18 times a night. Obsessive themes of dirt, disease, or contamination are common. Much compulsive behavior can be categorized as checking or cleaning behaviors. They are usually stereotyped, with little variation from one time to the next. Any relief from anxiety one can experience by performing these rituals is only short-term.

Perfectionism is another manifestation of a compulsive personality. A perfectionist, often plagued with feelings of self-doubt and guilt, works hard to overcome feelings of failure and sometimes, among professionals, to appease a considerable sense of responsibility. Some have inflated expectations and inflated self-worth so that personal beliefs in uniqueness and self-importance are formed.

Causes

Psychological roots may stem from trauma and/or abuse, and thus may be a coping mechanism for fears stemming therefrom. Anxiety reduction is thought to play an important role in the persistence of the ritualistic behavior. Studies of patients with obsessive-compulsive disorder exhibit significant reductions of anxiety and discomfort following completion of the repetitive behavior. Although some rituals lead to increased anxiety, it is postulated that such rituals are maintained in order to prevent still further increases in anxiety, or to prevent some other painful affect such as guilt or depression.

The fact that patients respond remarkably well to medication suggests that there may be a neurological basis for this disorder. The search for specific causes currently focuses on the interaction of neurobiological factors and environmental influences. Research indicates biochemical and/or hereditary predispositions. Specifically, serotonin deficiencies have been seen to produce these disorders in some cases.

There does seem to be an interesting relationship between obsessive-compulsive disorder and depression; obsessional traits are commonly found in the histories of depressed patients, and increased incidence of depression is found in obsessional persons. Depression is also frequently accompanied by obsessive-compulsive symptoms.

Attaining high grades for acceptance in professional schools of higher education; years of training amid high physical, mental and emotional demands; and the requirement of performing at high levels despite exhaustion—all these contribute to what may be considered a sense of exaggerated responsibility or perfectionism among many professionals.

Treatment

Psychotherapies, Behavioral Therapy, Psychopharmacological therapy, and even psychosurgery have all have been used in attempts to treat obsessive-compulsive behavior. Though this disorder has been notoriously difficult to treat, behavior therapy seems to offer the best documented success. One strategy of behavior treatments exposes the patient to ritual-inducing stimuli but prevents them from acting out the usual compulsive response. Exposure to stimuli may be gradually, incrementally increased, so as to minimize distress in the patient; or exposure may be abrupt and severe, as in maximal flooding.

Use of antidepressants as a treatment for obsessive-compulsive disorder has been a source of recent interest. The drug chlorimipramine has been successful in treating the disorder as well. This drug modifies the serotin level in the blood.

SEE ALSO:

Addictive Behaviors

Alcoholism

Alcohol Abuse in the Workplace

Anxiety

Behavioral Therapy

Compulsive Behavior

Drug Abuse in the Workplace

Gambling

Psychopharmacology

Psychotherapies

Stress Signals

Tobacco Use

BIBLIOGRAPHY

Cooper, A. M., Frances, A. J., & Sacks, M. H. (1986). *The personality disorders and neuroses.* Psychiatric Series (Vol. 1). Philadelphia: J. B. Lippincott.

Fals-Stewart, W., Marks, A. P., & Schaefer, J., (1993). A comparison of behavioral group therapy and individual behavior therapy in treating obsessive-compulsive disorder. *The Journal of Nervous and Mental Disease, 181,* 189–193.

Jenike, M. A. (1983). Obsessive compulsive disorder. *Comprehensive Psychiatry, 24,* 99–115.

Jenike, M. A., Baer, L., & Minichiello, W. E. (Eds.). (1990). *Obsessive-compulsive disorders: Theory and management* (2nd ed.). Chicago: Year Book Medical Publishers.

Marks, I. M. (1981). *Cure and care of neuroses: Theory and practice of behavioral psychotherapy.* New York: Wiley.

Schwartz, J. (1996). *Brain lock.* New York: ReganBooks.

Steketee, G., & White, K. (1990). *When once is not enough: Help for obsessive compulsives.* Oakland, CA: New Harbinger.

P
Pain–Psychotherapies

Pain

Description

Efforts to avoid or discontinue pain are probably the most powerful motivated behaviors. They take precedence over all our other needs and wants. When pain is acute, it *demands* immediate response. Intense pain comes across strongly to insist that we control its cause. *Pain signals the organism to stop doing what it is doing!*

Pain is a necessary part of living. It is a warning signal that we are being harmed. By learning that something can produce pain, we also learn to avoid (and in some ways to fear) it. Humans have learned to avoid oncoming trucks, but dogs stand fearlessly in front of them. Some people have been born without the ability to feel pain and are not warned of dangers. As a consequence, such individuals suffer many injuries that might be avoided if they were sensitive to pain and could express the caution that pain provides. They have, for instance, died of ruptured appendices. The child with congenital insensitivity to pain does not learn what fear is, cannot connect pain to punishment, and rarely lives long. However, sometimes pain has no value—for example, that experienced by a terminally ill person whose body has already suffered destruction and for whom additional pain cannot prevent further damage. If such pain has some kind of function, it certainly is not the usual one.

Self-reporting rating scales are frequently used to measure pain. For instance, the McGill Pain Questionnaire is composed of a series of adjective pain descriptors that reliably classify pain into the following three dimensions: sensory, affective, and evaluative. Patients lacking positive neurologic findings tend to be more vague and inconsistent in their pain descriptions on this questionnaire.

Causes

Pain sources are usually classified as organic or functional (behavioral, psychological). In organic sources, bodily injuries are sensed by stimulation of free nerve endings that function as pain receptors. A sharp jab to the skin, for example, causes complex reactions in various regions of the brain. Neuroscientists have traced separate pain pathways—bundles of nerve fibers that transmit signals from throughout the body through the spinal column and up into the brain. Distinct "pain centers" have been identified in various regions of the brain, each with a different function; for example, one region of the cortex collects information on the location, duration, and intensity of a painful event. Knowledge about pain centers increases our understanding of pain itself so that we may control it with various methods. The various regions of the central nervous system function with the accepted theory of pain known as the gate control theory.

Pain may be contributed to by poor overall health, stomach and digestive disturbances, various aches, disturbances in the sense of touch, irregular heartbeat, irrational worry about one's health, fatigue, and sexual difficulties. Whatever the source, pain is an unpleasant sensory or emotional experience that is normally associated with injury or threat of injury to the body.

To understand psychological influences on pain, picture yourself about to receive an injection or a drilling from a dentist. If you anticipate pain, especially if you fight it, you can intensify it. Your thoughts about what you expect can become a self-fulfilling prophecy. The effectiveness of suggestion to experience pain is illustrated in a study in which dummy (nonfunctional) electrodes were attached to subjects' heads. They were told that, through the electrodes, they were going to receive electric shocks that might induce headaches. Two-thirds of the subjects reported some degree of headache during the experiment event though no current was actually used. Just the word *pain* in the instructions influenced some subjects to rate a nonpainful stimulus as painful. Suggestion of pain has clinical importance. About one-third of patients who go to general medical practitioners report some kind of pain, principally from the abdomen, head, and back, although examinations reveal no apparent organic cause.

Treatment

There are many approaches to controlling pain such as the use of anesthetics or analgesic drugs (for example, aspirin and ibuprofen), electrical stimulation treatments, massage, and various behavioral methods. Recent findings, however, indicate that our society's obsession with pain relief is being diminished as a result of growing caution by physicians due to the increasing number of people who experience dangerous side effects from pain medication. The overuse of nonsteroidal anti-inflammatory drugs (NSAIDS), such as the family of medications containing ibuprofen, has recently led to an explosion in the number of cases of bleeding ulcers that required hospitalization and which have also led to death. Studies have revealed that about 25 percent of people who frequently use NSAIDS for chronic pain relief develop ulcers.

Behavior Therapy methods are major components of most of the multimodal treatment procedures. The two major groups of behavior therapy techniques are operant-conditioning methods, in which an attempt is made to change behaviors by modifying environmental consequences, and self-management techniques, in which the patient is taught to directly alter behavior. Since muscular tension exacerbates pain, relaxation of the striated muscles is effective in eliminating or alleviating many of the pain experiences. Much pain can be relaxed away. Fighting pain (overtensing) may worsen it so that the pain–tension relationship becomes a vicious circle such that the more tension the more pain, and so on.

Another response to pain that is being practiced is teaching the patient how to tolerate it in certain situations. For example, an approach to treating lower back pain is to do nothing. The idea is that lower back pain may be an injury similar to an ankle sprain and simply requires rest. Pain is an indication that one should not use an injured part. Sometimes it is advantageous to have a pain message around because it helps prevent a reinjury.

The body has evolved in many ways as a marvelous self-healing system. Biochemical events are closely integrated with the numerous neuromuscular phenomena involved in pain. For instance, the brain has developed its own pain-relieving system through the release of endorphins which, like morphine, mimic the body's own means of pain relief. Both morphine and endorphins create a euphoria. When opioids such as morphine are injected, the patients usually report that the pain is still there, but he or she does not care about it. Opioids are the most efficacious chemical agents available for relieving pain. They activate several descending pathways from the brain to inhibit pain.

SEE ALSO:

Behavior Therapy
Pain, Chronic
Stress Management Methods

BIBLIOGRAPHY

Bruno, F. J. (1993). *Psychological symptoms.* New York: Wiley.
Gottlieb, H. (1977). Comprehensive rehabilitation of patients having chronic pain. *Archives of Physical Medicine and Rehabilitation, 58,* 101–108.
Jamison, R. N. (1996). *Learning to master your chronic pain.* Sarasota, FL: Professional Resources Press/Professional Resource exchange.

Pain, Chronic

Description

Chronic pain is pain that persists beyond normal healing time after an accident or injury or that accompanies such diseases as arthritis. If one has multiple recurrent pains of at least several years' duration, it is considered to be a somatization ("body") disorder. But if pain is the only symptom ("psychological factors") and it apparently is not due to known organic causes, it is diagnosed as a conversion disorder. In conversion disorders the distribution of pain throughout the body is inconsistent and quite varied.

Chronic pain is one of the most frequent complaints made to physicians and is one of the leading medical problems in terms of hospitalization costs and disability payments. Chronic pain may be classified as a stress condition because it often causes the individual to be cranky—also because impaired movements may disrupt relationships due to frustration at inability to carry out daily life tasks. Often the patient becomes increasingly discouraged, helpless and even hypochondriacal. Chronic pain serves no beneficial purpose and usually there is prolonged suffering. The person may become somatically preoccupied, such as magnifying every day bodily occurrences out of proportion. He or she may become hypersensitive to the slightest possible pain.

Causes

Chronic pain often results from progressive degenerative diseases such as **Arthritis,** with common locations in the lower back, neck, and shoulders, joints, hands and feet, as well as from injuries that linger on, not healing. Diseases such as arthritis are often exacerbated by excessive muscle tension and sensory components within a patient's experience. Longevity of chronic pain can occur if patients are reinforced ("encouraged") to continue it, for example, they may seek to benefit from disability or insurance payments or by receiving special care and attention from others.

Treatment

There are many ways to attempt to control and relieve pain. Prominent is the use of anesthetics and analgesic drugs, such as aspirin and ibuprofen, and electrical stimulation treatments. While analgesics and narcotics may temporarily decrease pain, their long term use is contraindicated because of habituation and such side effects as constipation and addiction. Behavioral treatments for chronic pain have included such methods as **Progressive Relaxation, Biofeedback, Hypnosis,** guided imagery, **Operant Conditioning** techniques (e.g., removing the reinforcement) and cognitive-behavioral therapy. Turner (1982) found that relaxation training, and relaxation combined with cognitive behavioral therapy significantly improved measures of pain-related dysfunction, depression, pain relief, indicators of health care, and average number of visits to a physician for pain problems.

SEE ALSO:

Arthritis, Rheumatoid
Biofeedback
Conditioning, Classical and
    Instrumental (Operant)

Hypnosis
Hypochondriasis
Pain
Progressive Relaxation

BIBLIOGRAPHY

Azar, B. (1996, December). Behavioral interventions are proven to reduce pain. *Monitor of the American Psychological Association.*

Cains, D., & Pasiono, J. (1977). Comparison of verbal reinforcement and feedback in the operant treatment of disability due to chronic low back pain. *Behavior Therapy, 8,* 621–630.

Hanson, R. W., & Gerber, K. E. (1990). *Coping with chronic pain: A guide to patient self-management.* New York: Guilford Press.

Mcichenbaum, D., & Turk, D. (1976). The cognitive-behavioral management of anxiety, depression and pain. In P. O. Davidson (Ed.), *The behavioral management of anxiety, depression and pain* (pp. 1–34). New York: Brunner/Mazel.

Turner, J. A. (1982). Comparison of group progressive-relaxation training and cognitive-behavioral group therapy for chronic low back pain. *Journal of Consulting and Clinical Psychology, 50,* 757–765.

Panic Attacks

Description

Panic attacks occur when anxiety suddenly becomes overwhelming, leading to an intense disabling arousal of the autonomic nervous system, which creates an inability to function. Symptoms and signs include shortness of breath; becoming flushed; heart palpitations; feeling choked, dizzy, and lightheaded; chest tightness or pain; nausea or abdominal discomfort; sweating and weakness in the legs; headaches and blurred vision. The fear of having a heart attack is also common.

An estimated four to seven million people in the U.S. experience such panic attacks. Most of the sufferers are women in late adolescence or early adulthood, in times of choices, transitions, and added responsibilities. Those with panic attacks usually perceive their physical health to be poorer than comparison individuals. They tend to be frequent users of emergency, hospital, and ambulatory services; an accurate diagnosis of the presenting symptoms is difficult. It has been estimated that the average panic disorder patient may visit 10 physicians before an accurate diagnosis is made. The disorder may lead to phobias such as **Agoraphobia** (fear of going outdoors), and also insomnia, eating disorders, and **Post-Traumatic Stress Disorder** (PTSD).

Causes

Panic disorder patients often have a family history of anxiety disorder occurring during periods of great stress. This disorder may also have a biochemical basis. Strenuous activity has been known to intensify the chronic anxiety symptoms, along with their blood levels of lactic acid. The injection of sodium lactate has been shown to reduce the lactic acid and stop the panic.

Prolonged periods of anxiety-related stress contribute greatly to panic disorder attacks. The sudden withdrawal from alcohol, tobacco, or drugs as well as the experience of traumatic events such as natural disasters, combat trauma, or physical/sexual assault can be contributing factors.

In this disorder there is chronic, excessive muscular tension of which the patient may or may not be aware. In either case the original source of the anxiety may have been learned from a childhood experience or a more current event.

Treatment

Panic disorder is treated effectively with behavior therapies, especially **Progressive Relaxation** therapy, in which the overtense muscles that generate the anxiety may be relaxed. Adjusting the body through learning new behaviors can prevent or decrease the severity of panic disorder attacks. Medication, such as antidepressants, is advantageous when used in combination with behavioral therapy. Some biochemical research indicates that patients improve with the use of tricyclic antidepressants, monoamine oxidase inhibitors, or benzodiazepine. These medications act primarily in the central nervous system, which suggests that they control the disorder by modifying the central components of neuromuscular circuits.

SEE ALSO:

Agoraphobia
Anxiety
Phobic Disorders

Post Traumatic Stress Disorder (PTSD)
Progressive Relaxation
Social Phobia

BIBLIOGRAPHY

Asnis, G. M., & Meir van Praag, H. (Eds). (1995). *Panic disorder: Clinical, biological and treatment aspects.* New York: John Wiley.
Clark, D. A. (1996). Panic disorder: From theory to therapy. In P. M. Salkovskis (Ed.), *Frontiers of cognitive therapy* (pp. 318–344). New York: Guilford.
Wilhelm, F., & Margraf, J. (1997). A cognitive-behavioral treatment package for panic disorder with agoraphobia. In W. T. Roth, & I. D. Yalom (Eds.), *Treating anxiety disorders. The Jossey-Bass library of current clinical techniques* (pp. 205–244). San Francisco: Jossey-Bass.
Zal, M. N. (1990). *Panic disorder: The great pretender.* New York: Plenum.

Phobic Disorders

Description

A phobia is an irrational, obsessive, and intense fear that is focused on a specific circumstance, idea, or thing. Phobic disorders are a subcategory of anxiety disorders. The essential feature of a specific phobia is marked and persistent fear of clearly discernible, circumscribed objects or situations. Exposure to the phobic stimulus almost invariably provokes an immediate anxiety response. Some common phobias are fear of: public places, high places, closed spaces, social situations, death, the dark, animals, foreigners or other groups of people, meteorological events, and electricity. Phobia sufferers may experience a variety of symptoms, including dizziness, palpitations, nausea, and immobilization.

Phobic individuals can generally be identified according to two basic elements: (1) the phobia manifests as a specific, unreasonably excessive fear of something in the environment, and (2) the phobic individual spends much time and effort avoiding the feared object or situation.

Phobic disorders have been assigned to three subtypes:

1. Agoraphobia. Literally "fear of open spaces." Individuals experience marked fear of public places from which escape may be difficult or help not available in sudden incapacitation (e,g, crowds, tunnels, bridges, public transportation, elevators).

2. Social Phobia. Irrational fear of, and compelling desire to avoid a situation in which the individual is exposed to possible scrutiny by others and fears that he or she may act in a way that will be humiliating or embarrassing.

3. Simple Phobia. Irrational fear of, and compelling desire to avoid, objects or situations other than those described under agoraphobia or social phobia. Phobic objects are often animals, and phobic situations often involve heights or closed places.

Causes

Phobic disorder is caused by an external stimulus that is not necessarily threatening but is perceived as stressful. Phobias are learned according to conditioning principles wherein a nonthreatening stimulus is associated with one that evokes a fear response—as having been locked in a closet as a child could lead to claustrophobia. Genetic theory holds that there is a genetic predisposition to phobic disorders, but the connection has not been clearly discovered.

Treatment

Since most, if not all, phobias are learned by conditioning, reconditioning methods as applied in behavior therapy have achieved considerable success in eliminating them. **Progressive Relaxation** has also been successful, with particular attention given to relaxing the eye musculature during practice and thus eliminating unwanted visual images. The individual can be desensitized by exposure to the fear-provoking event/object at increasing levels of intensity while experiencing muscle relaxation. Another behavioral technique is "flooding," in which the person is exposed to the "worst case scenario" with no way out in order to recognize that the fear is truly unfounded. Flooding is risky and should be done only by a competent therapist. **Biofeedback, Hypnosis,** and **Stress Inoculation Training** have also been used to treat phobias.

SEE ALSO:

Anxiety   Progressive Relaxation
Behavior Therapy   Social Phobia
Biofeedback   Stress Inoculation Training

BIBLIOGRAPHY

American Psychiatric Association. (1994). *Diagnostic and statistical manual of mental disorders* (4th ed.). Washington, DC: Author.
Cooper, A. M., Frances, A. J., & Sacks, M. H. (1986). *The personality disorders and neuroses, Psychiatry Series* (Vol. 1). Philadelphia: J. B. Lippincott.
McGuigan, F. J. (1992). *Calm down: A guide for stress and tension control.* Dubuque, IA: Kendall/Hunt.

Police Stress

Description/Causes

The sources of stress for police are so numerous and commonly known that they will not be elaborated here. The effects of their jobs on their family lives and visa versa are especially deserving of attention.

Treatment

Typically, there are employee-assistance programs available in police departments. However, only a small percentage (only 15 percent in one study) were aware that such programs were available to them. Even so, police officers often believe that there is a stigma attached to mental health services, or they have concerns about the confidentiality of such services, or the like.

Police departments should counteract such conditions and offer well-validated **Stress Management** programs for their members.

SEE ALSO:

Stress Management Methods

BIBLIOGRAPHY

Sewell, J. D. (1994). The stress of homicide investigations. *Death studies, 18,* 565–582.
Yates, D. L., & Pillai, V. K. (1996). Attitudes towards community policing: A causal analysis. *Social Science Analysis, 33,* 193–209.

Post-Traumatic Stress Disorder (PTSD)

Description

Post-traumatic stress disorder is a frequently diagnosed, stress-induced psychological abnormality. PTSD results from rare and serious psychological traumas that are perceived as severe threats. Such traumas occur in military combat, rape, torture, assault, natural disaster and accidents. Witnessing harm or death to a loved one can evoke reaction symptoms after the immediate stressor is over.

This condition was referred to as "shell shock" during World War I and "battle fatigue" during World War II; PTSD was listed as a diagnostic category by the American Psychiatric Association in 1980.

Symptoms can include a complex set of intrusive, distractive feelings, ideas, and phobias related to the stressful event. Unwanted images are often visualized, as well as nightmares; and, in rare instances, dissociative states lasting for hours or even days can occur as the event is relived. Anxiety, depression, guilt, shame, and outbursts of rage are also common as a reaction to stimuli that may appear to others as minor or easy to cope with. The individual may have difficulty relaxing; be hypervigilant or hyperaroused; experience insomnia, rapid heartbeat, sweating, or hallucinations; and have an exaggerated startle response. PTSD has also been known to include the unexplained impairment of sensory functions such as sight and hearing as part of the reaction to witnessing war atrocities. Exposure to unusual or extended trauma during childhood may have an adverse impact on normal character development in the areas of cognition, attention, impulse control, and social interaction.

It is typical for weeks, months, or even years to pass after the trauma before the full syndrome of symptoms is experienced. The sufferer may go to great lengths to avoid exposure to the triggering stimuli and may attempt to cope in ways that lead to other disorders, such as excessive use of tobacco, alcohol, narcotics, or food.

Not all PTSD sufferers experience the full range of symptoms, but many suffer to the point that their lives are disrupted and they are in need of treatment. Passage of time itself usually does not bring relief.

However, relatively few who experience trauma develop PTSD. It is estimated that, among Vietnam War veterans, 8.5 percent of females and 15.2 percent of males were sufferers of PTSD 15 or more years after wartime service.

Causes

PTSD may develop in any person who undergoes a major traumatic experience, such as an accident or a battle. Many factors interact to cause PTSD, including the type of stressor, the social environment of the traumatic and post-traumatic period, and the personality (behavioral) characteristics of the person involved. The stressor is not itself sufficient to lead to this disorder, though prolonged catastrophic conditions such as torture as a prisoner of war have a high probability of doing so. Repeated traumas or chronic stress may lead to diminished function (depression) or aperiodic "false alarms" (anxiety).

Treatment

Various modes of therapy are used to deal with PTSD, including **Behavior Therapy,** supportive administration of sedating drugs, group therapy with other PTSD sufferers who are compatible, and individual **Psychotherapy.** The common aim of their use is to help the individual to understand and accept the traumatic experience and to restore normal functioning.

The individual experiencing PTSD should be informed that he or she is not "going crazy" and that symptoms could be typical, adaptive responding to some physical or psychological terror. Unhealed memories of injuries and so forth can be explored in psychotherapy. Usually, interventions are intended to increase the victim's control over his or her circumstances, build trust, clarify boundaries, and teach assertiveness, with the goal of restoring behavioral effectiveness.

Some individuals may have an inadequate external support network, and if they are out of control, may need hospitalization. Hospitalization may become involuntary if they are dangerous to themselves or others. PTSD patients who are victims of single-blow events, such as rape, may benefit from crisis intervention and short-term therapy. Long-term therapy is usually expected for the individual who has been a victim of long-term trauma.

SEE ALSO:

Behavioral Therapy
Phobic Disorders
Psychotherapies

BIBLIOGRAPHY

Eth, S., & Pynoos, R. S. (Eds.). (1985). *Post-traumatic stress disorder in children.* Washington, DC: American Psychiatric Press.
Pynoos, R., Nader, K., & March, J. (1991). Posttraumatic stress disorder. In J. Weiner (Ed.), *Textbook of child and adolescent psychiatry* (pp. 339–348). Washington, DC: American Psychiatric Press.
Saigh, P. A. (1991). The development of posttraumatic stress disorder following four different types of traumatization. *Behavior research and therapy, 29,* 213–216.

Pregnancy and Childbirth Stress

Description

During pregnancy and childbirth, a woman experiences dramatic physical changes, often with considerable physical discomfort and pain; for example, she will frequently suffer from **Fatigue, Backache,** weight gain, nausea, swelling, **Constipation, Hemorrhoids,** leg cramps, and dizziness. Physical changes including fluctuating hormone levels can also lead to changes in body image that can become a psychological stressor. Even successful childbirth can be stressful in the sense of **Eustress** (positive stress) due to overreaction with excess tension.

Cause

As the fetus grows, its increased weight and hormonal changes in the woman place a physical strain on the mother's body. After the birthing, the body's healing process and hormonal changes continue, which can be stressful, along with the mother's desire to return to her pre-pregnancy condition.

Treatment

General discomforts may be reduced by sufficient rest and sleep, a balanced diet, and regular mild exercise such as walking or swimming. Supporting the back and elevating the legs while sitting may help to comfort the back. Overall body tension that contributes to discomfort can be relieved by **Relaxation.** Due to the increased risk of birth defects, alcohol and tobacco should be eliminated during pregnancy. The use of drugs and medication should be avoided unless closely guided by a physician. During childbirth, the use of **Breathing** and relaxation procedures is encouraged to help alleviate some of the tension and pain caused by that activity.

SEE ALSO:

Backache
Breathing Techniques
Constipation
Eustress (Positive Stress)

Fatigue, "Nervous"
Hemorrhoids
Progressive Relaxation

BIBLIOGRAPHY

Good, R. S., Lederman, R. P., Osofsky, H. J., Youngs, D. D. (1990). Birth-related reactions as sources of stress. In J. D. Noshpitz & R. D. Coddington (Eds.), *Stressors and adjustment disorders.* New York: Wiley.

Hotchner, T. (1979). *Pregnancy and childbirth: The complete guide for a new life.* New York: Avon Books.

Jacobson, E. (1965). *How to relax and have your baby.* New York: McGraw-Hill.

McGuigan, F. J. (1992). *Calm down: A guide for stress and tension control* (2nd ed.). Dubuque, IA: Kendall/Hunt.

Ussher, J. M. (1989). *The psychology of the female body.* London, England: Routledge.

Verny, T. R. (Ed.). (1987). *Pre- and perinatal psychology: An introduction.* New York: Human Sciences Press.

Progressive Relaxation

Progressive Relaxation (PR) was developed by **Edmund Jacobson** starting in 1908, and he applied it for over 70 years. He was empirically guided through electromyographic scientific and clinical research, resulting in the most efficient method available for relaxing and controlling the entire body.

Tension is defined as contraction of striated muscle fibers, while relaxation is the lengthening of those fibers. The principles of this method of relaxation are (1) to identify and study a localized signal of tension (the classical muscle sense of Sir Charles Bell, reported in the last century) that is produced by muscular contraction; note that those tension signals are produced when muscles contract and generate afferent and efferent neural impulses that go to and from the brain (see **Tension Awareness**); then (2) to allow the tension signal to relax away; and finally (3) to study the contrast between the previous state of tension and the ensuing state of relaxation. Once the learner fully understands those basic notions, it is simply a matter of systematic repetition throughout all muscular regions of the body. Thoroughness is required, since almost half the body weight is comprised of some 1030 striated muscles.

Progressive Relaxation is designed so that one can control the entire striated musculature through which the other systems of the body can be largely controlled. Overtension of the striated muscles can affect the central nervous system, which in turn can have deleterious effects on other systems of the body. The clinical applications of progressive relaxation fall into two general categories, psychiatric and psychosomatic disorders. Psychiatric disorders include **Phobias, Depression, and Anxiety,** while psychosomatic (somatoform) disorders include **Esophageal Spasm, Hypertension, Spastic Colon, Headaches,** and **Backaches.** In either case, the appropriate therapy is to reverse the overtension process by relaxing the striated muscles (see figure in Introduction on page xiii). The therapeutic process to change behavior, both overt and covert, has three stages.

Stage One: In this stage, the patient specifies some contingent relationships between muscle responding and a complaint. This is achieved by identifying tension signals that control particular maladaptive thoughts or other disorders (e.g., one may relate tension in the abdomen with **Gastrointestinal Disorders** such as **Colitis, Ulcers, Diarrhea,** and **Constipation**).

Stage Two: The patient achieves control over the difficulty (complaint) by relaxing the relevant control (muscular tension) signals. If he or she has disturbing visual images such as crashing in an airplane, control can largely be obtained by relaxing the eye muscles so that the visual image is relaxed away. When the eyes are totally relaxed, there is no visual imagery, or visual perception either. The eyes must move before there can be visualization or perception (just as covert speech behavior is necessary for understanding what is being silently read).

Stage Three: The contingent relations with the therapeutic control of the problem are generalized to behavior in the external environment through **Differential Relaxation.** If, for example, the problem is pain in the abdomen due to spastic colon that occurs in social situations in everyday life, one learns to relax the abdominal muscles, along with muscles throughout the body, especially when entering into such social relationships.

In specifically learning the method, the first region of the body to be controlled is the arms (Jacobson, 1938, McGuigan, 1992). To start, the learner bends the hand at the wrist; the position is held for a minute or two while the tension signal is studied. This particular localized tension signal is found in the dorsal (upper) surface of the forearm and no doubt is the first time the learner has ever specifically recognized what localized tension feels like. Once there is a good clear image of that tension signal, the hand is allowed to relax like a limp dishrag—the hand simply collapses when support is removed. The learner thus allows the striated muscle fibers to elongate by "letting go." With practice, the tension signal can be relaxed or tensed to an appropriate degree at will, at which point it becomes a *control signal.*

The method calls for thoroughness; there are a number of control signals in each arm that need to be studied. After sufficient practice with the arms, the learner proceeds with the legs, in the same thorough manner, up through the buttocks, the trunk, the abdominal region, and through the chest, back, shoulders, neck, eyes, and the speech region. The muscles of the jaws are particularly vulnerable to tension control problems of **Bruxism,** and **Temporomandibular Joint Syndrome (TMJ),** and control of the tongue is especially effective for helping individuals to relax and go to **Sleep.**

Upon completion of this phase of training, the learner will have studied all of the 1030 or so muscles of the body in groups while learning to relax lying down. But to generalize control into everyday living, through successive approximation, the learner practices the preceding steps, relaxing all of those muscles while sitting, reading, writing, standing, and so on. This is the essential concept of differential relaxation.

Differential relaxation is the optimal contracting (tensing) of only those muscles that are necessary for successfully performing the act at hand. Those and only those muscles should contract and only to the extent required for the immediate purpose. All other muscles should be relaxed. Differential relaxation can be applied during various stressful situations as a form of **Self-Operations Control.**

Progressive relaxation is based strictly on physiological principles and is to be distinguished from **Hypnosis,** mysticism, suggestion, and trance phenomena. Progressive relaxation is in the same ballpark as **Biofeedback,** but differs substantially from it. For one, there is no need for external apparatus to observe one's tensions. Instead, the learner observes and controls tension signals within the body through internal (versus external) feedback systems. Furthermore, progressive relaxation is designed to relax all of the individual muscles. Usually in biofeedback, only one muscle, such as the brow, is relaxed, and learning to relax one muscle does not generalize to other muscles.

With particular regard to **Pain,** tension exacerbates pain so that the more one tenses, the greater the subjective experience. In turn, the greater the discomfort, the more one tenses. To break the pain–tension–pain cycle, one can learn to effectively control and relax the striated musculature so as to alleviate, eliminate, or prevent pain.

To apply progressive relaxation in a clinical practice, one needs first to become proficient in the method. For learning it, there are sources such as those specified in the bibliogaphy, available from the publishers.

SEE ALSO:

Anxiety
Backache
Biofeedback
Bruxism
Depression
Differential Relaxation
Esophageal Spasm/Globus Hystericus
Gastrointestinal Disorders
Headache, Migraine and Tension
Hypertension, Essential (High Blood
   Pressure)

Pain
Phobias
Self-Operations Control
Insomnia (Sleep Difficulties)
Spastic Colon
Temporomandibular Joint Syndrome
   (TMJ)
Tension Awareness
Stress Management Methods

BIBLIOGRAPHY

Jacobson, E. (1938). *Progressive relaxation* (Rev ed). Chicago: University of Chicago Press.
McGuigan, F. J. (1992). *Calm down: A guide for stress and tension control.* Dubuque, IA: Kendall/ Hunt.
McGuigan, F. J. (1993). Progressive relaxation: Origins, principles, and clinical applications. In Paul M. Lehrer and Robert L. Woolfolk (Eds.), *Principles and practice of stress management* (2nd ed., pp. 17–52). New York: Guilford Press.

Psychoimmunology

Psychoimmunology is the study of how the immune system is influenced by psychological factors and, how, in turn, diseases develop. Behavior, "lifestyle," and emotional factors have been implicated in disease development.

Early research indicated that brain activity influenced the body's ability to fight infections; since **Conditioning** was thought to be a brain phenomenon, early Russian physiologists sought to control immune reactions by developing relevant conditional reflexes. However, the results have been both positive and negative, so the issue remains controversial.

There are two theories of immune systems functioning: The selection theory holds that antibodies combat invading organisms by surrounding and consuming them; the conditioning theory holds that killer cells are increased to combat the invader.

The immune system has a large number of different kinds of antibodies that are produced, in response to foreign substances, to protect the body against invading organisms. Antibodies released into fluids of the body also may coat bacteria so that the bacteria can be ingested by scavenger cells of the immune system. All animals are born with a complete repertoire of antibodies. Stimulation of the central nervous system can increase the effectiveness of immune processes, whereas inhibition can reduce its effectiveness.

The immune system fights disease by *humoral* responses (*humoral* refers to such fluids of the body) wherein B cells are generated by bone marrow. Slower *cell-mediated* responses, carried out by T cells that are generated by the thymus, fight slower diseases such as cancer. They also assist in fighting viruses and help the body to accept transplants.

Variables that have been shown to affect the immune system include increasing age, poor nutrition, uncomfortable temperatures, irradiation, various drugs, genetic characteristics, and circadian rhythms. Psychological reactions to stress can deleteriously influence the immune system, as well as the progress of cancers. Those influences apparently affect the central nervous system through neurotransmitter and hormonal activity.

When threatening information is received by the receptors, the entire body is activated in the startle reaction. Complex neuromuscular circuits direct messages between the muscles and the brain and circuits between muscles, the cortex, the limbic system, and posterior hypothalamus of the limbic system are activated. With these interactions, the body is in a state of **Distress** and the effectiveness of the immune system is reduced. When distress situations are chronic, there can be atrophy of lymph node tissue and enlargement of adrenal glands.

On the other hand, positive stress (**Eustress**) may actually facilitate the immune system. Perhaps laughter and pleasant occasions release beta endorphins that create pleasant feelings and beneficial physiological effect by activating opiate receptors that mimic opiate drugs.

Behavioral variables do have physiological effects on the immune system, but the effects are extremely complex. The immune system is integrated with other systems to maintain homeostatic conditions. There are complex interactions among immune, genetic, neural, and endocrine systems with behavioral-emotional responses. Behavioral interventions through **Stress Management** can alter specific and nonspecific aspects of immune function.

SEE ALSO:

BIBLIOGRAPHY

Antoni, M. H., Schneiderman, N., Fletcher, M. A., Goldstein, D. A., Ironson, G., & Laperriere, A. (1990). Psychoneuroimmunology and HIV-1. *Journal of Consulting and Clinical Psychology, 58,* 38–49.

Kiecolt-Glaser, J. K., & Glaser, R. (1992). Psychoneuroimmunology: Can psychological interventions modulate immunity? *Journal of Consulting and Clinical Psychology, 60,* 569–575.

Solomon, G. F. (1987). Psychoneuroimmunology: Interactions between central nervous system and immune system. *Journal of Neuroscience Research, 18,* 1–9.

Psychopharmacology

Psychopharmacology is an interdisciplinary field that is concerned with the effects of drugs on psychological (including psychiatric) processes, as well as the effects of psychological factors in determining responses to drugs. "Psychoactive" and "psychotropic" are among the terms most commonly used for drugs that have psychological effects. The major classes of psychotropic drugs are antipsychotic, antidepressant, and antianxiety drugs. Some of these drugs are, in effect, muscle relaxants and operate on the internuncial neurons, while others also work through the midbrain and reticular activating system of the brain. When mixed with alcohol or other central nervous system depressants, a number of these drugs may become hypotensive and may result in death.

Drugs per se cannot cure a mental or emotional illness, but evidence indicates that florid symptoms can be controlled and severe psychotic anxiety abated. Schizophrenic behavior can be managed more effectively with medication, while manic depressive states and other affective disorders, such as depressions, also frequently become responsive to appropriate medication. Debilitating anxiety, as a symptom of severe neurosis, is usually ameliorated through the administration of carefully selected and monitored tranquilizers. Effective psychopharmacological treatment depends on accurate diagnosis, the availability of suitable medications, and a cooperative patient. Constant or definite signs and symptoms and a predictable course enhance the reliability of prescribing appropriate drugs. Unfortunately, patients often present a cluster of symptoms that at times make a clear-cut diagnosis difficult. Further, the clinical picture is often complicated by more than one pathological process and medications that do not have single actions; moreover, effective dosages vary from one person to another due to individual physiological differences.

Both the function and response of neurotransmitters have gained much prominence in recent years as potential avenues for dramatic breakthroughs in the understanding and treatment of mental disorders. The metabolites of serotonin, noradrenalin, and dopamine, in particular, have been the focus of the study in depressive disorders.

Affective disorders account for disturbances in mood or emotional tone and include excitability, as well as depression. Some drugs that help to control anxiety are of value in dealing with heightened emotional states, such as mania and hypo-mania. Antidepressants are generally classified into their principal groups—tricy-clic agents, monoamine oxidase inhibitors, and selective serotonin reuptake inhibitors. Stimulants are inhibitors sometimes used to combat depression.

Lithium salts were initially thought to be useful largely for manic states, but they have been shown to be of some value for depressive states as well.

Sleep-inducing and sedative drugs, used before recent psychoactive drugs came on the market, are now still prescribed for nighttime use when sleep is desired.

Most psychoactive drugs have been developed for their clinical properties, for their ability to ease personal distress and make overt behavior more socially acceptable. Some drugs have had the effect of reducing the experience of stress, but also may reduce the person's ability to cope with reality.

Antipsychotic drugs may protect the psychotic patient by decreasing respon-siveness to the environment, thus decreasing the likelihood of exhibiting psychotic behaviors. By delaying responses, the antipsychotic drugs thereby can lead the patient to process stimuli more effectively and to assure a more rational behavior.

Drugs have long been used to alleviate the experience of stress either as adjuncts to other types of therapy or as a therapy in themselves. Drugs do provide a powerful way of changing cognitive appraisal and may do so by distorting a number of important perceptions, as well as the perception of demand, capability, and consequences of attempts at coping. Although a particular drug may reduce the immediate experience of stress, it may also reduce the person's ability to cope both cognitively and behaviorally.

Two general difficulties exist with this form of therapy. First, the drugs may have a paradoxical effect of both reducing and enhancing the person's difficulties. Second, because the drug reduces the experience of stress, taking it as a reward may form the basis for the development of psychological and then possibly phys-ical dependance. Many people also believe that drugs only cause more stress; these people use relaxation techniques, or even meditation and yoga in effort to lessen their stresses.

SEE ALSO:

Anxiety
Drug Abuse in the Workplace

BIBLIOGRAPHY

Bowden, C. L., and Giffen, M. B. (1990). *Psychopharmacology for primary care physicians.* Baltimore: Williams & Wilkins.
Corsini, R. J. (Ed.). (1987). *Concise encyclopedia of psychology.* New York: Wiley.
Klein, D. F., Rowlend, L. P. (1996). *Current psychotherapeutic drugs.* New York: Brunner/Mazel.

Psychosomatic Illness

Psychosomatic (somatoform) illnesses are commonly thought of as those physiological disorders produced by psychic or mental stresses. For example, many believe that people who chronically worry can develop as a psychosomatic illness a peptic ulcer. However, this is a dualistic model that holds that nonphysical psychic events can influence physical, bodily phenomena—a model that is untenable. A realistic model is that psychic or mental processes themselves are actually bodily events—see **Mind** and **Mental Events**. Hence, we interpret *psycho* in the word "psychosomatic" as *physicalistic behavior*, which is the common interpretation in modern psychology: Psychology is defined as the science of behavior. Behavior, of course, is an activity of the body, involving muscular, neural, chemical, and other events. *Somatic* in the term "psychosomatic" literally means body. Therefore, "psychosomatic illness" may be interpreted to mean that the illness resulted because activity of one or more systems of the body affected other systems of the body. Consequently, if you are told that you have a psychosomatic illness, what this really can mean is that chronic overtension of the striated muscular system resulted in pathological conditions in other bodily systems. In the figure in the Introduction on page xiii, we noted that an increase in skeletal musculature tension can produce undesirable consequences for the gastrointestinal system, the cardiovascular system, and so on. Conversely, systematic relaxation of skeletal musculature brings a state of tranquility to the autonomic and other systems. Psychosomatic illnesses such as **Irritable Bowel Syndrome** can thus be treated by relaxing the skeletal muscles and in turn the gastrointestinal tract. With reduction of resulting spasticity in the bowels, the gastrointestinal complaint can be eliminated. A basic principle of medicine is to not intervene unnecessarily into the body's functions, as one should not surgically remove a portion of a colon because of its spasticity. Rather one should give the body an opportunity to heal itself. To repeat, to help the body heal itself, an effective treatment for a psychosomatic illness is to reduce tension of the skeletal musculature. The body can thereby heal pathological conditions in other systems.

S E E   A L S O :

Irritable Bowel Syndrome
Mind and Mental Events
Stress Management Methods

B I B L I O G R A P H Y

Bloona, R. (1996). *Coping with stress in a changing world.* New York: Mosby.
Hall, S. S. (1989, June). A molecular code links emotions, mind and health. *Smithsonian, 20,* 67–71.
Hall, N. R. S., Altman, F., & Blumenthal, S. J. (1996). *Mind-body interactions and disease and psychoneuroimmunological aspects of health and disease.* Orlando, FL: Health Dateline.

O'Leary, A. (1990). Stress, emotion, and human immune function. *Psychological Bulletin, 108,* 363–382.

McGuigan, F. J. (1992). *Calm down: A guide for stress and tension control* (2nd ed.). Dubuque, IA: Kendall/Hunt.

Rice, P. L. (1992). *Stress & health* (2nd ed.). Pacific Grove, CA: Brooks/Cole.

Psychotherapies

Psychotherapies are methods of relating with patients (clients) for the purpose of improving their behavior in everyday living. Usually, the patient's behavior interferes with his or her effectiveness, as when the individual is victimized by a psychiatric disorder. The purpose of psychotherapy may also be to improve an already satisfactory life.

There are numerous psychotherapeutic techniques, including psychoanalysis, client-centered therapy, **Behavior Therapy, Systematic Desensitization,** aversive therapy, family therapy, **Cognitive-Behavioral** techniques, group therapy, psychoeducation, orgone therapy (the attempt to manipulate a biological energy named after orgasm), and over 460 other varieties.

Traditionally, psychotherapies have used verbal techniques, as in the classic work of Sigmund Freud. The method and assumptions of Freud's classical psychoanalysis are that the patient attend perhaps four sessions weekly for 4 to 5 years. The patient lies on a couch so that no eye contact is made with the analyst and, through a process of free association, the patient recreates some early childhood conflicts. The analyst adopts a neutral (anonymous) stance so that the patient's feelings are associated with other significant people. The analyst interprets the significance of the patient's reactions and explores unconscious reactions, defenses, and resistance in an attempt to thus allow the patient to discard old thought patterns and adopt a new mode of being.

Today, what is called a psychodynamic approach assumes that anxiety is reduced by an unconscious process whereby the ego is protected from being overwhelmed by biological urges. This ego defense system can be adaptive or maladaptive. The quality of these defenses depends on the type of early interactions that the individual had with his or her biological mother. Later problems have their origins in a problematic early mother–child relationship. The purpose of therapy is to have the patient regress to those early disruptions and, through insight, create a more adaptive response pattern.

Basically, regardless of the type of therapy, the effort in any psychotherapy is to *modify* the patient's *behavior* in some way. Consequently, when effective, psychotherapy is a learning experience. This realization has led to a revolutionary movement in psychotherapy in which **Behavior Therapies** have emerged based on the scientific principles of learning theory. Classical verbal psychotherapies have assumed the medical model in which an attempt is made to trace the patient's contemporary behavioral problems to earlier experiences, for example, improper toilet training in childhood. Behavior therapies, on the other hand, focus on the current maladaptive behavior. Once the appropriate methods of learning and relearning are applied, the improvement of behavior allows the individual to assume a more effective life, regardless of the original causes of the maladaptive behavior.

Methodological Problems in Validation

A tremendous amount of research has been conducted to attempt to meet demands to demonstrate the validity of psychotherapies. In part, because of the great complexity of the problem, however, the results have often been disappointing. A large amount of psychotherapy research has been methodologically unsound, so that there have been few valid conclusions. Singer and Lalich (1997), in their book entitled *Crazy Therapies*, identified between 400 and 500 untested, dubious therapies. Margaret Singer, a professor at the University of California, Berkeley, pointed out that there was an upsurge in psychoanalysis at the end of World War II that led people to think there was a magic solution to psychological problems if patients could determine who or what was to blame for their problems. Out of this grew numerous therapies, often based on only one case; this is so in part because, typically, anybody can call himself or herself a psychotherapist. However, in order to call oneself a psychologist or a psychiatrist, one must meet all the criteria of stringent licensing laws.

Another problem is that the establishment of a legitimate control group may be thought unethical because it may deny patients the help that they need. At issue is the question of whether doing nothing more than giving a placebo treatment is actually less effective than administering a psychotherapy, especially when the particular method may be destructive itself, as in false memory syndrome (see below).

Yet another difficulty in validating psychotherapy is that psychotherapies are so numerous and varied that a conclusion with regard to one may have nothing to do with the others.

A common phenomenon in psychotherapy is that the therapist misdiagnoses the patient's behavioral problem. For instance, whatever issue the patient may mention—such as referring to a sexual matter—if the therapist suddenly expresses interest, the therapist thereby may reinforce the patient to continue to discuss and elaborate on that particular issue as one of maladjustment, even if it does not constitute a problem. Consequently, the patient and therapist reinforce each other and may develop a strong, false belief system, when only tentative thoughts were originally expressed by the patient. What happens is that the therapist and patient create a folie à deux in which they both develop and share the same delusional beliefs. The therapist is a very powerful reinforcing agent and can do great harm by misapplying learning principles. For example, psychotherapists have tragically influenced some clients to falsely "recall" instances of childhood abuse by the parents (false memory syndrome), even as early as three months of age, sometimes leading them to sue their parents. John Kihlstrom (1981) explains that we do not remember much of anything from the first 5 to 7 years of life because before that the brain is not sufficiently mature to effectively record memories.

SEE ALSO:

Behavior Therapy
Cognitive-Behavioral Therapy
Systematic Desensitization

BIBLIOGRAPHY

Kihlstrom, J. F. (1981). On personality and memory. In N. Cantor & J. F. Kihlstrom (Eds.), *Personality, cognition, and social interaction* (pp. 123–149). Hillsdale, NJ: Erlbaum.

O'Donohue, W., & Krasner, L. (1995). *Theories of behavior therapy: Exploring behavior change.* Washington, DC: American Psychological Association.

McGuigan, F. J. (1994). *Biological psychology: A cybernetic science.* Englewood Cliffs, NJ: Prentice Hall.

Pope, K. S., & Brown, L. S. (1996). *Recovered memories of abuse: Assessment, therapy, forensics.* Washington, DC: American Psychological Association.

Singer, M. T., & Lalich, J. (1997). *Crazy therapies: What are they? Do they work?* San Francisco: Jossey-Bass.

Spanos, N. P. (1996). *Multiple identies and false memories: A sociocognitive perspective.* Washington, DC: American Psychological Association.

Wachtel, P. L. (1997). *Psychoanalysis, behavior therapy and the relational world.* Washington, DC: American Psychological Association.

R Raynaud's Disease–Running, Relaxed

Raynaud's Disease

Description

In Raynaud's disease there is severely restricted blood flow to the periphery of the body because of spasms of the peripheral blood vessels. This disease has potentially very deleterious consequences, including the possibility of gangrene and the loss of fingers and toes.

Causes

This disease usually occurs as a reaction to cold when the small arteries that supply the fingers or toes with blood become extrasensitive to cold and suddenly contract. Lack of oxygenated blood makes the affected area pale, often with a bluish tinge. However, Raynaud's disease may also occur as a secondary effect of conditions other than cold. It is sometimes an occupational disorder of people who work with vibrating equipment such as chain saws or pneumatic drills. It can be caused by a disorder of the connective tissue such as scleroderma, pulmonary hypertension, Buerger's disease, an emotional disturbance, stress, or a nerve disorder. It can also be brought on by sensitivity to certain drugs that can affect the blood vessels.

Treatment

Some stress management techniques have been beneficial in the treatment of Raynaud's disease. Behavioral approaches in the treatment of this disease are favored because of their noninvasive nature. Most behavioral research has focused on **Biofeedback** and **Relaxation** strategies.

SEE ALSO:

Biofeedback
Progressive Relaxation

BIBLIOGRAPHY

Freedman, R. R. (1994). Mechanisms and treatment of Raynaud's disease. In J. C. Carlson, A. R. Seifert, & N. Birbaumer (Eds.), *Clinical applied psychophysiology*. New York: Plenum.

Taub, E. (1976). Feedback: In self-regulation of skin temperature. In F. J. McGuigan (Ed.), *Tension control: Proceedings of the Third Meeting of the American Association for the Advancement of Tension Control.* Louisville: American Association for the Advancement of Tension Control.

Schwartz, M. S., Kelly, M. F. (1995). Raynaud's disease: Selected issues and considerations in using biofeedback therapies. In M. S. Schwartz (Ed.), *Biofeedback: A practitioner's guide* (2nd ed., pp. 429–444). New York: Guilford Press.

Repetitive Stress Injuries

Description

Workers' compensation claims for stress are categorized as repetitive stress injuries. A worker typically complains of soreness and tenderness of the wrists and fingers, and it is especially common in computer operators.

Causes

Carpal tunnel syndrome is a common form of repetitive stress injury, characterized by numbness of the hand and weakness of the limb due to keeping the wrist in a constant position for repetitive keying at the computer. Pressure is thereby placed excessively on the palm. The carpal tunnel of the wrist leads to painful swelling and tenderness and loss of strength in the hand, wrist, and arm.

Cumulative trauma disorder is an associated disorder that is due to motions similar to those causing carpal tunnel syndrome. Cases occur in individuals working on certain machines for lengthy periods of time; sewing and similar industry-related activities are said to account for perhaps 50 percent of all such occupational disorders.

Treatment

An appropriate job stress management program can prevent the causes and contributing causes of job stress injuries by changing the ways the jobs are performed. Examples are improved management style and designing the work environment to be less conducive to such stress-related disorders. Experts in the field have held that this is an outstanding way for helping workers to cope with this kind of job stress.

Humphrey (1998) discussed stress-management programs for this purpose, and Charlesworth (1981) tested a stress-management program involving visual imagery, deep muscle relaxation, autogenic training, and systematic desensitization for ten sessions over a five-week period. They found that trait anxiety and state anxiety declined over a period of time.

SEE ALSO:

Technostress
Workplace Stress

BIBLIOGRAPHY

Humphrey, J. H. (1998). *Job stress.* Boston: Allyn & Bacon.

Charlesworth, E. (1981). Stress management for nursing students. *Journal of Clinical Psychology, 37.*

Lynch, R. T., & Rodriquez, A. (1992). Carpal tunnel syndrome: Considerations for rehabilitation. *Journal of Applied Rehabilitation Counseling, 23,* 23–29.

Thomas, R. E., Vaidya, S. C., Herrick, R. T., & Congleton, J. J. (1993). The effects of biofeedback on carpal tunnel syndrome. *Ergonomics, 36,* 353–361.

Road Rage

Description

If you are a law-abiding citizen driving to work in the morning on an interstate or freeway, carefully obeying the posted speed limit, you may look with horror in your rearview mirror at the oncoming traffic. Cars whiz past you on either side and you must carefully dodge those cutting in front of you with reckless abandon. You can momentarily observe possessed drivers with satanic countenances: furrowed brow, gritted teeth, fixed eyes, determined expression, vigorously grasping the steering wheel, hunched forward in the seat exuding a sense of urgency.

"Road rage" is the term used to describe the attitude of extremely angry, hostile, and aggressive drivers toward other road users. Angry drivers tend to become excessively aggressive when they get behind a wheel and engage in dangerous driving practices such as abrupt braking, unsignaled lane changes, and tailgating—behavior that leads to fatalities, injuries, assault, and even murder. The AAA Foundation for Traffic Safety reported that aggressive driving was responsible for 218 deaths and 12,610 injuries between 1990 and 1996.

While many of the drivers involved in fatalities and injuries were young males between the ages of 18 and 26, the problem is not confined to them. Both genders and all age groups are prone to allow anger to dictate driving behavior. A national survey on driver behavior found that 80 percent of respondents report being angry most or all of the time when driving. Everyday events such as traffic congestion, stoplights, or passengers alighting from or entering cars are sufficient to act as triggering stressors.

Causes

Factors associated with "road rage" include road congestion and deficient skills in driving, poor time management, and lack of anger control in drivers. Road congestion has become worse in the past 10 years due to an increase in both the number of cars and total miles driven, without a commensurate expansion in the amount of road space available. This congestion adds to the amount of time a driver spends on the road and frequently causes delay as well as late or missed appointments. This is an added stressor for individuals whose schedules are already overloaded due to work and family responsibilities. Such constraints on time increase the tendency to overreact to what otherwise might be considered slight inconveniences. Thus, the angry, stressed driver is likely to perceive the mere presence of others on the road as "unreasonable" behavior and an excuse to disregard legal and safety regulations so that she or he can get past the "morons".

Treatment

The anger that underlies aggressive driving is a learned behavior and can be unlearned by recognizing the triggers that elicit it. **Stress Management Techniques** and courses in **Anger** management help drivers adapt to stressors and control responses, thus enabling the development of defensive driving skills. **Time Management** teaches drivers to plan ahead, to prioritize, and to set realistic goals that can be achieved within time constraints available—hence, reducing the "need" to engage in risky driving behavior. Proficiency in **Progressive Relaxation** enables a driver to focus solely on driving and to be an observer of—rather than a participant in—"road rage." It also has an added advantage in that it can be practiced while stopped in traffic. Hence, what once was the source of irritation can be transformed into an opportunity to manage stress.

SEE ALSO:

Commuting Stress, Automobile
Driving (Automobile) Stress
Progressive Relaxation

Stress Management Methods
Time Management

BIBLIOGRAPHY

AAA Foundation for Traffic Safety (1997). *Aggressive driving: Three studies.* Washington, DC: Author.
AAA Foundation for Traffic Safety (1997). *Road rage: How to avoid aggressive driving.* Washington, DC: Author.
Ferguson, A. (1998, January 12). Road rage. *Time, 151,* 64–68.
Larson, J. A. (1996). *Steering clear of highway madness.* Wilsonville, OR: Book Partners.
McGuigan, F. J. (1992). *Calm down: A guide to stress and tension control* (2nd ed.). Dubuque, IA: Kendall/Hunt.

Role Conflict

Description

Chronic role conflict poses a great threat to our adaptive mechanisms. Role conflict (incompatible modes of behavior demanded of one) and role ambiguity are two stressors that have been researched and linked to health and physical outcomes and consequences. Researchers have found that men whose roles were in conflict experienced more tension and were less satisfied in their jobs than were

men whose roles did not conflict. As a stressor, role conflict can produce job dissatisfaction and anxiety and contribute to physiological changes that have both
personal and organizational costs.

Causes

Role conflict can arise when two or more pressures occur together so that comply-
ing with one should make doing the other more difficult. There is a variety of
causes for role conflict, such as conflicting messages: The conflict may be between
the deadline and the request for high-quality work. Another type of role conflict is
the difference between our self-expectations and the perception of others' expectations of us. Role conflict can also occur with promotion: A new manager may
experience a conflict between new responsibilities and loyalty to former coworkers. An individual's personal values and beliefs may clash with role requirements;
for instance, a used-car salesman may be torn between telling the truth about a car
and trying to make a sale. Some women are often caught between the conflicting
demands of a family and a job.

Treatment

Role conflict can be lessened to some degree by lowering or adjusting the expectations we have of ourselves and the standards we think we must live up to.
Researchers report that participative decision making is an important factor that
can help to reduce role conflict and role ambiguity among blue collar, secretarial,
and professional employees.

Various forms of **Psychotherapy** may help, either directly or indirectly, to
resolve the conflict.

One way that conflict resolution can proceed is by gradually increasing the
strength of the approach gradient toward a goal. For example, if a person wishes
to be promoted to the next position in a company, he or she could first practice
accomplishing one of the behaviors appropriate for that position; successful
behavior for that component would constitute a reinforcement that would
increase the strength of the gradient toward the goal of being promoted. Then one
would accomplish another component in the job description of that position and,
on successful completion, would again be reinforced, further strengthening the
approach gradient, and so on until one is vigorously moving to accomplish the
goal. So strengthening the approach gradient should gradually reduce the anxiety
created by the conflict. Successfully reinforcing the approach steps can give rise to
confidence, independence, and success.

A related method of conflict resolution is to gradually reduce the strength of
the avoidance gradient toward a goal. One may fear the responsibilities that
would come with the promotion. To reduce that avoidance gradient toward the
promotion, one can gradually develop the concept of job performance responsibility in that position. One can, for instance, imagine the feared aspect of the responsibility and then imagine or project success in overcoming that fear. Gradually,

one comes to approach the total responsibility of the new position through these small steps. Each closer step is taken only after the individual's fear is eased at each step. Eventually he or she may learn to actually confront the feared responsibility with greatly eased or eliminated fears.

Other examples abound, such as how to reduce stage fright (**Public Speaking Anxiety**). For this, one can first imagine being near a place where a speech is to be given, until he or she feels comfortable with that thought. Then one can gradually move closer and closer to actually speaking and performing on a stage in front of an audience. This is successive approximation, which is done in **Progressive Relaxation** therapy. The avoidance reduction method is practiced to make the person more willing to approach the formerly feared or avoided condition or object. For objects that are feared, one could first show the individual pictures of the feared object, then gradually (from a distance) bring that individual closer to the actual object. Each closer step is taken only after the individual's fears ease at each step. Eventually he or she can actually confront the feared object with greatly eased or eliminated fears.

Both approach and avoidance strategies can work together, neither being wholly dominant, but each more salient at a given time.

SEE ALSO:

Progressive Relaxation
Psychotherapies
Speaking Anxiety (Public)

BIBLIOGRAPHY

Corsini, R. J. (Ed.). (1987). *Concise encyclopedia of psychology.* New York: John Wiley.
Havlovich, S. J., & Keenan, J. P. (1995). Coping with work stress: The influence of individual differences. In R. Crandall & P. L. Perrewe (Eds.), *Occupational stress: A handbook* (pp. 179–192). Philadelphia: Taylor & Francis.
Van der Velde, M., & Class, M. D. (1995). The relationship of role conflict and ambiguity to organizational culture. In S. L. Sauter & L. R. Murphy (Eds.). *Organizational risk factors for job stress.* Washington, DC: American Psychological Association.

Running, Relaxed

Description

Many inexperienced distance runners have a tendency to involve themselves totally in the running movement. Regardless of the pace, these runners often think that all body parts must be exerted with maximum force. What they don't realize is that they are not achieving efficiency. Theirs is seldom a smooth, rhythmical, relaxed style of running since the upper body and facial muscles, in particular, are needlessly tensed to a high degree, beyond the point of muscular efficiency for the desired pace.

Causes

Without **Muscular Tension** awareness, inexperienced long-distance runners expend energy that should be conserved for a prolonged pace. Energy sources deplete quickly when muscles are exerted beyond an optimal tension level. In addition, some upper body muscles may be overly tensed to the point where the runner moves in a jerky motion.

Treatment

One way to conserve energy resources and to relax muscle groups properly is for runners to learn to differentially relax the major muscles of the upper body while running. Time and concentration are key elements in practicing **Differential Relaxation** while running. That is, in differential relaxation one optimally tenses only those muscles required for performing the act at hand, in this case running. A runner should reserve a portion of each workout to practice relaxation, particularly in the upper body muscles, but elsewhere too.

There are three stages to this practice. During the first stage the runner concentrates on developing muscular awareness during a ten-minute jog. Specifically, the runner practices "loosening up" or "letting go" the taut muscles during the jogging period. The second stage is during the warm-up jog, in which the runner alternately tenses and relaxes the major muscles of the upper body. Finally, in the third stage the runner practices total body relaxation. After the runner learns to relax individual muscle groups, he or she begins to focus on a combination of body parts, such as the face and neck muscles, the arm and shoulder muscles, or the entire back. Eventually the runner incorporates all the upper body muscles into a single unit to be relaxed, and practices this differential relaxation until it becomes habitual.

SEE ALSO:

Differential Relaxation   Tension Awareness
Exercise, Benefits of
Sports Performance, Bodily Conditioning,
    and Injuries

BIBLIOGRAPHY

American Podiatry Association. *Jogging advice from your podiatrist.* Washington, DC: Author.

Burke, T. R. (1975). Relaxed running. In F. J. McGuigan (Ed.), *Tension control: Proceedings of the First Meeting of the American Association for the Advancement of Tension Control*. Blacksburg, VA: University Publications.

Greenberg, J. S. (1996). *Comprehensive stress management* (5th ed.). Chicago: Brown & Benchmark.

Seaward, B. L. (1994). *Managing stress: Principles and strategies for health and wellbeing*. Boston: Jones & Bartlett.

Taylor, J. (1995). A conceptual model for integrating athletes' needs and sport demands in the development of competitive mental preparation strategies. *Sports Psychologist, 9*, 339–357.

Williams, T. J., Krahenbuhl, G. S., & Morgan, D. W. (1991). Mood states and running economy in moderately trained male runners. *Medicine and Science in Sports and Exercise, 23*, 727–731.

S | Schizophrenia and Stress–Systematic Desensitization

Schizophrenia and Stress

Description

Schizophrenia is the most common of the psychoses. But the syndrome is quite ambiguous in that there are few features in common among those diagnosed as schizophrenics. The syndrome was first described as a single disorder by German psychiatrist Emil Kraepelin in 1896. He called it "dementia praecox," "dementia" referring to intellectual deterioration and "praecox" to the fact that the symptoms first occur in early adulthood. Swiss psychiatrist Eugene Bleuler renamed the disorder "schizophrenia" to express his view that a prominent feature is a splitting of psychic functions; for example, ideas and feelings are isolated from one another—a patient may express frightening or sad ideas in a happy manner.

Contrary to some popular accounts, however, schizophrenic persons do not have a "split personality" in the sense of different personalities on different occasions, as in the rare syndrome of multiple personality.

The symptoms of schizophrenia include delusions, hallucinations, thought disorders, loss of boundaries between self and nonself, blunted or inappropriate emotional expression, socially inappropriate behavior, loss of social interests, and deterioration in areas of functioning such as social relations, work, and self-care. The symptoms fluctuate in occurrence and in severity.

Causes

Because there are so many different characteristics among schizophrenic persons, it is not possible to specify a common cause. Until we achieve a better-defined syndrome, efforts to find "the cause" are doomed to failure. There must be many causes for what we loosely refer to as "schizophrenia."

However, one major psychosocial factor in the development of schizophrenia in American culture is stress. Research suggests that individuals who have a predisposition for schizophrenia or are in what is termed the premorbid phase, the active phase, or the residual phase may have an increase in symptoms under stress. For example, family stress is significantly correlated in the development of this psychopathology; the expression of emotions causing stress on the individual has a significant relationship in the development of schizophrenic symptoms. Thus, if a person is predisposed to, or is suffering from, schizophrenia and is in a critical and hostile family environment, symptoms can be expected to commence or increase in severity.

Most researchers hold to a diathesis–stress theory: Both a biological predisposition and environmental factors interact to determine who becomes schizophrenic.

Treatment

For many years, psychotherapy was the preferred mode of treatment of schizophrenia, and it continues to be used. Electroconvulsive therapy (ECT) was introduced in 1937 and became the prevalent mode of treatment until the late 1950s; it is still used in some cases. Psychosurgery (lobotomy and lobectomy), however, which became common in the 1940s and 1950s, is now in disrepute.

Since the late 1950s, schizophrenia has been treated primarily with the antipsychotic medications that block the action of dopamine in the brain. They do not cure schizophrenia, but they help to control the symptoms. However, using some drugs at high dosages for long periods may have severe negative side effects.

The recent trend has been toward outpatient treatment, because of the belief that prolonged hospitalization is deleterious. This trend is controversial, however, and its popularity may be based on civil libertarian concerns as much as on evidence concerning its usefulness.

Up to one-third of diagnosed schizophrenia sufferers substantially recover and manage their conditions, especially patients who had a good social and sexual adjustment prior to the illness. Significant numbers improve even after years of severe illness, but some residual signs of the disorder almost invariably remain.

Some research indicates that family stress is more a predictor of the onset of schizophrenia than a schizophrenic person's biological disposition. As a result, family therapy may be helpful. Teaching the families of schizophrenic patients social skills—which include communication skills—may benefit the schizophrenic patient more than other types of psychotherapies. Therapeutic interventions such as teaching families to become more loving and to reframe their negative communication patterns in a more loving perspective may be beneficial.

SEE ALSO:

Chemicals of the Body and Stress

BIBLIOGRAPHY

Benes, F. M. (1997). The role of stress and dopamine-GABA interactions in the vulnerability for schizophrenia. *Journal of Psychiatric Research, 31,* 257–275.

Eaton, M. C. (1996). The psychotherapy of schizophrenia. In W. R. Breakey (Ed.), *Integrated mental health services: Modern community psychiatry.* New York: Oxford University Press.

Farhall, J., & Gehrke, M. (1997). Coping with hallucinations: Exploring stress and coping framework. *British Journal of Clinical Psychology, 36,* 259–261.

Goldstein, J., Faraone, S., Chen, W., Toomiczenko, G., & Tsuang, M. (1991). Gender differences in the familial transmission of schizophrenia. *British Journal of Psychiatry, 161,* 1185–1198.

Henn, F. A., & Nasrallah, H. A., (Eds.). (1982). *Schizophrenia as a brain disease.* New York: Oxford University Press.

Lewine, R. R. J. (1998). Schizophrenia. In E. A. Blechman & K. D. Brownell, *Behavioral medicine & women: A comprehensive handbook* (pp. 778–782). New York: Guilford Press.

Pallanti, S., Quercioli, L., & Pazzagli, A. (1997). Relapse in young paranoid schizophrenic patients: A prospective study of stressful life events, P300 measures, and coping. *American Journal of Psychiatry, 154,* 792–798.

Tarrier, N. (1996). A psychological approach to the management of schizophrenia. In M. Moscarelli, A. Rupp, & N. Sartorius (Eds.). *Handbook of mental health economics and health policy* (Vol. 1, pp. 271–285). New York: Wiley.

School/College Stress

Description

Many students experience stress in a wide variety of ways. In Japan, the problem has become increasingly serious, to the point at which the truancy rate has increased consistently for the last two decades. Truants in Japan have traditionally been considered "psychologically ill, social misfits with character defects." Some were taken to therapists or hospitals, locked in a room, or given high doses of medicine. Truancy is a major problem in the United States also. About 6.6 percent of American junior high school students are absent from school on any given day. In Japan, the percent is just over 1 percent.

Student stress at the college level is even more serious.

Causes

Often, in public school, stress is caused by the student's inability to do the class assignments due to any number of reasons. Some students simply stay away from school because of fear of failure, teasing by other students, and the like. A major reason for truancy in Japan is that students are bullied by other students; this has even resulted in suicide in some cases. There are strict rules governing behavior, dress, and hair styles, and corporal punishment by teachers is allowed. There is such great pressure to achieve that even some elementary school students begin activities early in the morning and conclude late at night.

American college students are frequently stressed about finances, grades, and getting ahead. As a result, more are smoking and feeling depressed and overwhelmed; the trend is an increasing one of experiencing greater emotional strain. The depression sometimes becomes so great that it leads to self-destructive behavior.

Depression that leads to self-destruction is especially hard to understand in college students—they are privileged, young, intelligent, and educated. Yet they commit **Suicide** at a greater rate than their noncollege peers. Research has shown that suicidal students are differentiated from their classmates in various ways: The suicidal group is older, contains a greater proportion of language majors and foreign students, more frequently reports the experience of emotional disturbance, and demonstrates academic achievement superior to that of fellow students.

Contrary to the popular belief that suicides frequently occur during final examinations week, studies have indicated that the peak danger period for student suicides is the beginning (first six weeks), not the middle or end, of the semester. Most suicidal students give recurrent warnings of their suicidal intent. Many of them have a similar pattern marked by loss of appetite, insomnia, and periods of despondence. Among the major precipitating factors are worry over schoolwork and chronic and bizarre concerns about physical health. They often have difficulties with interpersonal relationships because of emotional withdrawal, social isolation, and romantic rejections.

Treatment

There is a need for behavioral analysis as to why the children with school problems do not go to school. Then an analysis needs to be specialized for each child to determine what causes should be eliminated and what behaviors incompatible with success need to be reinforced, as in **Behavior Therapy.**

For both school and college students, coping with stressors needs to be enhanced through the application of **Stress Management Methods.** For students in lower grades, the application of **Progressive Relaxation,** as explained by Marshall & Beach (1976), should be considered.

SEE ALSO:

Behavior Therapy
Medical School Stress
Nursing Stress in Students
Progressive Relaxation

Student Control (Achieving Classroom Discipline)
Suicide

BIBLIOGRAPHY

Hale, J. F., Greenberg, J. S., & Ramsey, S. A. (1990). Assessment of college students' stress and stress-management needs: A pilot study. In J. H. Humphrey (Ed.), *Human stress: Current selected research* (Vol. 4, pp. 77–88). New York: AMS Press.

Humphrey, J. H. (1993). *Stress management for elementary schools.* Springfield, IL: Charles C. Thomas.

Marshall, M. G., & Beach, C. W. (1975). A method for teaching tension control in the elementary school. In F. J. McGuigan (Ed.), *Tension control: Proceedings of the Second Meeting of the American Association for the Advancement of Tension Control* (pp. 7–18). Chicago: University Publications.

Sears, S. J., & Milburn, J. (1990). School-age stress. In E. Arnold (Ed.), *Childhood stress* (pp. 224–246). New York: Wiley.

Sciatica

Description

The pain of this disorder is especially prominent along the sciatic nerve that runs from the lower back along the legs. Broadly (the term is sometimes not used technically), it is pain in the lower back, buttocks, hips, and at the back of the thigh that can be intensified by movement, sneezing, or coughing. When touched, the muscle area around the sciatic nerve is very tender and sore.

Causes

Organic Causes. The primary cause is the compression of the sciatic nerve from a prolapsed (or slipped) disk or osteoarthritis of the spine. Among older people, a common cause is deterioration of intervertebral discs, which causes pressure on the sciatic nerve, which causes pain. Other causes in the general population include tumors, infection, and spinal fracture. Improper lifting of objects may also create pressure on the sciatic nerve.

Stress Causes. Emotional stress may cause what the brain interprets as "pain" in the lower back. In response, the back muscles go into spasm to protect themselves. This spasm may contract the muscles in such a way as to produce pressure on the sciatic nerve.

Treatment

If pain is chronic for more than three to five days, one might consult a physician to determine whether there is a physical problem such as misalignment or disc injury. Stress-caused sciatica often disappears without treatment, but tends to recur. Pain killers, muscle relaxants, anti-inflammatory agents, vitamin B-12, antibiotics, or other medication (as prescribed by a physician) may counteract the pain–spasm cycle. **Relaxation** can help with the emotional stress that causes lower-back pain. Bed rest, hot or cold packs, chiropractic treatment, physiotherapy, and massage (by a professional) may also alleviate the pain and, perhaps, the stress. In extreme cases, surgery may be necessary.

S E E A L S O :

Backache   Progressive Relaxation
Pain   Spondylitis

BIBLIOGRAPHY

Barlow, H. H., Macey, S. J., & Struthers, G. R. (1993). Control-related cognitions, chronic disease and gender. In H. Schroder, K. Reschke, M. Johnson, & S. Maes (Eds.). *Health psychology: Potential in diversity* (pp. 154–164). Regensburg, Germany: S. Roderer Verlag.

Deyo, R. A., Rainville, J., & Kent, D. L. (1992). What can the history and physical examination tell us about low back pain? *Journal of the American Medical Association, 268*, 760.

Friedman, M. (1995, Nov.). Your aching back. *Parents' Magazine, 70*, 57.

Kunz, J. R. M., & Finkel, A. J. (1987). *The American Medical Association family medical guide.* New York: Random House.

Massey, E. W. (1991). Disorders of bones, ligaments, cartilage and meninges. In W. G. Bradley, R. B. Daroff, G. M. Fenichel, & C. D. Marsden (Eds.), *Neurology in clinical practice* (Vol. 2, pp. 1625–1660). Boston: Butterworth Heinemann.

Self-Mutilating Behaviors

Description

Self-mutilating behaviors are sometimes found in individuals displaying **Obsessive-Compulsive** behaviors. This is especially true of those afflicted with Borderline Personality Disorder (see the Diagnostic and Statistical Manual of Mental Disorders Case Book IV). The self-mutilating behavior found most frequently is that of scratching a skin surface until it bleeds. The scratching continues, thus not allowing the wound to heal. Other behaviors include cutting oneself.

Causes

This condition may arise and persist as a maladaptive response to stressors. The individual may experience ego-dystonic special feelings, such as one's attempt to relieve bodily stress, or to distract himself or herself, by self-mutilation. The individual typically inadequately copes with environmental stressors, that is, has a highly "nervous style" (excessively tense).

Treatment

Treatment could well aim at changing the individual's ineffective ("nervous") coping style. With astute treatment, self-mutilating behaviors can be reduced and eventually extinguished. **Progressive Relaxation** has been shown to relieve this condition. (See, for instance, Case 4, pp. 403–404, Jacobson, 1938.) In treatment, attention should be called to the individual's overt expressions of nervousness and excitement as well as to any other fidgeting; the individual should then be taught how to relax these behaviors (Jacobson, 1938).

SEE ALSO:

Compulsive Behavior
Obsessive-Compulsive Behavior
Progressive Relaxation

BIBLIOGRAPHY

American Psychiatric Association. (1994). *Diagnostic and statistical manual of mental disorders* (4th ed.) Washington, DC: Author.

Favazza, A. R., & Simeon, D. (1995). Self-mutilation. In E. Hollander & D. J. Stein (Eds.), *Impulsivity and aggression* (pp. 185–200). Chichester, England: Wiley.

Hawton, K., & Cowen, P. J. (1990). *Dilemmas and difficulties in the management of psychiatric patients.* Oxford, England: Oxford University Press.

Jacobson, E. (1938). *Progressive relaxation* (Rev. ed.). Chicago: University of Chicago Press.

Walsh, B. W., & Rosen, P. M. (1988). *Self-mutilation: Theory, research and treatment.* New York: Guilford Press.

Self-Operations Control

Self-operations control, a synonym for **Progressive Relaxation,** has two self-programming general phases: (1) wherein you set yourself to meet specified objectives and (2) in which you carry out your objectives in the most efficient way possible.

SEE ALSO:

Progressive Relaxation

BIBLIOGRAPHY

Alman, B. M., & Lambrou, P. (1992). *Self-hypnosis: The complete manual for health and self-change* (2nd ed.). New York: Brunner/Mazel.

Jacobson, E. (1964). *Self-operations control: A manual of tension control.* Chicago: National Foundation for Progressive Relaxation.

Jacobson, E. (1938). *Progressive relaxation* (Rev ed.). Chicago: University of Chicago Press.

Hans Selye (1907–1982) and the General Adaptation Syndrome (GAS)

Known as the father of stress, Hans Selye conducted experiments in Montreal on animals defining what he referred to as the general adaptation syndrome (GAS). The GAS proposes that all humans manifest the same bodily response patterns to stress—thus he defined stress as a biologic bodily reaction. No matter what the stress, the general biologic reaction, he held, is quite similar among different organisms. With prolonged stress, the excessive chronic activity of the sympathetic nervous system results in some specific organs breaking down. Following such prolonged stress, Selye held that the events of the GAS—alarm, resistance, exhaustion and death—follow. In the alarm stage maximum energy production is achieved by activating all of the physiological responses, including the release of stress hormones, increasing blood sugar level, accelerating heart and breathing rate. The next stage (resistance) is entered if the stress continues such that breathing rate and heart rate return to prestress levels and the individual appears to have returned to normal; however, the elevated hormone and sugar levels continue and the body becomes particularly vulnerable to infection. Further continuation of stress leads to the exhaustion stage, in which the bodily processes start to break down—the organs required to generate energy become so depleted that the body becomes exhausted and the final stage (death) may follow.

While Selye's research on this multistage GAS reaction to prolonged stress was validated on animals, further research is required on humans.

SEE ALSO:

Distress (Negative Stress)
Eustress (Positive Stress)

BIBLIOGRAPHY

Monat, A., & Lazarus, R. S. (Eds). (1991). *Stress and coping: An anthology* (3rd ed.). New York: Columbia University Press.
Selye, H. (1978/1956). *Stress of life*. New York: McGraw-Hill.
Selye, H. (1987). Stress without distress. In L. Levi (Ed.), *Society, stress and disease: Old age* (Vol. 5, pp. 257–262). Oxford, England: Oxford University Press.
Selye, H. (1993). History of the stress concept. In L. Goldberger (Ed.), *Handbook of stress: Theoretical and clinical aspects* (pp. 7–17). New York: Free Press.
Shannon, C. (1994). Stress management. In D. K. Granvold (Ed.), *Cognitive and behavioral treatment: Methods and applications* (pp. 339–352). Pacific Grove, CA: Brooks/Cole.

Sexual Dysfunction in Men

Description

The physiology of male sexual functioning is incredibly complex, and as a result, there are a number of ways in which reproductive mechanisms can go awry, for example, impotence, premature ejaculation, diminished concentration of testosterone, lower levels of sperm production, and decreased sex drive.

Causes

Stressors can produce problems in male sexual functioning. The onset of a stressor may cause a decline in luteinizing hormone releasing hormone (LHRH) concentrations, whereupon the release of LHRH is inhibited by the release of endorphins and enkephalins (mostly endorphins); endorphins play a role in blocking pain and are secreted in response to exercise as well as to physical or psychological distress. The increase in endorphins thus results in reduced concentrations of testosterone. In addition, the increase in glucocorticoid brought on by stress blocks the response of the testes to LHRH. With chronic stress, the testes may diminish in size, produce less mobile sperm, and decrease sex drive.

It is obviously important to establish that a sexual dysfunction results from psychological causes ("stress," etc.) and is not organic. It is further important to identify these stressors as a causative of the sexual dysfunction. Many, if not most, men who complain of impotence achieve automatic erections during REM sleep states, indicating that these causes may be stress-related and not the result of physiological impairment.

Exercise, when done excessively, can contribute to male **Impotence;** endorphins are released during exercise (accounting for the so-called "runner's high" that joggers often describe), and may suppress testosterone.

Often, temporary situations such as marital conflict, **Fatigue,** or **Anxiety** may lead to impotence. It is common for problems of impotency and premature ejaculation also to result from the onset of stressors. The parasympathetic nervous system must function properly for erection to occur; the parasympathetic nerves of the male member cause the muscles in the arterial walls of the penis to relax and expand so that blood may fill the spongy tissue of the penis; sympathetic nerves, on the other hand, constrict the arterial walls, thereby depriving the penis of erection.

Stress makes it difficult for the body to effectively influence parasympathetic activity; because erection is dependent on the parasympathetic system, the result can be impotence. In addition, nervousness and anxiety can result in quick shifts from parasympathetic (erection) to sympathetic activity (ejaculation), which may result in premature ejaculation.

In other cases the stressor may be the sexual dysfunction itself. Men who cannot perform sexually may experience great **Frustration** about disability. Impotence may also accompany severe **Depression.**

Treatment

Psychological counseling can help the patient identify the stressors and learn to cope appropriately. Such counseling could consist of psychotherapy, especially of **Progressive Relaxation** for coping skills. It is important to reassure the patient that all men experience sexual dysfunction at some point in their lives, and that stress-related sexual dysfunctions are generally temporary conditions.

SEE ALSO:

Anxiety
Depression
Fatigue, "Nervous"
Frustration

Impotence
Infertility
Progressive Relaxation
Stress Management Methods

BIBLIOGRAPHY

Bancroft, J. (1989). *Human sexuality and its problems* (2nd ed.). Edinburgh, Scotland: Churchill, Livingstone.

Bruce, T. J., & Barlow, D. H. (1990). The nature and role of performance anxiety in sexual dysfunction. In H. Leitenberg (Ed.), *Handbook of social and evaluation anxiety.* New York: Plenum.

Katchadourian, H. A. & Lunde, D. T. (1982). *Fundamentals of human sexuality.* New York: Holt, Rinehart and Winston.

LoPiccolo, J. (1990). Sexual dysfunction. In A. E. Bellack, M. Hersen, & A. Kazdin (Eds.), *International handbook of behavior modification and therapy* (2nd ed., pp. 547–564). New York: Plenum.

Rosen, R. C., & Leiblum, S. R. (1995). Treatment of sexual disorders in the 1990's: An integrated approach. *Journal of Consulting and Clinical Psychology, 63,* 877–890.

Vandereycken, W. (1995). The behavioral management of sexual dysfunctions. In G. R. Caddy & D. G. Byrne (Eds.), *Behavioral medicine: International perspectives (Vol. 3); Development in clinical psychology* (pp. 107–133). Norwood, NJ: Ablex.

Sexual Dysfunction in Women

Description

Women often report an increase of sexual satisfaction as a result of successful experience with sex, as one would expect. However, sexual dysfunction in women is often a problem, especially when individual distress and its negative impacts on a relationship are reported. Such problems in sexual functioning are deficits in sexual desire or responsiveness, and disorders in which penetration is painful, difficult, or impossible. The most commonly reported disorders are dyspareunia (painful intercourse), anorgasmia, and vaginismus.

Vaginismus is a condition in which the outer muscles of the vagina involuntarily contract, causing penetration problems. The severity of this condition may range from mild, inducing some tightness and discomfort, to severe, whereby penetration is impossible. It is reported more frequently in younger women than in older women, and especially in women who have negative attitudes toward sex. It is usually discovered when intercourse is first attempted or during a gynecological examination.

Causes

Stressors such as relationship problems, sexual abuse experienced as a child, and adult sexual trauma have been associated with impairment of female sexual functioning. Other psychological antecedents are lack of sexual assertiveness, discomfort with masturbation, and exposure to negative attitudes toward sex during upbringing.

Those who have been sexually abused as children have a higher level of stress hormones in their blood than is normal for them, and it seems that the negative effects of such experiences continue long after the abuse has ceased. As a group they tend to experience puberty earlier than nonabused children.

Physical symptoms such as pelvic inflammatory disease, vulvar vestibulitis, vaginal irritations, growths, and reactions to contraceptive devices can cause dyspareunia. When a painful condition such as dyspareunia has persisted over a long period of time the patient can associate pain with sexual activity and, consequently, may have anxiety about resuming sex after the physical complaints have subsided.

Changes in hormonal levels and side effects from medications are also associated with sexual problems. A deficiency of hormones such as estrogen has been associated with lack of libido, inadequate lubrication during sexual arousal, and anorgasmia. Women also report such deficits after menopause, when the level of estrogen decreases.

Treatment

It is important that the causes of sexual difficulties be established and that appropriate medical and/or psychological interventions be made. **Systematic Desensitization** is frequently used in the treatment of orgasmic disorders, dyspareunia, and vaginismus. In systematic desensitization, the patient is first taught **Progressive Relaxation.** When the individual is in a deeply relaxed state she is presented with anxiety-inducing stimuli on a graduated basis.

SEE ALSO:

Child Sexual Abuse, Stress of
Female Stress
Infertility

Progressive Relaxation
Systematic Desensitization

BIBLIOGRAPHY

Andersen, B. L., & Cyranowski, J. M. (1995). Women's sexuality: Behaviors, responses and individual differences. *Journal of Consulting and Clinical Psychology, 63,* 891–906.

Epps, R. P., & Stewart, S. C. (Eds.). (1996). *The American Medical Woman's Association guide to sexuality.* New York: Dell.

Rosen, R. C., & Leiblum, S. R. (1995). Treatment of sexual disorders in the 1990s: An integrated approach. *Journal of Consulting and Clinical Psychology, 63,* 877–890.

Stotland, N. L. (1996). Women and psychiatry. In R. E. Hales & S. C. Yudofsky (Eds.), *The American Psychiatric Press synopsis of psychiatry.* Washington, DC: American Psychiatric Press.

Sickle Cell Disease

Description

Sickle cell disease (SCD) is a major concern, especially for African Americans, whom it affects with a frequency of about 1 in 400 to 1 in 600. It results in chronic anemia, pain, and organ damage. Many individuals with SCD experience vaso-occlusive pain, which is unpredictable in its course and severely painful.

Causes

SCD is part of a group of genetic disorders that include chronic anemia and result in both acute and chronic organ damage. Stressful life conditions exacerbate the symptoms.

Treatment

Currently there is no known cure or prevention for SCD. Patients typically are administered pain medications and advised to consume considerable fluids. However, some stress management techniques have been found to be beneficial. For example, adults in a study by Gil et al. (1996) who reported dysfunctional coping and negative thought patterns also had relatively intense pain, considerable depression and anxiety, decreased ability to work, and lowered social activity, and they used relatively more health care. They were instructed in coping skills and how to use six **Progressive Relaxation** and distraction strategies. Those patients reported that the training increased their ability to cope, that they had less negative thinking and a lower tendency to report pain.

S E E   A L S O :

Pain
Stress Management Methods

B I B L I O G R A P H Y

Gil, K. M., Wilson, J. J., Edens, J. L., Webster, D. A., Abrams, M. A., Grant, M., Orriginger, E., Clark, W. C., & Janal, M. N. (1996). Effects of cognitive coping skills training on coping strategies and experimental pain sensitivity in African American adults with Sickle Cell Disease. *Health Psychology, 15,* 1, 3–10.
Hill, S. A. (1996). Caregiving in African American families: Caring for children with sickle cell disease. In S. L. Louise Logan (Ed.), *The Black family: Strengths, self-help, and positive change* (pp. 39–52). Boulder, CO: Westview.
Lemanek, K. L., Buckloh, L. M., Woods, G., & Butler, R. (1995). Diseases of the circulatory system: Sickle cell disease and hemophilia. In M. C. Roberts (Ed.), *Handbook of pediatric psychology* (2nd ed., pp. 286–309). New York: Guilford Press.
Sturges, J. W., & Drabman, R. S. (1995). Psychophysiological disorders. In A. R. Eisen, C. A. Kearney, & C. E. Schaefer (Eds.), *Clinical handbook of anxiety disorders in children and adolescents* (pp. 383–411). Northvale, NJ: Aronson.

Skin Disorders/Diseases

Description

Numerous skin diseases, such as acne, psoriasis, hives, eczema, and herpes, as we shall see, can be aggravated by stress.

Causes

Emotional stress can add years to one's appearance, according to dermatologist Eugene Farber, M. D., director of the Psoriasis Research Institute in Palo Alto, California. As he put it, the skin and the psyche are very much in communication; consequently, stress plays a huge role in a number of skin diseases. A person's stressed physiology sends blood to the most vital organs—the brain, heart, and lungs—rather than the skin. A result is a pale ashen look that makes under-eye circles prominent. Also skin-cell turnover slows down, exacerbating dryness, and allows a buildup of metabolic by-products that can make skin look yellow. And due to a decrease in the production of the proteins that provide elasticity in the skin, skin under stress can become lax. Environmental factors such as temperature, humidity, cosmetics, toiletries, and clothing can contribute to skin problems. However, their effects are more severe when an individual simultaneously experiences environmental **Stressors.** In addition, genetic factors seem to influence the incidence and severity of skin problems. Stress can also upset the care and feeding of the body, upon which youthful skin depends. Insufficient rest, a poor diet, and little attention to skin care may contribute to puffy eyes and the dry skin that can accentuate fine lines and wrinkles. Frowns and furrows on the face are signs of excessive muscular tension; continuous stress can make them permanent.

Eczema and its recurrence are correlated with high-stress life events; for example, itching, a common symptom of eczema, often increases while people discuss stressful events in their lives. Attendant scratching may become habitual, even though not triggered by an itching sensation.

Acne often occurs among teenagers, but is not limited to that age group. Theories concerning acne have varied throughout the years. Measurements of the quantity of sebum, or oil, have been performed on acne subjects during periods of relative calm and during intense periods of anger. The sebum increased between two and five times during anger.

The stressful teenage years, combining rapid hormone changes and the need for adaptation to a more adult life pattern, along with the demands from parents and peers, are a fertile time for development of excess tension. While the chemical changes brought on by tension and anxiety may not themselves cause skin diseases, they can trigger an outbreak of them.

Rosacea, the skin reddening that often accompanies aging, can also be aggravated by stress, due to the tendency for blood vessels to dilate when one is under duress.

One current theory suggests that the nervous system may play a role in skin diseases such as psoriasis and neurodermatitis. The sensory nerves are thought to secrete molecules called neuropeptides that can cause local inflammation when released. It has been found that stressed psoriasis patients have higher-than-normal levels of a neuropeptide called substance P.

Treatment

Distractions such as working at hobbies have been shown to sometimes help clear the skin of diseases. Other treatments that have been successful include **Progressive Relaxation** and medications (prescribed and over-the-counter).

S E E   A L S O :

Asthma and Stress   Progressive Relaxation
Chemicals of the Body and Stress   Stress, Defined

B I B L I O G R A P H Y

Folks, D. G., & Kinney, F. C. (1995). Dermatologic conditions. In A. Stoudemire (Ed.), *Psychological factors affecting medical conditions* (pp. 123–140). Washington, DC: American Psychiatric Press.
Friedman, S., Hatch, M., & Paradis, C. I. (1993). Dermatological disorders. In R. J. Gatchel & E. B. Blanchard (Eds.), *Psychophysiological disorders: Research and clinical applications* (pp. 205–244). Washington, DC: American Psychiatric Press.

Sleep, Healthy and Unhealthy

Description

Sleep is a biological rhythm that follows a systematic cycle during each 24-hour period (called a circadian pattern). In human adults, sleep occurs in four stages that occur sequentially throughout the night. Depth of sleep increases with each stage, with the deepest sleep known as rapid-eye-movement (REM). Although the amount of sleep required is different for everyone, getting less than is necessary can lead to irritability and stress.

The amount of sleep that each person gets is influenced by many factors: the degree of relaxation versus excessive tension, what is eaten, what is done physically, what resolution of psychological conflicts is achieved, what events are to be faced the next day, as well as the type of bed and the room temperature. All these can influence the depth of sleep.

Healthful sleep must not be disturbed by nightmares, extraneous stimulation, or unresolved conflicts, or any other condition that leads to excessive tension. Fitful and incomplete rest leads to an energy drain and biological disequilibrium. Difficulty falling asleep and waking too early (INSOMNIA) can be signs of anxiety, depression, and psychological disturbances. They may also be signals of stressful lifestyle habits, such as overeating. All are signals of excessive tension.

If sleep is too brief, fitful, or disrupted, then we awaken irritable, tired, cranky, and less able to cope. Chronic sleep disturbances can lead to physical and psychological exhaustion, depression, and a general feeling of anxiety.

The seriousness of sleep disorders is indicated by the estimate that in one form or another they affect every person every year. There may be transient sleep disorders that can last for days or weeks as a result of various temporary stressors, or sleep disorders may be chronic and relatively long-lasting. More than 100 centers throughout the United States study the two major categories of sleep disorders: Dyssomnias include insomnia disorders and maladaptive sleep/wake schedules. Parasomnias include sleep terrors, nightmares, and sleepwalking. Nightmares usually occur in the REM stage of sleep. In contrast, night terrors typically occur when dreams are absent. In night terrors, the individual often panics and wakes up screaming. Studies have found that anxious people do not have more nightmares than nonanxious people, though they may be more likely to remember and more likely to complain about nightmares.

Sleep disorders are often associated with other behavioral disorders such as **Worrying, Obsessive-Compulsive Behavior,** and **Anxiety** and with such organic conditions as Parkinson's disease.

Three disorders of initiating and maintaining sleep are (1) falling asleep, defined as taking more than 30 minutes for sleep onset; (2) maintaining sleep, defined as awakening for more than 30 minutes; and (3) terminal insomnia—awakening early in the morning and not getting back to sleep. All three types may occur together or singly, but they all contribute to daytime fatigue. A sleep problem is serious when it starts to affect daytime performance.

Causes

Many sleep disorders are due to excessive stress. The overly tense individual thinks about problems and carries the stresses of life over into bedtime. Excessive muscular tension is incompatible with good sleep. Other contributing factors are biological predisposition, drugs and alcohol, and medical problems (produced by **Arthritis, Ulcers, Headache, Asthma,** irregular heartbeat, and sleep apnea, in which there are brief bouts of breathing cessation). Drug and alcohol dependency have been established as the primary cause in 12.4 percent of patients with chronic insomnia.

Sleep disorders often follow a positive feedback model in which physiological arousal (rapid heartbeats, high bodily temperature, etc.) decreases sleep, whereupon poor sleep leads to worry and increased physiological arousal.

Treatment

The development of healthy sleep patterns is vital to the maintenance of energy reserves. It is important to develop reliable habits so that there is the expectation of sound sleep. Some of the more common contributors to insomnia are the expectations of having difficulty falling asleep, nightmares, and feeling poorly upon waking. The expectation of negative events typically generates anxiety and tension. These in turn create a self-fulfilling prophecy. Once sound sleep habits have been established, the expectation of full sleep facilitates that event.

There are a number of guidelines that have been found to encourage sound sleep habits:

- Keep a regular sleeping schedule.
- Eat three regular meals a day at a regular time.
- Exercise regularly (though not too close to bedtime).
- Take time to unwind, at least two hours before going to bed (this is a good time to practice relaxation techniques).
- Curtail ingestion of caffeine in the evening.
- Don't take sleeping drugs or drink alcohol to help sleep.
- Approach sleep with a positive attitude, being ready both physically and psychologically to get a full night's restful sleep (see **Mind and Mental Events**).

Other treatments include medication, which is not a permanent solution, and **Progressive Relaxation.** Rapid mental activity, sometimes described as a "racing mind," interferes with sleep. By learning ways to relax, especially to relax the speech musculature that is especially involved in generating thoughts, the racing mind can be relaxed (see **Mind and Mental Events**).

SEE ALSO:

Anxiety
Arthritis, Rheumatoid
Asthma and Stress
Headache, Migraine and Tension
Insomnia (Sleep Difficulties)

Mind and Mental Events
Obsessive-Compulsive Behavior
Progressive Relaxation
Ulcers, Peptic, Gastric and Duodenal
Worry

BIBLIOGRAPHY

Friedman, L., Brooks, J. O., III., Bliwise, D. L., Yesavage, J. A., & Wicks, D. S. (1995). Perceptions of life stress and chronic insomnia in older adults. *Psychology and Aging, 10, 3,* 352–357.
McGuigan, F. J. (1992). *Calm down: A guide for stress and tension control.* Dubuque, IA: Kendall/Hunt.
Pressman, M. R., & Orr, W. C. (1997). *Understanding sleep: The evaluation and treatment of sleep disorders.* Washington, DC: American Psychological Association.
Ogilvie, R., & Harsh, J. (1994). *Sleep onset: Normal and abnormal processes.* Washington, DC: American Psychological Association.

Social Phobia

Description

Social phobia describes the excessive fear that an individual experiences on being exposed to possible scrutiny by others, fear of behaving in a way that is embarrassing or humiliating, and so forth. Those with social phobia share a common feature of excessive fear of negative evaluation, though of course there is considerable heterogeneity among them. Although socially anxious people in general fear that their anxiety will be visible to others, some focus almost exclusively on a particular physical reaction or anxiety symptom such as blushing, voice or hand tremors, head shaking, perspiration, or palpitations. Usually the fear is that others will see the symptoms and draw some negative conclusion about the person. Situations commonly feared include talking or performing in front of a group (see **Speaking Anxiety, Public**), being the center of attention, attending meetings, eating/drinking/writing while others observe, dating, attending a party, using a urinal, using a telephone, being assertive, and shaking hands.

Causes

The causes of social phobia vary, but as with any kind of phobia, conditioning of a past noxious experience is the probable source. Some have lived under isolated conditions, and have become overly anxious in group environments. Others have never developed social skills, and their deficit contributes to social anxiety; or their extreme anxiety may interfere with the execution of skills the person does possess. One fear often reported revolves around some terrible secret they are afraid will be revealed.

Treatment

Research suggests that exposure-based treatment (as in **Behavior Therapies**) is likely to be very effective, but a number of factors may make this kind of treatment difficult for the patient as well as for the therapist. Most individuals with social phobia have arranged their lives in such a way that they have little contact with other people. When they finally decide to take a risk to enter social environments, they may perform in a manner that will result in negative consequences. Because of this, the use of imaginal or simulated exposure followed by relaxation of muscles is often helpful as initial steps to approach exposure to the feared situation (see especially **Progressive Relaxation** and **Systematic Desensitization**). The patient needs opportunities to allow habituation to occur. The situations used in simulated exposures may be unrealistic or extremely unlikely to occur but may represent a fear of what could happen.

BIBLIOGRAPHY

Heimberg, R. G., Liebowitz, M. R., Hope, D. A., & Schneier, F. R. (Eds.). (1995). *Social phobia: Diagnosis, assessment and treatment.* New York: Guilford Press.
Juster, H. R., & Heimberg, D. G. (1995). Social phobia: Longitudinal course and long-term outcome of cognitive-behavioral treatment. *Psychiatric Clinics of North America, 18,* 821–842.
Juster, H. R., Heimberg, R. G., Frost, R. O., & Holt, C. S. (1996). Social phobia and perfectionism. *Personality and Individual Differences, 21,* 403–410.
Stein, M. B., Baird, & A., Walker, J. R. (1996). Social phobia in adults with stuttering. *American Journal of Psychiatry, 153,* 270–278.
Trower, P., & Turland, D. (1984). Social phobia. In S. M. Turner (Ed.), *Behavioral theories and treatment of anxiety* (pp. 321–367). New York: Plenum.

Social Support

Social support research has been increasing at a rapid rate during the past few decades. This research has been in vogue because it appears to help buffer the effects of the stressors of life on health and well-being; also, because it suggests facilitating adjustments for "stressed" individuals. However, the data are not definitive, so the role of social support for adjustment to stressors is in need of yet further research.

One difficulty associated with the study of social support is the precise meaning of this term. Some investigators regard it as perceptions of support available to the person under stress. Others, however, define support as what actually is received. Still others consider social network variables such as the number of living children and siblings, marital status, and so on, as the definition of social support. There is even further complexity, inasmuch as value of support provided specifically by family, friends, confidants, and so forth needs to be distinguished.

It is therefore not surprising that different researchers find different relations between social support and adverse health reactions to stress. One somewhat consistent finding, though, is that only perceived, as opposed to actually received, social support seems to serve as a buffer to stress.

BIBLIOGRAPHY

Lehrer, P. M., & Woolfolk, R. L. (1993). *Principles and practice of stress management* (2nd ed.). New York: Guilford.

Pierce, G. R., Sarason, B. R., & Sarason, I. G. (Eds.). (1996). *Handbook of social support and the family.* New York: Plenum.

Sarason, I. G., & Sarason, B. R. (1985). Life change, social support, coping and health. In R. M. Kaplan & M. H. Criqui (Eds.), *Behavior epidemiology and disease prevention. NATO ASI Series A: Life Sciences, Vol. 84* (pp. 219–236). New York: Plenum.

Seeman, T. E., Berkman, L. F., Blazer, D., & Rowe, J. W. (1994). *Social support and neuroendocrine function. Annals of behavioral medicine, 16,* 95–106.

Wills, T. A. (1998). Social support. In E. A. Blechman & K. D. Brownell, *Behavioral medicine & women: A comprehensive handbook* (pp. 118–123). New York: Guilford.

Wills, T. A., Blechman, E. A., & McNamera, G. (1996). Family support, coping and competence. In E. M. Hetherington & E. A. Blechman (Eds.), *Stress, coping and resiliency in children and families* (pp. 107–133). Mahwah, NJ: Erlbaum.

Spastic Colon

Description

Spastic colon is a serious disorder of the gastrointestinal tract. It usually begins during adulthood, and is more frequent in women. It is related to **Esophageal Spasm,** mucous colitis (colitis with secretion of mucous), and other gastrointestinal disorders; its symptoms are similar to appendicitis so that it is important to make a differential diagnosis. Spastic colon frequently is accompanied with constipation, alternating with normal bowel movement and diarrhea. Additional symptoms include attacks of pain and tenderness of the colon which can particularly be revealed by palpation. An X ray with a barium enema can assist in diagnosis.

Causes

Spastic colon is most often caused by emotional upset (nervous hypertension), due to continuous stressful life styles. Such continuous confrontation with stressors evokes striated muscle reactions throughout the body (see the figure in the Introduction on page xiii), and those tensions cause the smooth muscles as in the colon to constrict. It can be expected that such chronic overtension can wreak havoc on the colon; overtense muscles, especially in the abdomen, contribute greatly to the condition.

Treatment

Spastic colon has been successfully treated with **Progressive Relaxation.** There is usually amelioration of symptoms within the first couple of months of treatment. During treatment, symptoms sometimes reoccur temporarily, which may discourage the patient. Here as in other chronic medical disorders there are ups and downs, but where the patient continuously practices relaxation, in the long run success can be achieved.

SEE ALSO:

Gastrointestinal Disorders
Esophageal Spasm/Globus Hystericus
Progressive Relaxation

BIBLIOGRAPHY

Folks, D. G., & Kenney, F. C. (1995). Gastrointestinal conditions. In A. Stoudemire (Ed.), *Psychological factors affecting medical conditions.* Washington, DC: American Psychiatric Press.
Jacobson, E. J. (1938). *Progressive relaxation* (Rev. ed.). Chicago: University of Chicago Press.
McGuigan, F. J. (1992). *Calm down: A guide for stress and tension control.* Dubuque, IA: Kendall/Hunt.
Thompson. W. G. (1993). *The angry gut: Coping with colitis and Crohn's disease.* New York: Plenum.

Speaking Anxiety (Public)

Description

Fear of public speaking, a major anxiety of some Americans, is an emotional reaction triggered by anticipation of performing before an audience. Some manifestations are a quavering voice, stuttering, inappropriate laughing, speech blocks, swallowing repeatedly, vomiting, rapid shallow or heavy breathing, fast heart rate, avoiding eye contact, tense face muscles, clenching the teeth, rigid posture, fidgeting hands, cold and sweaty hands, trembling, pacing, sweating, dry mouth, facial redness, blacking out, or fainting. These manifestations may begin as early as when the individual first learns he or she will be speaking in public; and the maladjustments can continue even after the speaking has been completed. **Fear** of making a mistake in front of an audience may be so great as to produce a complete avoidance of any social speech.

Causes

Common causes of public speaking anxiety include fears of making a mistake, of being unattractive, of criticism, of the known, and of the unknown, and the excitement from anticipation. Lack of ability, preparedness, and knowledge of speech-making techniques is a contributing cause. The result includes secretion of stress hormones, especially adrenaline, that eventually may overload one to the extent of experiencing emotional reactions, as if the body is hyperactive and there is nothing to be done about it. These fears contribute to the speaker's wavering sense of self-confidence and to the various physical and emotional manifestations of stressful situations.

Treatment

Since the maladaptive reactions to speech making are learned, the solution for speech stress is to control the discomfort behaviorally. Widely used treatments are

Hypnosis, Biofeedback, visualization, **Assertiveness Training,** goal setting, cognitive restructuring, **Systematic Desensitization,** and skills training.

Systematic Desensitization uses a three-step procedure in which the client is taught to relax by contracting and releasing large muscle groups; the therapist assists the client in building a hierarchy of anxiety-producing stimulus situations; and the client is slowly taught to associate relaxation with his or her identified stimulus situations.

An integrated approach is a multimodal plan that uses techniques of relaxation, deep breathing, and visualization, with mental rehearsal to transform the negative anxiety experience into a positive one.

Results suggest that **Stress Management Methods** involving **Progressive Relaxation, Breathing,** and visualization are effective in reducing stress and anxiety associated with public speaking anxiety, although they do not necessarily enhance the speaking ability of the anxious client.

There are also some behavioral adjustments that help to alleviate some of the physical symptoms of this stress: Drinking water just before making the speech will help combat dry mouth, but drinking milk may coat the throat with phlegm. Eating before making a speech might contribute to upset or "nervous" stomach. Eating sugar or salt before speaking may make the tongue feel swollen and/or dry. Drinking caffeine only contributes to shakiness. Drinking alcohol impairs concentration and fine motor skills. One could wear lightweight clothing to ease overheating and sweating. Going to the bathroom before making a speech aids in physical comfort.

SEE ALSO:

Anxiety

Biofeedback

Hypnosis

Progressive Relaxation

Social Phobia

Stress Management Methods

Stuttering

Systematic Desensitization

BIBLIOGRAPHY

Ayres, J., Hopf, T., & Ayres D. M. (1994). An examination of whether imaging ability enhances the effectiveness of an intervention designed to reduce speech anxiety. *Communication Education, 43,* 252–258.

Burnley, M. C. E., Cross, P. A., Spanos, N. P. (1992–1993). The effects of stress inoculation training and skills training on the treatment of speech anxiety. *Imagination, Cognition, and Personality, 12,* 355–366.

Kaiser, J., Hinton, J. W., Khrone, H. W., Stewart, R., & Burton, R. (1995). Coping dispositions and physiological recovery from a speech preparation stressor. *Personality and Individual Differences, 19,* 1–11.

Rossi, A. M., & Seiler, W. J. (1989–1990). The comparative effectiveness of systematic desensitization and an integrative approach in treating public speaking anxiety: A literature review and a preliminary investigation. *Imagination, Cognition and Personality, 9,* 49–66.

Spondylitis

Description

Spondylitis, a progressive disease of the spine, exists in two forms, ankylosing and tuberculous spondylitis.

Causes

Ankylosing spondylitis is a disease of unknown cause, but with evidence of genetic transmission, occurring nine times more frequently in males than females. It is a progressive form of arthritis and begins in the lower back—a common cause of pain in men in their twenties and thirties; in addition it is a common cause of stress among young males. The disease is characterized by degeneration of vertebral joints, calcium and bone deposition in associated ligaments, and inflammation of surrounding tissues. Vertebrae tend to fuse as a result of bone deposition between them (ankylosis). Associated compression of spinal nerves causes pain to radiate to other areas. As the disease spreads up the spine, substantial stiffening and deformity can develop over a period of 10 years or more.

Tuberculous spondylitis, or Pott's disease, is caused by tuberculosis in a vertebra, where the infection can destroy intervertebral discs and spread to adjacent vertebrae. Infectious agents other than tuberculosis can produce similar effects.

Treatment

Patients are treated with anti-inflammatory drugs for the symptoms and with exercise programs for maintenance of posture. Treatment includes antibiotic therapy and sometimes surgical drainage of abscesses and fusion of affected vertebrae. Relaxation is recommended where the injured muscle can be gently treated so that the patient can practice its function gradually and thus relieve pain.

SEE ALSO:

Backache   Progressive Relaxation
Pain   Sciatica

BIBLIOGRAPHY

Barlow, H. H., Macey, S. J., & Struthers, G. R. (1993). Control-related cognitions, chronic disease and gender. In H. Schroder, K. Reschke, M. Johnson, & S. Maes (Eds.), *Health psychology: Potential in diversity* (pp. 154–164). Regensburg, Germany: S. Roderer Verlag.

Massey, E. W. (1991). Disorders of bones, ligaments, cartilage and meninges. In W. G. Bradley, R. B. Daroff, G. M. Fenichel, & C. D. Marsden (Eds.), *Neurology in clinical practice* (Vol. 2, pp. 1625–1660). Boston: Butterworth Heinemann.

Sports Performance, Bodily Conditioning, and Injuries

Description

The old motto "the more effort you put into something the better the results" is not necessarily true when it comes to sports. In most athletic situations, the more tense you are the more your performance and satisfaction decrease. When athletes tense the wrong muscles required for the activity and if they tense their muscle groups too much, they lose an essential source of the body's natural energy, adenosine triphosphate. The loss of energy and elasticity creates a crash-and-burn syndrome. The athlete may start with a big bang but fizzle out quickly with a quiet whimper or a scream because of a torn muscle or ligament. When it comes to high-contact sports, such as boxing, martial arts, or football, it is best for the individual not to be tense when he or she is hit. The extra-tensed muscles create a more powerful impact from the hit than if they were more relaxed. In addition, when one is tense and gets hit, the muscles are hypertensively contracted to their maximum point. On impact the tense muscle pulls or tears other muscles because it is not able to give and take, creating extra strain on the system.

Causes

The cause of many poor performances and injuries in sports activities is the fact that many athletes are not able to contract only the appropriate muscles that are needed for optimal functioning in a particular sport. Instead, they contract more muscles than are needed for the activity. Also, many athletes overtense these muscles, losing elasticity and energy. Endurance, coordination, flexibility, concentration, speed, and dexterity are all essential qualities that should be at an optimal level to achieve the best results.

Treatment

To attain maximum results in performance, the athlete must try to maintain a state of relaxation that is optimal for the performance required. Practice in **Progressive Relaxation** can improve the performance of the athlete and help to protect the body. In one study, it was found that progressive relaxation training decreased injuries: Swimmers had a 52 percent decrease in injuries; there was also a significant reduction in injuries on the varsity football team. This program taught the individuals to contract only those muscles that are needed at optimal levels to get the most efficient results for the intended purpose. The program included educating the individuals about their muscle groups, teaching them both to recognize where the muscles are and that gaining control over them is essential for the over-tense athlete. In order to obtain this control over the muscles groups, the athletes practiced progressive relaxation one hour a day. They learned to recognize the muscle tensions, where they were, how they feel and how to rid themselves of the tension in specific muscle groups. At the end of the program the athletes were more relaxed, efficient, and resilient.

S E E   A L S O :

Exercise, Benefits of   Running, Relaxed
Progressive Relaxation   Sports Stress

B I B L I O G R A P H Y

Druckman, D., & Bjork, R. A. (1991). *In the mind's eye: Enhancing human performance.* Washington, DC: National Academy Press.
Kerr, G., & Goss, J. (1996). The effects of stress management program on injuries and stress levels. *Journal of Applied Sport Psychology, 8,* 109–117.
Jones, J. G., & Hardy, L. (Eds.). (1990). *Stress and performance in sport.* Chichester, England: Wiley.
van Raalte, J. L., & Brewer, B. W. (Eds.). (1996). *Exploring sport and exercise psychology.* Washington, DC: American Psychological Association.

Sports Stress

Description

Inappropriate physical tension in the form of anxiety can interfere with accomplishments on the playing field. Experts note that as stress begins to increase, performance improves up to an optimal amount; but then following an inverted U-shaped function, as it continues to increase further, performance levels off and rapidly deteriorates. Symptoms of excessive stress can include fatigue, dizziness, confusion, panic, loss of control, fear, and overexcitement. There may be excessively high heart rate and blood pressure, rapid breathing, high blood sugar levels, and perspiration. One may experience a need to urinate, have loose stools, and make nervous movements; there may be insomnia and nausea associated with high levels of stress. The result can be failure to focus attention, feelings of nausea, fears of failure and of injuries, depression, lack of self-confidence, distractibility, and poor regulation of thought processes.

Causes

Excessively high sports stress may be produced by high levels of **Anxiety,** in which there is abnormally high general tension throughout the muscles that interferes with good athletic performance. One may perform well in practice, but in games tend to tense up and fail to perform effectively.

Treatment

When the athlete is well trained, his or her confidence can increase so that the negative effects of stress can often be prevented. Mental and emotional training can be helpful in reducing anxiety and thus increasing performance levels.

One expert (Silva, 1982) counsels pulling oneself together by calling upon some stress-coping strategies designed for sports psychology. One is a cognitive behavioral intervention program in which one targets problems and restructures attitudinal changes in cognitions; the learner thus replaces the faulty ideas that led to negative consequences in the past. One way that this can be accomplished is by pairing a word cue with a new behavior by covertly rehearsing the word and the new behavior. Later one can use the word to evoke the new behavior. A similar procedure is to pair the imagery of a good performance that was achieved in practice with the word "relax." For example, in a game, one can recall successful free throws that were achieved in practice that had been preceded by the imagery evoked by the word "relax." By thus having covertly rehearsed relaxed free-throw shooting, one can in a real game step up to the free-throw line, say "relax" to oneself, use that as the cue to **Differentially Relax,** and successfully swish the shots. Several different studies have proven the efficacy of this approach. To elaborate on these matters, consider the nature of cognitions that interfere with successful sports performance.

Interfering Cognitions.   Cognitions during athletic performance may be beneficial or detrimental; undesired cognitions can interfere with and disrupt the goal activity. To understand this, note that irrelevant cognitions are actually neuromuscular activities. During irrelevant (undesired) thoughts there are actual covert speech muscle responses, eye muscle responses, and somatic responses that interfere with optimal performance. Irrelevant cognitions are neuromuscular activities that generate neural impulses that are widespread throughout the body. When such nervous activity interacts with the muscular activities of the athlete, performance deteriorates. Examples abound, as in the tennis player who was thinking of the last point when receiving a serve, the sprinter who is concerned with the runner next to him, and the wide receiver in football who thinks that his hands might fail him as the football comes over his shoulder. To successfully perform athletic activities, the individual must control those cognitions that are irrelevant to and interfere with the primary purpose of the behavior.

Controlling Irrelevant Cognitions.   Since cognitive activities are generated when neuromuscular circuits reverberate, they can be eliminated when the neuromuscular circuits cease to be active. To silence those circuits and thus stop the reverberations, a person can differentially relax the relevant striated muscle components. When one is so relaxed, there is optimal contraction of only those muscles necessary to perform the task at hand. Through practice, one can thus eliminate interfering tensions (be they cognitive or otherwise) so that desired behaviors become effective and habitual.

The more one understands differential relaxation and learns how to do it, the more successful such a program to control athletic stress can be.

SEE ALSO:

Anxiety
Differential Relaxation
Exercise, Benefits of
Running, Relaxed

Sports Performance, Bodily
    Conditioning, and Injuries
Tension Awareness

BIBLIOGRAPHY

Jones, J. G., & Hardy, L. (Eds.). *Stress and performance in sport.* Chichester, England: John Wiley.
Nideffer, R. M. (1976). *The inner athlete: Mind plus muscle for winning.* New York: Crowell.
Onestak, D. M. (1991). The effects of progressive relaxation, mental practice, and hypnosis on athletic performance: A review. *Journal of Sports Behavior, 14,* 247–282.
Silva, J. M. (1982). Competitive sport environments: Performance enhancement through cognitive intervention. *Behavior Modification, 6,* 443–463.
Smith, R. E. (1984). Theoretical and treatment approaches to anxiety reduction. In J. M. Silva, III, & R. S. Weinberg (Eds.), *Psychological foundations of sport* (pp. 157–176). Champaign, IL: Human Kinetics.
van Raalte, J. L., & Brewer, B. W. (Eds.). (1996). *Exploring sport and exercise psychology.* Washington, DC: American Psychological Association.
Weinberg, R. S. (1984). Mental preparation strategies. In J. M. Silva, III, & R. S. Weinberg (Eds.), *Psychological foundations of sport* (pp. 145–156). Champaign, IL: Human Kinetics.

Stress, Defined

Description

While no definition of stress has been universally accepted, three common classes of definitions are as follows. One is as a stimulus, an environmental event, usually a threat, that affects the body in complex ways; in this interpretation, stress is referred to as a "stressor," one that evokes complex reactions of the various systems of the body.

A second kind of definition is that stress is a bodily reaction to stressors; consequently, complex interactions of systems of the body can result in deleterious consequences to those systems and their organs to the point of a person's becoming "stressed out"; serious illness can follow. This class fits Hans Selye's definition of stress as the nonspecific response of the body to any demand. The demands, Hans Selye (1978/1956) held, can be positive ones (**Eustress**) or negative ones (**Distress**).

A third class is an interactive one between environmental events (stressors) and bodily reactions such that stressors affect systems of the body and the resulting behavior feeds back to affect the environmental stressors. Richard Lazarus

(1984) depicted such a relationship by describing stress as the interaction between the person and the environment, which is appraised as exceeding the person's resources and endangering the person's well-being.

For an elaboration of stress and stress management, see the Introduction on pages xi–xiv.

Whatever the definition of "stress" one adopts, it should be differentiated from **Anxiety** and **Burnout;** both of these topics are developed as separate entries in this encyclopedia.

By any definition, stress is a normal part of life, and some producers of stress such as physical exercise, positive emotional states, and creative activities are usually considered healthy. Prolonged and unwanted stress (distress), however, can have undesirable effects on mental and physical health, although reactions to such pressure can vary greatly among individuals. A person in a physically or mentally demanding or dangerous situation is said to be under stress. Internal diseases such as acidosis, cirrhosis, and other conditions can also produce stress. Chronic repetition of certain emotions, such as anger or despair, as well as changes in work or home situations or a reaction to surgery are just a few of the further ways in which distress can occur. And more than one factor causing stress can be present at one time.

Mental states (see **Mind and Mental Events**) such as severe melancholic depression are closely linked with stress-inducing anxiety, and the complex syndrome known as **Post-Traumatic Stress Disorder** is produced by traumatic situations such as war and other disasters.

Physiological effects linked with stress include **Gastrointestinal Disorders, Hypertension, Cardiovascular Disease** and so forth. Stress can also adversely affect the **Immune System,** causing the body to be less resistant to a wide range of health problems.

Causes

While the effects of stress are complex, they all are caused by a certain group of basic bodily responses including those of the startle reaction pattern (see **Tension Awareness**). These responses developed in the course of evolution, as organisms met situations of physical danger.

When a person perceives danger (whether real or imagined), increased muscle tension in concert with the brain activates the pituitary gland to release a hormone called adrenocorticotropic hormone. This hormone then triggers the adrenal glands to release epinephrine and various other hormones that speed up heart rate, raise blood pressure, and so forth. These effects are all part of the "fight or flight" response of the body to a threatening environment as one engages in the startle pattern.

These same effects are observed in social situations of occupational or emotional stress, even though one's life is not in any danger. Usually such responses are of short duration. If these effects persist beyond a reasonable length of time, however, they can also lead in complex ways to a variety of mental or physical problems, as detailed throughout this encyclopedia.

Treatment

Though there are many ways to avoid stressful situations and resultant excess tension, we cannot fully eliminate them from our lives. Therefore, treatment includes a number of **Stress Management Methods** which are developed individually as described in this encyclopedia.

SEE ALSO:

Anxiety

Burnout

Cardiovascular Disease

Distress (Negative Stress)

Eustress (Positive Stress)

Hypertension

Post Traumatic Stress Disorder (PTSD)

Stress, Environmental

Stressful Life Events

Stress Management Methods

Stress Signals

BIBLIOGRAPHY

Adams, J. D. (Ed.). (1980). *Understanding and managing stress*. San Diego: University Associates.

Burchfield, S. R, (Ed.). (1985). *Stress: Psychological and physiological interactions*. Washington, DC: Hemisphere.

De Vries, J. (1985). *Stress and nervous disorders*. Edinburgh, Scotland: Mainstream.

Gray, J. A. (1987). *The psychology of fear and stress* (2nd ed.). Cambridge, England: Cambridge University Press.

Lazarus, R. S., & Folkman, S. (1984). *Stress, appraisal and coping*. New York: Springer-Verlag.

Lehrer, P. M., & Woolfolk, R. L. (1993). *Principles and practice of stress management* (2nd ed.). New York: Guilford Press.

Seaward, B. L. (1994). *Managing stress: Principles and strategies for health and wellbeing*. Boston: Jones and Bartlett.

Seyle, H. (1978/1956). *The stress of life*. New York: McGraw-Hill.

Sutterly, D. C., and Donnelly, G. F., (Eds.). (1982). *Coping with stress: A nursing perspective*. Rockville, MD: Aspen Systems.

Stress, Environmental

Description

The stressors of our modern lifestyle can kill. As mortality due to infectious diseases decreased since the beginning of the twentieth century, there was a corresponding increase in deaths attributed to behavior and lifestyle. Major killers changed to heart disease, cancer, and cerebrovascular diseases, with each related to lifestyle. Psychological factors play a powerful part in health and illness.

Causes

Environmental stressors, acting singly or in combination, produce physiological changes that manifest clinically in psychosomatic and/or psychiatric disorders. These stressors include infectious agents, chemical agents, changes in climate or language, physical trauma, allergens, and the like. Three of the most critical "behavioral pathogens" are (1) smoking, (2) being overweight by at least 20–30 percent of normal weight, and (3) working and living a chronically stressed lifestyle (e.g., Type A behavior). The risk of premature death is twice the average of other individuals for persons who engage in any one of these behaviors.

In a study that followed a group of middle-aged Swedish men for seven years, life events were significantly associated with mortality, even after such variables as smoking or occupational class were controlled for. Life events included bereavement, legal trouble, being forced to move, financial problems, and job insecurity.

Treatment

Emotional support appears to buffer the effects of life events. Adequate emotional support may strengthen the psychobiological resistance to stress. Treatment, then, would need to involve assessment of an individual's actual and perceived social support; where lacking, support groups would be recommended, as well as training in assertiveness and/or other social skills to facilitate establishing a support network.

Behaviors that can protect one from the effects of life stressors are (1) maintain a desirable weight, (2) rarely eat fattening snacks, (3) eat breakfast daily, (4) do not smoke, (5) get adequate sleep, (6) exercise regularly, and (7) do not drink alcohol excessively. Research indicates that men who engaged in four or five of these health practices had a mortality rate four times lower than men who engaged in zero to three of these behaviors.

Clearly, the interaction of physiological and psychological stressors can have enormous impact on one's health. People need to find ways to change their behavior so as to prevent or control the effects of lifestyle stressors.

S E E   A L S O :

Stress, Defined
Stress Signals
Stressful Life Events

B I B L I O G R A P H Y

Halpern, D. (1995). *Mental health and the built environment: More than bricks and mortar?* London, England: Taylor & Francis.
Linsky, A. S., Bachman, R., Straus, M. A. (1995). *Stress, culture and aggression.* New Haven, CT: Yale University Press.

Matarazzo, J. D. (1994). Health and behavior: The coming together of science and practice in psychology and medicine after a century of benign neglect. *Journal of Clinical Psychology in Medical Settings, 1,* 7–39.

McAndrew, F. T. (1993). *Environmental Psychology.* Galesburg, IL: Knox College.

Rosengren, A., Orth-Gomer, K., Wedel, H., & Wilhelmsen, L. (1993). Stressful life events, social support, and mortality in men born in 1933. *British Medical Journal, 307,* 1102–1111.

Svenson, A., & Maule, M. (Eds.). (1993). *Time pressure and stress in human judgement and decision making.* New York: Plenum.

Stress, Legal Redress for?

There is a lively legal debate and interplay between stress litigation and the disability discrimination acts. Workers recognize the growth of stress-induced claims. There is no general rule as to whether an employee who suffers stress on the job is entitled to legal remedies or protection. Each state has its own workers compensation laws that provide compensation for work-related injuries or occupational diseases. However, there is great variance between how different states treat work-induced stress. Some states provide compensation for the psychological or mental suffering caused by stress at the workplace; some states require that the claimant suffer from some physical injury caused by stress. California requires that the claimant suffer psychiatric injury causing disability or requiring medical treatment. Other states preclude compensation for stress unless the claimant demonstrates that the stressors he or she was exposed to at work were unusual or unique to his or her occupation. Claims based on stress that is considered to be the natural part of any job may be denied. Some cases have denied compensation for stress that was caused by lawful employer actions, such as when an employee has been disciplined in a reasonable manner or terminated for just cause.

Post-traumatic stress disorder induced by a work-related event (such as a school bus driver's witnessing an accident in which children were killed) is generally compensable.

If a rule can be stated, it is that an employee is more likely to receive compensation for the physical injuries or disorders caused by work-induced stress, rather than compensation for stress per se. In any case, the employee must be able to demonstrate at least a casual connection between the work environment and the stress he or she suffers.

A federal employee whose job-related stress resulted in dizziness, high blood pressure, and severe stomach pain with hyperventilation and gastroenteritis was entitled to disability retirement even though he was not suffering from a specific disease or injury. However, federal employees who suffer from stress will be denied disability retirement regardless of the subjective complaints if they are still able to perform their jobs in a satisfactory manner or unless they first attempt to undergo medical and drug treatment.

The United States Equal Employment Opportunity Commission (EEDC) has stated that stress, by itself, is not a handicapping condition entitling the employee workplace accommodation under the Americans with Disabilities Act (ADA). A United States Court of Appeals has held that workplace stress that resulted from a personality conflict between an employee and her supervisor was not a qualifying disability under the ADA, and therefore did not entitle the employee to protection against termination. "Such a conflict is not disabling," the Court wrote, "at most it requires the employee to get a new job." The court noted, however that if the stressful workplace conflict triggered "serious mental illness," the employee may be entitled to protection from discrimination under the ADA. However, employees who engage in threatening or violent workplace behavior precipitated by stress-induced mental illness were not protected from termination by the ADA.

SEE ALSO:

Workplace Stress

BIBLIOGRAPHY

American Jurisprudence 2d, 339, 340.
Broida, P. *A guide to merit systems protection board law and practice.* (Dewey, 1997) at 2514-15.
EEOC Enforcement Guidance. (March 25, 1997). *The Americans with Disabilities Act and Psychiatric Disabilities.*
Palmer v. Circuit Court of Cook County, Illinois, 117 F.3d351 (7th Cir.1997).

Stressful Life Events

In an extensive series of studies, Rahe (1990) followed up on the classic life-event scale (Social Readjustment Rating Scale) of Holmes and Rahe (1967). He found that the order of magnitude for stressful life events was quite consistent, regardless of individual differences in age, sex, marital status, education, social class, generation category, religion, or race. Furthermore, Rahe found that life changes based on the rating scale accounted for some past significant disorders and illnesses in individuals. For example, life changes were particularly apparent during depressive episodes, prostatitis, and severe tonsillitis. Rahe then used the life changes to predict near-future illnesses of a sample of 84 resident physicians. Those physicians who showed elevated life changes suffered considerably more illnesses than did those lower on the scale. That is, 49 percent of subjects who showed elevated life changes also experienced 24 illnesses. Those whose life changes were less stressful suffered considerably less illness (eight of 32 subjects had eight illnesses). Of those who had very low changes, only one of 11 subjects had one illness. The general conclusion from these data is strikingly obvious: Those individuals who suffer severely stressful events tend to develop a variety of illnesses and psychiatric disorders.

Hobson et al. (1998) comprehensively revised and updated the Holmes and Rahe (1967) scale so that their new scale contains fifty-one major life events as presented in the accompanying table.

Major results of the Hobson et al. research included: (1) there were practical and significant differences in mean ratings for the 51 life events; (2) there were five overlapping themes in the top 20 rated life events—death and dying, health care, crime and the criminal justice system, financial/economic issues, and family-related issues; and (3) an amazing level of agreement existed concerning perceived life event stressfulness of the items in the Rank-Ordered Life Events table, regardless of gender, age, or income level.

Rank-Ordered Life Events (Means)

Life Event	Mean = 1
1. Death of spouse/mate	87
2. Death of close family member	79
3. Major injury/illness to self	78
4. Detention in jail or other institution	76
5. Major injury/illness to close family member	72
6. Foreclosure on loan/mortgage	71
7. Divorce	71
8. Being a victim of crime	70
9. Being the victim of police brutality	69
10. Infidelity	69
11. Experiencing domestic violence/sexual abuse	69
12. Separation or reconciliation with spouse/mate	66
13. Being fired/laid off/unemployed	64
14. Experiencing financial problems/difficulties	62
15. Death of close friend	61
16. Surviving a disaster	59
17. Becoming a single parent	59
18. Assuming a responsibility for sick or elderly loved one	56
19. Loss or major reduction in health insurance/benefits	56
20. Self/close family member being arrested for violating the law	56
21. Major disagreement over child support/custody/visitation	53
22. Experiencing/being involved in auto accident	53
23. Being disciplined at work/demoted	53
24. Dealing with unwanted pregnancy	51
25. Adult child moving in with parent/parent moving in with adult child	50
26. Child develops behavior or learning problem	49
27. Experiencing employment discrimination/sexual harassment	48
28. Attempting to modify addictive behavior of self	47
29. Discovering/attempting to modify addictive behavior of close family member	46
30. Employer reorganization/downsizing	45

Rank-Ordered Life Events (Continued)

Life Event	Mean = 1
31. Dealing with infertility/miscarriage	44
32. Getting married/remarried	43
33. Changing employers/careers	43
34. Failure to obtain/qualify for a mortgage	42
35. Pregnancy of self/spouse	41
36. Experiencing discrimination/harassment outside the workplace	39
37. Release from jail	39
38. Spouse/mate begins/ceases work outside the home	38
39. Major disagreement with boss/coworker	37
40. Change in residence	35
41. Finding appropriate child care/daycare	34
42. Experiencing a large unexpected monetary gain	33
43. Changing positions (transfer, promotion)	33
44. Gaining a new family member	33
45. Changing work responsibilities	32
46. Child leaving home	30
47. Obtaining a home mortgage	30
48. Obtaining a major loan other than home mortgage	30
49. Retirement	28
50. Beginning/ceasing formal education	26
51. Receiving a ticket for violating the law	22

SEE ALSO:

Stress, Defined
Stress, Environmental
Stress Signals

BIBLIOGRAPHY

Hobson, C. J., Kamen, J., Szostek, J., Nethercut, C. M., Tiedmann, J. W., Wojnarowicz, S. (1998). Stressful life events: A revision and update of the social readjustment rating scale. *International Journal of Stress Management, 5,* 1–23.

Holmes, T. H., & David, E. M. (Eds). (1989). *Life change, life events, and illness: Selected papers.* New York: Praeger.

Holmes, T. H., & Rahe, R. H. (1967). The social readjustment scale. *Journal of Psychosomatic Research, 11,* 213–218.

McLean, D. E., & Link, B. G. (1994). Unraveling complexity: Strategies to refine concepts, measures, and research designs in the study of life events and mental health. In W. R. Avison & I. H. Gotlib (Eds.), *Stress and mental health: Contemporary issues and prospects for the future.* New York: Plenum.

Miller, T. W. (Ed.). (1989). *Stressful life events.* (International Universities Press Stress and Health Series, Monograph No. 4.) Madison, CT: International Universities Press.

Monroe, S. M., & McQuaid, J. R. (1994). Measuring life stress and measuring its impact on mental health. In W. R. Avison & I. H. Gotlib (Eds.), *Stress and mental health: Contemporary issues and prospects for the future* (pp. 43–73). New York: Plenum.

Monroe, S. M., & Simons, A. D. (1991). Diathesis-stress theories in the context of life stress research: Implications for depressive disorders. *Psychological Bulletin, 110,* 406–425.

Rahe, R. H. (1990). Life change, stress responsivity, and captivity research. *Psychosomatic Medicine, 52,* 373–396.

Stress Inoculation Training

This technique helps individuals cope with stress by developing a tolerance for it. It is based on the concept that stress tolerance is achieved by exposing individuals to graded stressors so that they learn to tolerate the experiences. This technique has been applied to people with phobias, chronic pain, test anxiety, alcoholism, and the like.

The technique was developed by Donald Meichenbaum in 1977 and involves components such as teaching individuals that negative self-evaluations and ruminations over decisions increase the stress response, teaching individuals to monitor their own self-defeating cognitions, and teaching new cognitive strategies. Meichenbaum viewed **Fear** and **Anxiety** as being caused by awareness of excessive physiological arousal and by specific thoughts. To relax and change the anxiety, the stress inoculation techniques are rehearsed mentally and then used in actual stressful situations, such as in an unpredictable electric shock. In this way the learner comes to control anxiety in the face of stressful activities without letting them overwhelm him or her.

SEE ALSO:

Anxiety
Fear
Stress Management Methods

BIBLIOGRAPHY

McGuigan, F. J. (1994). *Biological psychology: A cybernetic science.* Englewood Cliffs, NJ: Prentice-Hall.

Meichenbaum, D. (1993). Stress inoculation training: A 20-year update. In P. M. Lehrer & R. L. Woolfolk (Eds.), *Principles and practice of stress management* (pp. 373–406). New York: Guilford Press.

Meichenbaum, D., & Deffenbacher, J. L. (1988). Stress inoculation training. *Counseling Psychologist, 16,* 69–90.

Meichenbaum, D., & Fitzpatrick, D. (1993). A constructivist narrative perspective on stress and coping: Stress inoculation applications. In L. T. Goldberger & S. Breznitz (Eds.). *Handbook of stress: Theoretical and clinical aspects* (2nd ed., pp. 706–723). New York: Free Press.

Stress Management Methods

The need for individuals and organizations to learn how to manage stress is a crucial and an expanding one. Our society is becoming ever faster paced and more complex, with increasing pressures to become and stay financially solvent. Our technology, originally created to help us, now sometimes rules us—and oftentimes even deprives us of our jobs. As a result, more individuals and more organizations are experiencing greater stress; as a result of this, more individuals, both singly and within organizations, are reacting in ways that are not always beneficial to themselves or their organizations. The American culture has widely accepted the use of medicine such as tranquilizers in an attempt to cope with stress and anxiety; however, chemical strategies have drawbacks, such as addiction and the return of the original anxiety as the drug wears off. Thus, alternative stress management methods have been utilized.

Stress management is typically a behavioral (psychological) procedure offered or undertaken that deliberately attempts to alter beneficially any aspect of the stress process; this broad definition includes altering the environment and the subjective, behavioral, and physiological responses to the stressful experiences of life. Numerous programs have been developed to help both individuals and organizations in stress management. For an elaboration of the concept of **Stress,** see the Introduction on page xi–xiv.

Stress management strategies that have been thought to be beneficial are listed in the cross-reference list below. Other stress-release efforts have included laughing, crying, writing; healthful eating habits; scheduled time for rest and relaxation; organizational wellness programs, employee assistance programs; stress-reduction clinics, massage services, and exercise programs; counseling services; self-help books, tapes, cassettes, and software programs; and health educators.

For an outstanding presentation of various stress management methods, see especially Lehrer and Woolfolk (1993).

SEE ALSO:

Assertiveness Training	Psychotherapies
Biofeedback	Social Support
Crying—A Stress Management Method?	Stress, Defined
Exercise, Benefits of	Stress Inoculation
Hypnosis	Time Management
Meditation	Yoga
Progressive Relaxation	

BIBLIOGRAPHY

Berger, B. G. (1994). Coping with stress: The effectiveness of exercise and other techniques. *Quest, 46,* 100–119.

Lehrer, P. M., & Woolfolk, R. L. (Eds.). (1993). *Principles and practice of stress management* (2nd ed.). New York: Guilford Press.

Monat, A., & Lazarus, R. S. (Eds). (1991). *Stress and coping: An anthology* (3rd ed.). New York: Columbia University Press.

Rice, P. (1992). *Stress and health* (2nd ed.). Pacific Grove, CA: Brooks/Cole.

Stress Signals

We often do not notice in ourselves when we become overloaded with "stress," which means we are excessively tense and lack **Tension Awareness.** It may take another person to point that out to us. Some "signals of stress" displayed by those who are experiencing excessive levels of stress are as follows. These behaviors have been identified by participants in stress-management workshops and are similar to behaviors identified in studies of **Burnout** among human-service professionals:

1. Dangerous driving behavior, as in tailgating

2. Disregarding priority tasks

3. Redrawing boundaries at work or home to shift or avoid responsibilities

4. Refusing to take in new information relevant to one's work

5. Being only superficially involved in work; appearing to give up

6. Consistently expressing negative or cynical attitudes about customers/clients/others

7. Appearing depersonalized, detached

8. Rigidly "going by the book"

9. Being more precise than the work demands

10. Displaying inappropriate humor

11. Stealing or using other means of "ripping off" the organization

To control stress signals, one needs to effectively apply a stress management method.

SEE ALSO:

Burnout

Executive Stress

Stress Management Methods

Tension Awareness

Workplace Stress

BIBLIOGRAPHY

Keita. G. P., & Hurrell, J. J. (1994). *Job stress in a changing workplace.* Washington, DC: American Psychological Association.

Sauter, S. L., & Murphy, L. R. (1995). *Organizational risk factors for job stress.* Washington, DC: American Psychological Association.

Stroke

Description

Stroke is one of the most common causes of death in North America. A cerebrovascular accident, stroke involves damage to the brain because of impaired blood supply; as a result, the physical and mental functions influenced by the injured area deteriorate. A stroke may be mildly incapacitating or involve a sudden loss of consciousness, followed by headache, nausea, confusion, and stupor. The symptoms include sudden weakness or numbness of the face or limbs on one side of the body (hemiplegia); loss of speech or comprehension; dimness or loss of vision, particularly in one eye; and unexplained dizziness, unsteadiness, or sudden falling. The symptoms may persist for about 24 hours, though they usually last much longer.

About one in three strokes is fatal, one in three causes permanent damage or disability, and one in three apparently has no lasting ill effects. If someone survives a stroke, he or she may be partially paralyzed for many weeks before improvement becomes apparent. Even a mild stroke is a danger signal; it may be the first of a succession of increasingly severe attacks.

Causes

Strokes may be due to one of three types of vascular disorders: cerebral thrombosis, cerebral embolism, or cerebral hemorrhage. Cerebral thrombosis can occur if an artery that supplies blood to the brain is narrowed, usually due to atherosclerosis. A plaque, or large deposit of fatty tissue, at the narrowed and roughened portion of the artery may break open and make a place where the blood can coagulate and form a thrombus, or clot. This thrombus may grow until it partially or completely blocks the artery.

A cerebral embolism is also a block, but it is caused by some type of foreign material, or embolus. The embolus may be a bit of arterial wall, or a small blood clot from a roughened artery or a diseased heart. It is carried in the bloodstream until it becomes wedged in a place where it obstructs the flow of blood to the brain.

In a cerebral hemorrhage, the artery is not blocked; it bursts or leaks. Blood seeps from the rupture into surrounding brain tissue and continues to do so until the seepage is prevented by a pressure buildup as the blood "backs up" outside of the rupture, and by the blood's clotting. The initial effects of a hemorrhage may be more severe than those of a thrombosis or embolism, but the long-term effects of all three types of stroke are similar.

Whatever the cause, the results of a stroke depend on which part and how much of the brain is affected.

Stroke is often influenced by high blood pressure (**Hypertension, Essential**), which can be exacerbated by **Stressful Life Events.** Most people who have strokes are over age 65 (more often men than women); people over 65 are more likely to have high blood pressure and blood vessels that are narrowed by atherosclerosis. However, abnormally high blood pressure at any age can cause a stroke by weakening cerebral arterial walls. Smokers are more likely to suffer a stroke than nonsmokers. Strokes also seem to be more prevalent among diabetics and people with a high level of low-density lipoprotein cholesterol in their blood.

Treatment

Immediate medical help is required for someone who develops symptoms that suggest a stroke. Although general treatment of all three forms of stroke is essentially the same, different types of investigation may be needed to determine the cause and location of the disturbance and its treatment.

One can guard against strokes or prevent them from recurring by having blood pressure checked regularly, following a physician's advice about medications and behavior, not smoking or eating too much fatty food, and exercising moderately and regularly.

SEE ALSO:

Cardiovascular Disease
Hypertension, Essential (High Blood
    Pressure)

Stressful Life Events
Type A Behavior

BIBLIOGRAPHY

Birkett, D. P. (1996). *The psychiatry of stroke.* Washington, DC: American Psychiatric Press.
Skilbeck, C. (1996). Psychological aspects of stroke. In R. T. Woods (Ed.), *Handbook of the clinical psychology of ageing* (pp. 283–301). Chichester, England: Wiley.

Student Control (Achieving Classroom Discipline)

Description

A major problem for teachers is achieving discipline in the classroom and thus reducing stress for teachers and students alike. Discipline is a habit difficult to cultivate, particularly among children. The absence of discipline leads to numerous problems that manifest themselves throughout the life span. These problems include approaching tasks in a disorderly manner, resulting in wasted time, effort, money, and, more seriously, antisocial behavior. This could lead the individual to blame society for lack of success, causing the individual to act out his or her frustration on society.

Lack of discipline is more noticeable in the early school years. Yet some individuals continue to display discipline problems throughout their school years and beyond.

Causes

The causes for a lack of discipline are multidimensional, but at its roots lies the lack of training or inappropriate training due to parents' or care givers' poor child-raising skills. There are also numerous sociological, environmental, educational, economical, psychological, and physiological factors. Of these, the physiological factors may be the most salient. Specifically, excessive levels of neuromuscular activity, along with unbalanced endogenous systems, can greatly diminish control. Differential levels of chronic **Tension** may help to explain why some children become disciplined with no or minimal guidance and others do not, even with the aid of professional help.

Treatment

Discipline in the schools can be improved by teaching both children and teachers **Stress Management Methods.** Marshall and Beach (1974) developed and applied **Progressive Relaxation** for public schools. Their program was designed to instruct children and teachers how to detect and control tension. The authors conducted an initial instruction session and prepared a program consisting of 16 ten-minute sessions. Children were taught during physical education and in the classroom. The authors also assigned each child to one of three groups according to the child's abilities to control residual tension (as identified during the initial instruction period). Group one consisted of children who could not effectively control their tension; group two consisted of children who sometimes controlled their tensions; and group three consisted of children who could generally control their tensions. The benefits to society from such a program being universally implemented in the lower grades (as Edmund Jacobson hoped) could be enormous. Not only could teachers achieve effective discipline in their classrooms, but also the longer term positive effects could have their origins in the school years.

SEE ALSO:

Medical School Stress

Progressive Relaxation

School/College Stress

Self-Operations Control

Stress Management Methods

Tension Awareness

BIBLIOGRAPHY

Cohen, J. J., & Fish, M. C. (1993). *Handbook of school-based interventions: Resolving student problems and promoting healthy educational environments.* San Francisco, CA: Jossey-Bass.

Marshall, M. G., & Beach, C. W. (1974). Tension control at Michigan State University. In F. J. McGuigan (Ed.), *Tension control: Proceedings of the First Meeting of the American Association for the Advancement of Tension Control.* Chicago, IL: University Publications.

Ridley, D. S., & Walter, B. (1995). *Creating responsible learners: The role of a positive classroom environment.* Washington, DC: American Psychological Association.

Stuttering

Description

Stuttering (stammering) is the interruption or blockage of fluent speech, or the prolonging or repetition of certain sounds; volume levels are also often abnormal. Secondary characteristics, such as tremors of the lips and jaws, are largely due to efforts not to stutter. This speech disorder is ancient and widespread, occurring in about 17 percent of the population. It usually begins in childhood by age seven and occurs three to four times more often in males. Stuttering can lead to increased anxiety, tension, feelings of inferiority, embarrassment, self-consciousness, and fear of social awkwardness.

Research has suggested that some stutterers are unable to automatically self-monitor their speech using the sound of their own voice. Although they are able to speak fluently when their voice is masked by other loud sounds so that they are unable to hear their own voice, when the masking sound is removed, stuttering returns.

Causes

Stuttering is primarily a disorder in which the vocal folds are pulled together with abnormal levels of force, so that they resist their normal patterns of motion. The larynx has powerful muscles that draw the vocal folds together and can prevent their proper usage, thus halting speech if the person is "stuck" on a sound or syllable. The tongue can also be involved as normal muscular movement is disrupted by opposing muscle pairs working in conflict with each other. There is some evidence that stuttering has a genetic link.

Stuttering can also be a symptom of the body's reaction to acute or special stress, such as frightening experiences or tension in relationships.

Treatment

Stuttering often can be "outgrown" by the age of twelve. If the problem persists by about age twelve, it is probable that stuttering will continue unless effective therapy is applied. Traditional therapies have been about 25 percent effective and usually consist of attempts to build self-confidence, self-understanding, and training in speech movement control. Attempts have also been made to resolve unconscious conflicts assumed to be the cause of stuttering. Therapy known as Precision Fluency Shaping, developed by Professor Ronald Webster, has been found to be more reliably effective. This therapy consists of a three-week program focusing on movement control and voice control. Movement control involves the physical formation of very slight movements of the tongue, soft palate, and lips and their integration into the speech flow. Voice control involves training the individual to use the muscles that control the vocal folds effectively. The individual can be aided by a Voice Monitor, a computer that signals accuracy of speech and provides essential feedback; this allows the stutterer to become aware of exactly when fluent speech is produced, an awareness that can become permanent without the devices.

SEE ALSO:

Anxiety
Speaking Anxiety, Public

BIBLIOGRAPHY

Bobrick, B. (1995). *Knotted tongues: Stuttering in history and the quest for a cure.* New York: Simon & Schuster.

Kirshner, H. S. (Ed.). (1995). *Handbook of neurological speech and language disorders. Neurological disease and therapy,* (Vol. 33). New York: Marcel Dekker.

Webster, R. (1991). Fluency enhancement in stuttering: Advances in self-regulation through sensory augmentation. In J. G. Carlson & R. Seifert (Eds.), *International perspectives on self-regulation and health. Plenum series in behavioral psychophysiology and medicine.* New York: Plenum.

Webster, R. (1992). Stuttering: A statement from Ronald Webster. In F. J. McGuigan, *Calm down: A guide for stress and tension control* (2nd ed., pp. 123–129). Dubuque, IA: Kendall/Hunt.

Success, Excessive Drive for

Description

The drive for success is encouraged by desire for such things as money, knowledge, love, and recognition. However, in much of today's society, the motivation to succeed and the importance of achieving material wealth may be counterproductive. Although it is good to have goals and to work hard to reach these goals, many people strive excessively for success, some even to the point of breakdown. Stress, tension, anxiety, and depression are some of the outcomes people experience as the result of an overemphasis on succeeding. In working to obtain our goals, some individuals are overwhelmed by the energy requirements and the hard work needed for success. Many crave power and strive for fame and recognition to the point of self-destruction. Although the drive for success may appear harmless, failure to learn how to **Differentially Relax** while working, and failure to look at work and life with a positive perspective, can result in physical and mental damage.

Causes

When the success sought is finally attained or when there is failure to reach one's expectations, a person may become "stressed out." Fluctuations in joy of accomplishment, in hope, and in despair can exacerbate stressful reactions if an individual does not know how to cope with such subjective feelings. Without effective strategies for coping with an overemphasis on reaching material success, fame, and so forth, personal disaster can result. Many very successful millionaires, even billionaires, have ultimately ruined their lives by not being satisfied with their accomplishments.

Treatment

An effective approach to handling this stress may be to reevaluate goals to be sure they are realistic and reasonable. When a person is satisfied with what has been achieved, the goals may then be raised slightly. The key is not to be greedy.

The most obvious way of avoiding stress due to an exaggerated drive for success would be for individuals not to succumb to excessive pressures to achieve. However, in a capitalist society such as ours, this may be almost impossible. Therefore, learning ways to deal with stressors, and consequently the resulting tension, can be a viable solution. Changing one's "mindset" on life (one's behavior) might be a start. People can learn to be satisfied with what they have when that is sufficient.

By retraining our modes of thinking with stress management methods, the excessive drive for success can be controlled. One can work hard and achieve much while still maintaining the body's integrity if one learns to differentially relax.

SEE ALSO:

Compulsive Behavior   Stress, Defined
Differential Relaxation   Stress Management Methods
Money (Financial) Stress   Type A Behavior
Obsessive-Compulsive Behavior

BIBLIOGRAPHY

Friedman, M. (1996). *Type A behavior: Its diagnosis and treatment.* New York: Plenum.
Spielberger, C. D., Sarason, I. G., & Strelau, J. (Eds.). (1991). *Stress and anxiety* (Vol. 13). New York: Hemisphere.

Suicide

Description

Suicide is the intentional taking of one's own life. Some forms are direct, such as shooting oneself; other forms are indirect, such as refusing to take actions necessary for self-preservation.

Over the past three decades in the United States, the number of suicides among white and black males has increased about 4 percent; among white females it has decreased almost 2 percent; and among black females it has decreased three-tenths of 1 percent. The number of elderly in the United States who commit suicide has increased over the past 15 years. Suicide is the third leading killer of 15- to 24-year-olds in the United States, up 200 percent over the past four decades. Worldwide suicide rates for the early 1990s show there were 89.8 suicides per 100,000 people in Denmark, 36.9 in Britain, 12.0 in the United States (which is a slight rise from a report six years earlier).

Causes

Nineteenth-century sociologists thought the source lay in the ups and downs of society itself. Some modern researchers put more emphasis on genetic influences and neurotransmitters. Common assertions are that the primary cause of suicide is **Stressful Life Events.**

There is a wide range of potential suicide triggers, from loss of employment or loved ones to aging and physical impairment. Most scientists today agree that in almost all cases there is an underlying psychiatric illness—depression, alcoholism, substance abuse, and the like. Clinically depressed people are at a 50 percent greater risk of killing themselves than are the non-clinically depressed. Schizophrenia and antisocial personality disorder are other important factors often leading to suicide.

Recent scientific findings implicate the chemical serotonin in suicides: A variety of violent, impulsive behaviors, including some suicides, have been associated with low levels of serotonin. Although it is not clear why some people have low levels of this chemical—causes may be genetic, developmental, or environmental—it does seem that a person's serotonin level reveals some sort of vulnerability to suicide. This may lead to chemical screening as well as treatment for patients suffering from depression, which is associated with suicidal behavior.

Sociologists have emphasized the importance of both the social structure and the personal relationships individuals face as possible causes of suicide. Cross-cultural comparisons of adolescents indicate that teenage stress is largely a manifestation of cultural developmental demands; that is, there is a positive correlation between levels of teenage stress and the magnitude of culturally designated adjustments that must take place between late childhood and early adulthood.

The symptoms of a potential suicide must be taken seriously. Talk about suicide should always be treated as the serious symptom it is. A number of other signals can alert the careful observer:

1. continued depression, escalating to feelings of hopelessness, eating and sleeping disturbances, declining school or work performance
2. gradual social withdrawal and isolation
3. breakdown in communication with people important in the person's life
4. a history of previous suicide attempts or accidents; the fatal potential of past suicide attempts are particularly serious warning signs (e.g., attempts at hanging or shooting oneself as opposed to mild overdoses of aspirin)

Treatment

Although an initial period of hospitalization and medication may occasionally be necessary for the self-protection of some seriously depressed suicide attempters, hospitalization alone will not solve the life problems the person is experiencing. Proper treatment should deal with both the immediate events as well as the long-term conflicts that can make suicide seem a viable solution. The clinician should demonstrate the warmth and true concern that the suicidal person typically finds lacking in other relationships, let the patient know that the clinician is there to help, and, in so doing, offer a glimmer of hope for resolution.

Because troubled family relationships are often at the heart of teenage suicide, inclusion of parents in the teenager's psychotherapeutic program is often required.

In terms of long-term treatment, **Stress Management Methods** might help the individual develop the ability to control his or her life and responses to life's stressors.

SEE ALSO:

Cancer and Suicide

Depression

School/College Stress

Stress, Defined

Stressful Life Events

Stress Management Methods

BIBLIOGRAPHY

Clark, D. C. (1993). Suicidal behavior in childhood and adolesence: Recent studies and clinical implications. *Psychiatric Annals, 23*, 271–283.

Conger, J. J. (1973). *Adolescence and youth: Psychological development in a changing world.* New York: Harper & Row.

Gelman, D. (1994, April 18). The mystery of suicide. *Newsweek*, 44–49.

Jurich, A. P., & Collins, O. P. (1996). Adolescents, suicide and death. In C. A. Corr & D. E. Balk (Eds.), *Handbook of adolescent death and bereavement* (pp. 65–84). New York: Springer.

Schuckit, M. A. (1997, February). Suicide: A preventable catastrophe. *Drug abuse & alcoholism newsletter.* San Diego: Vista Hill Foundation.

Sprang, G., & McNeill, J. (1995). *The many faces of bereavement: The nature and treatment of natural, traumatic and stigmatized grief.* New York: Brunner/Mazel.

U.S. Bureau of the Census (1991). *Statistical abstract of the United States:* Washington, DC: Author.

Systematic Desensitization

Description

Joseph Wolpe used the technique of relaxation with increasing levels of anxiety-evoking stimuli. In the first three to six sessions, the patient is taught to relax for about 10 minutes. Next, the patient practices relaxing at home for 10 to 15 minutes a day. Eventually, the patient is asked to sit down, close the eyes, and relax as much as possible in accordance with training; then the instruction is to imagine the weakest stimulus that provokes anxiety; for example, if the fear is of strangers, the patient imagines being in the presence of *one* stranger. After several repetitions of imagining in the relaxed state, the patient no longer reacts with anxiety when asked to imagine one stranger. The next imagining in the hierarchy is of being in the presence of *two* strangers, and so on, progressively increasing the amount of stimulation by imagining more and more strangers. However, one only advances to the next number when a given number has ceased to evoke any anxiety (see **Speaking Anxiety, Public**).

Wolpe reports that transfer usually occurs from the imaginary to the real; about 85 percent of people can use the imagining technique. For the remaining 15 percent, real stimuli must be used. "The two main advantages are that the amount of relaxation training is relatively small, and that the therapist has complete control over the exposure to the things that are disturbing" (Wolpe, 1975, p. 29).

Systematic desensitization depends on the fact, Wolpe states, that relaxation produces autonomic effects that counteract anxiety. This was demonstrated by Jacobson in his method of **Progressive Relaxation** and has been confirmed many times since.

Systematic desensitization has been amply validated empirically. Wolpe reports that over 90 percent of phobias are overcome in an average of 10 sessions. According to Wolpe, because patients often respond to therapists, *every* type of psychotherapy will yield anything from a 40 percent to 50 percent success rate. Consequently, for a specific technique to be validated, the recovery rate must be significantly better than that range. **Behavior Therapy,** he points out, has consistently achieved such satisfactory success rates.

SEE ALSO:

Anxiety	Progressive Relaxation
Behavior Therapy	Speaking Anxiety (Public)
Phobic Disorders	Stress Management Methods

BIBLIOGRAPHY

Freuh, B. C., de Arellano, M. A., & Turner, S. M. (1997). Systematic desensitization as an alternative exposure strategy for PTSD. *American Journal of Psychiatry, 154,* 287–288.

King, N. J., & Ollendick, T. H. (1997). Treatment of childhood phobias. *Journal of Child Psychology and Psychiatry and Allied Disciplines, 38,* 389–400.

Seaward, B. L. (1994). *Managing stress: Principles and strategies for health and wellbeing.* Boston, MA: Jones and Bartlett.

Willshire, D. (1996). Trauma and treatment with hypnosis. *Australian Journal of Clinical and Experimental Hypnosis, 24,* 125–136.

Wolpe, J. (1961). The systematic desensitization treatment of neurosis. *Journal of Nervous Mental Disorders, 112,* 189–203.

Wolpe, J. (1975). Relaxation as an instrument for breaking adverse emotional habits. In F. J. McGuigan (Ed.), *Tension control: Proceedings of the First Meeting of the American Association for the Advancement of Tension Control.* Blackburg, VA: University Publications.

Wolpe, J. (1990). *The practice of behavior therapy* (4th ed.). London, England: Pergamon.

T

Technostress–
Type B Behavior

Technostress

Description

The computer revolution has created a new form of stress that is threatening the physical and mental health of many workers. "Technostress" is a modern disorder caused by an inability to cope in a healthy manner with the new computer technology.

Technostress manifests itself in several distinct but related ways. It can surface as the individual struggles to learn how to adapt to computers in the workplace, which often provokes anxiety. Some individuals develop fears about such modern technology that require professional intervention to alleviate and eliminate.

Technostress can also surface as overidentification with computer technology. Some individuals develop a machine-like mind-set that reflects the characteristics of the computer itself; some who once were warm and sensitive human beings become cold, lose their friends, have no patience for the easy exchange of informal conversation, and watch television as a major—or only—recreational activity.

Further, "technostress" is the term used for such physiological stress reactions as computer-related eyestrain, headaches, neck and shoulder tension, and backache. Also, many people who use computer keyboards frequently and for long periods of time develop carpal tunnel syndrome, another technostress reaction.

Causes

These various reactions often develop from long-term use of computers. If someone spends most of his or her working hours interacting only with a computer screen and keyboard, that person may easily develop any of the mentioned symptoms.

Eyestrain develops from focusing continuously on a screen at close range. The individual who focuses for a long time on one specific colored screen may see the complementary color when looking up at a blank wall or ceiling. This color reversal effect is a normal part of the way vision works and usually subsides in a few minutes.

Headaches, though sometimes caused by eyestrain, are most often due to tension involving muscles of the brow, temples, jaw, upper neck, and base of the skull. These headaches can be exacerbated by improper height of the chair and/or screen and even lack of arm rests (which causes the arms to pull down on the shoulders, creating, in turn, tension at the shoulder tip and base of the skull, and spasms radiating up into the head).

Carpal tunnel syndrome, a numbness, tingling, or burning sensation in the fingers or wrists, may be induced by inflammation of the synovial membrane lining ligaments and tendons in fingers and wrists. This inflammation may be caused by trauma as well as by chronic muscular tension.

Treatment

Preventing or eliminating technostress can be a cooperative venture, involving the sufferer as well as his or her supervisor or mate. Organizational leaders should both implement a human policy regarding introduction and use of computer technology and plan for a process of adaptation that people will pursue.

To avoid becoming a technocentered person, one may engage in self-appraisal and be alert to some warning signs of technostress—becoming less patient with people and losing sensitivity to others. Be open to honest feedback from leaders, fellow workers, and friends.

Alleviating eyestrain is relatively simple. One can routinely break his or her gaze away from the computer screen to focus on something in the distance. This can help the tense eye muscles relax and lessen the strain. Some improved computer screens can ease this common symptom.

Computer-related **Headaches** can be treated in various ways. If the headache is moderate, rest and/or a mild pain killer may help. One should check the furniture to be sure the height of the computer screen is at a level that allows the user to read it without stretching or retracting his or her neck. Also, one should make sure the height of the chair is appropriate for the desk-top and that the chair has arm rests to help ease the downward pull of the shoulders. Taking periodic breaks in the routine to stand up and do some simple neck, shoulder, and arm-stretching exercises may help. Some headaches can be triggered by poor lighting. That can usually be individually adjusted.

Regularly implementing **Progressive Relaxation** has been shown to alleviate and even prevent headaches. Through **Differential Relaxation** one learns to avoid misusing muscles so as to prevent many aspects of technostress.

SEE ALSO:

Differential Relaxation
Headache, Tension and Migraine
Progressive Relaxation

Stress Management Methods
Tension Awareness

BIBLIOGRAPHY

Cooper, C. L. (1981). *The stress check: Coping with the stresses of life and work.* Englewood Cliffs, NJ: Prentice-Hall.

House, J. S. (1992). *Technostress.* Boston: Houghton Mifflin.

McGuigan, F. J. (1992). *Calm down: A guide for stress and tension control.* Dubuque, IA: Kendall/Hunt.

Sauter, S. L., & Murphy, L. R. (Eds.). (1995). *Organizational risk factors for job stress.* Washington, DC: American Psychological Association.

Seppala, P. (1995). Experiences on computerization in different occupational groups. *International Journal of Human Computer Interactions, 7,* 315–327.

Zapf, D. (1995). Stress oriented analysis of computerized office work. In J. M. Peiro, F. Prieto, J. L. Melia, & O. Luque (Eds.), *Work and organizational psychology: European contributions of the nineties* (pp. 61–76). Hove, England: Erlbaum (U.K.), Taylor & Francis

Temporomandibular Joint Syndrome (TMJ)

Description

TMJ is one of several disorders under the category of myofacial pain dysfunction syndrome. TMJ is often caused by complex muscle contractions around the temporomandibular joints (the two joints on either side of the jaw). In this disorder the jaw muscles are very sensitive, and it may be painful to fully open the jaw.

While the pain is in the joints and muscles of the jaw, it may be referred to other parts of the face and head. Sometimes TMJ pain is experienced as a headache between the eyes and the forehead, near the temples, or as a pain in the shoulders and neck. TMJ pain may also be referred to the ears and experienced as earaches. Other symptoms are popping or clicking sounds in the jaws. Chronic TMJ pain often can be debilitating and can lead to depression.

Causes

TMJ can be produced in a normal person by yawning and opening the mouth wide, or the person can use the muscles of the face in abnormal ways. Sometimes TMJ **Pain** results from biting the fingernails or clenching and grinding the teeth together, habits that put stress on the jaws. Most people who have spasmodic pain in the jaw muscles have TMJ syndrome.

X rays and laboratory tests carried out on people with this syndrome often reveal no abnormality. Possible causes may include arthritis, malocclusion (bad bite), **Bruxism** (grinding of the teeth), and muscle tension or psychological stress.

The chronic overextension of the jaw muscles, for whatever reason, is a primary direct cause. Another cause of pain and stiffness in the temporomandibular joints is rheumatoid arthritis. However, with this latter condition the symptoms are most severe the first thing in the morning, which is not generally the case with temporomandibular joint syndrome.

Treatment

Treatment is primarily to relax the jaw muscles, which helps to correct the mechanical problem and to break the pain cycle. In learning to relax, patients avoid excess tension in such ways as not chewing gum, clenching teeth, biting fingernails, or yawning excessively. Eating soft food may help, as might applying moist heat to relieve sore muscles.

Treatment to relieve the painful spasms may include local heat therapy, injections or sprays of local anesthetics, and simple analgesics, such as aspirin or ibuprofen. Patients who do not respond to **Progressive Relaxation** therapy may use a splint (usually at night), which is a device placed over teeth to keep them from grinding.

SEE ALSO:

Bruxism   Progressive Relaxation
Muscular System Discomfort   Tension Awareness
Pain

BIBLIOGRAPHY

Gevirtz, R. N., Glaros, A. G., Hopper, D., & Schwartz, M. S. (1995). Temporomandibular disorders. In M. S. Schwartz (Ed.), *Biofeedback: A practitioner's guide* (pp. 411–428). New York: Guilford Press.

Glaros, A. G., & Glass, E. G. (1993). Temporomandibular disorders. In R. J. Gatchel & E. B. Blanchard (Eds.), *Psychophysiological disorders.* Washington, DC: American Psychological Association.

McGuigan, F. J. (1992). *Calm down: A guide for stress and tension control* (2nd ed.). Dubuque, IA: Kendall/Hunt.

McGuigan, F. J. (1994). *Biological psychology: A cybernetic science.* Englewood Cliffs, NJ: Prentice-Hall.

Tension Awareness

Description

Tension is defined as contraction (shortening) of striated muscles, and relaxation is lengthening of striated muscles. If one lacks the necessary skills in identifying tensions throughout the body, relaxation is severely hampered. A key, then, to relaxation is learning to be aware of the tensions in one's body. For proper relaxation, there are two basic elements: identification of striated muscle tension and the release of that tension.

Proven methods of muscle relaxation have been validated as successful in the treatment of a number of psychiatric disorders (such as **Phobias, Depression** and **Anxiety**) and **Psychosomatic** disorders (such as **Headaches, Hypertension, Insomnia, Spastic Colon, Pain, Asthma,** and teeth grinding [**Bruxism**].

The most thoroughly validated method for becoming aware of tension and for controlling it is **Progressive Relaxation.** The task of learning to become aware of tension throughout the body is enormous, if one wishes to become really accomplished. This is because of the massive amount of striated muscle in the body, comprising almost half the body weight; also, because people typically misuse their muscles by inappropriately contracting them, usually for as long as they have lived. In this regard, see especially **Differential Relaxation.** There are, however, a variety of other, perhaps less well-validated, suggestions for becoming aware of muscular tension. Some of these are summarized below.

To Become Aware: First, focus attention on the outside world. Start sentences with, "I am aware of…."

After becoming aware of everything that is going on around you, shift the focus of attention to your body and your physical sensations.

Mentally, shuttle back and forth between internal and external awareness.

To "Let Go" of Your Body: Lie down on a rug or firm bed and get comfortable. Pull your feet up until they rest flat on the floor.

Close your eyes. Check yourself for comfort. This may require some shifting around. Become aware of your breathing. Feel the air move into your nose, mouth, and down your throat into your lungs.

Focus on your body and let all the parts come into your awareness spontaneously. What parts come into awareness first? What parts are you less aware of? Become aware of which parts of your body you can easily feel and which parts have little sensation. Do you notice any difference between the right and left side of your body?

Now become aware of any physical discomfort you are feeling. Become aware of this discomfort until you can describe it in detail. Focus and become aware of any changes that happen to this discomfort. Let your body go for 5 to 10 minutes.

Stress Awareness Diary

Some times of the day elicit more tension than others, and some stressful events are more likely to produce physical and emotional symptoms. It might be useful to keep a record of stressful events, as well as symptoms that may occur as stress reactions to them. Maintaining a stress awareness diary, perhaps for two weeks (with columns for time, event, and symptom) might offer valuable insights by charting how particular stresses result in predictable symptoms.

SEE ALSO:

Anxiety
Asthma and Stress
Bruxism
Depression
Differential Relaxation
Headache, Tension and Migraine
Hypertension, Essential (High
   Blood Pressure)

Insomnia (Sleep Difficulties)
Pain
Phobic Disorders
Progressive Relaxation
Psychosomatic Illness
Spastic Colon

BIBLIOGRAPHY

Bakal, D. A. (1992). *Psychology and health* (2nd ed.). New York: Springer.

Lehrer, P., & Carr, R. (1997). Progressive relaxation. In W. T. Roth & I. D. Yalom (Eds.), *Treating anxiety disorders. The Jossey-Bass library of current clinical technique* (pp. 83–116). San Francisco: Jossey-Bass.

McGuigan, F. J. (1992). *Calm down: A guide for stress and tension control.* Dubuque, IA: Kendall/Hunt.

Stevens, J. O. (1971). *Awareness.* New York: Real People Press.

Thought Stopping

The perceptions we have of ourselves and of the world around us plays a crucial role in how we manage life's stressors. When these perceptions are negatively distorted, they serve only to complicate coping and add appreciably to the stressful experience.

Irrational self-talk is a stream of negative and overgeneralized perceptions of self and environment. For instance, while driving to work, overresponding to a traffic delay with thoughts such as "My whole day will be ruined" or "Why does the worst always happen to me?" are two examples of irrational self-talk. Erroneous negative thought patterns such as these can elicit reflexive emotional reactions characteristic of anxiety; the person can become increasingly nervous, the skeletal muscles tense, and breathing may take place high in the chest. Irrational self-talk is largely the result of learned responses and thought processes derived from any combination of past experience, cognition of past experience, learned methods of coping, and perceived control over one's environment.

One technique that has been thought to be beneficial in the treatment of irrational self-talk is thought stopping. Using thought stopping to eliminate self-defeating thoughts was popularized by behavior therapist Joseph Wolpe in the 1950s. Basically, one version of the technique consists of two components:

1. Learning to yell "stop" to oneself immediately following an unwanted thought, and

2. Immediately following the thought stopping, substituting a desirable alternative thought. For instance, instead of thinking "I am late for work. My whole day is ruined," one could perceptually counteract with "Being late will not affect my whole day. I'll phone to work to tell them I'll be late, and if necessary, reschedule any appointments." Similarly, the thought "Why does the worst always happen to me?" can be more realistically restated as "I did manage to get to work on time every day last month. Being late once in a month is not too bad."

Another form of thought stopping is to have the individual imagine a situation in which unwanted thoughts are likely to occur—as in obsessive thinking. After about three minutes, the person or therapist firmly commands "Stop"; next the individual is supposed to keep the mind blank for about 30 seconds, repeating the word "Stop" if the undesired thoughts reoccur. Eventually, the learner attempts to substitute positive statements for the unwanted obsessive thoughts. Berger (1994) held that thought stopping is particularly effective in treating a variety of stress-producing thoughts, such as **Worry** and thoughts of failure.

SEE ALSO:

Exercise, Benefits of   Stress Management Methods
Mind and Mental Events   Worry

BIBLIOGRAPHY

Berger, B. G. (1994). Coping with stress: The effectiveness of exercise and other techniques. *Quest, 46,* 100–119.
Cautela, J. R., & Kearney, A. J. (Eds.). (1993). *Covert conditioning casebook.* Pacific Grove, CA: Brooks/Cole.
Lehrer, P. M., & Woolfolk, R. L. (Eds.). (1993). *Principles and practice of stress management* (2nd ed.). New York: Guilford Press.
Wolpe, J. (1958). *Psychotherapy by reciprocal inhibition.* Palo Alto, CA: Stanford University Press.

Time Management

Many people believe that there is not enough time for them to do all that they feel is demanded of them. There are always many small and seemingly less important components to any job—interruptions, meetings, a variety of fragmented activities that seem to take over. However, the problem may be not too many demands, just an unbalanced way of dealing with them. It is better to realize that the many little demands often represent only the means, not the ends, to achieving our goals. The small matters may be, however, the ones that cause stress, and too much attention to them may result in lessened productivity. To take stock of one's time management practices, consider the following questions:

1. How can I be more productive?
2. What are the most important activities I should be doing?
3. Why do the most important tasks often seem to be postponed for trivial (but perceived as urgent) ones?
4. How do I find balance between my personal and work lives?

There is an "80/20 rule" that states, generally, that 80 percent of our productivity will come from 20 percent of our time, if our focused effort is accurate and timely. The key to improving productivity, therefore, is to reserve at least 20 percent of our time for focused effort on "high-pay-off" activities; these are not those on our daily to-do list, but are those three or four critical functions on which our jobs may hinge. The question is how to focus on those high-pay-off activities. Some helpful thoughts for a solution are: (1) Identify the few high-pay-off activities that will especially help productivity; (2) Relegate some of the many trivial, less meaningful, activities; (3) Focus effort by arranging the working environment so as to concentrate on productivity with limited or no interruptions; (4) Find a retreat to use for vital tasks, uninterrupted work; (5) Develop effective self-management habits in planning and organizing, so that at least the important tasks get accomplished.

The next issue is how to keep the everyday happenings that may seem urgent from preventing attention to high-priority tasks. Good time management is *effective* use of time, which requires one to distinguish between the important and the less important; also, between the urgent and the less urgent.

Four uses of one's working time have been classified by Gmelch (1996) as: (1) The important, but not urgent: This category consumes little of our time but should consume much, as for long-range planning. If we ignore this category, and fail to plan ahead, we may drive activities into the next category, thereby increasing the sense of urgency and time pressure. (2) Important and urgent: This is where we plan in order to prevent some of our important activities from becoming urgent. Yet we cannot completely control our work environment, and some important tasks are thrust on us, for immediate action, which we cannot ignore. (3) Not important but seemingly urgent: This constitutes deception—apparent urgency can create an illusion of importance. These activities may seem important to others, but they are really not in the general perspective. They can consume considerable time and effort when they should account for only little. As one wit's sign said "Your lack of planning is not my crisis." (4) Not important and not urgent: Time wasters include gossiping, busywork, and avoidance activities such as sorting and organizing. Many such activities should not be happening; while time wasters can be fun, they don't contribute to productivity.

Many people spend the majority of their time in the "urgent" arenas (2 and 3). If urgency is driving us, we can count on high stress, maybe even burnout. We need to ask ourselves what activities contribute significantly to our professional and personal goals. Probably our answers would fit into the first arena of important, but not urgent, tasks. But to find more time to spend in this activity, eliminate some of the activities from the third category of not important, but deceptively urgent. If category 1 activities should have a high priority, why do some of us postpone them? First, because they are not urgent, they're easy to push aside. Second, these activities are not critical to maintaining the status quo. Third, no one really forces us to work in this arena, as the tasks here are typically self-imposed.

Unfortunately, the urgent but not important activities often take over because we often lack clear, purposeful goals, so that unimportant activities become the path of least resistance—since we need to keep busy, they keep us active.

In order to increase time on our important but not urgent tasks and be more productive and healthy (less stressed), some suggestions Gmelch (1996) offered were: Schedule a daily time for planning, so that pressures do not determine daily task priorities. Identify your activities and periodically ask, "Why am I doing this?" Once you assess your activities, drop everything no longer productive. Finally, update goals for both professional and personal activities. Time management also is for our everyday lives. Therefore, conduct personal time audits so as to plan strategies for more effective, productive, and enjoyable time use. Managing time effectively in work and personally can provide satisfaction, growth, and development, and what some call a "well-balanced life."

SEE ALSO:

Stress Management Methods
Time Pressure

BIBLIOGRAPHY

Britton, B. K., & Glynn, S. M. (1989). Mental management and creativity: A cognitive model of time management for intellectual productivity. In J. A. Glover, R. R. Ronning, & C. R. Reynolds (Eds.), *Handbook of creativity. Perspectives on individual differences* (pp. 429–440). New York: Plenum.

Feather, N., & Bond, M. (1994). Structure and purpose in the use of time. In Z. Zaleski (Ed.), *Psychology of future orientation. Scientific Society of the Catholic University of Lublin, 32* (pp. 120–140). Lublin, Poland: Wydawnictwo Towarzystwa Naukowego Katolickiego Uniwersytetu Lubelskiego.

Gmelch, W. H. (1996). It's about time. *Academe, bulletin of the American Association of University Professors, 82*, 22–26.

Time Pressure

Description

Personal burdens and work problems, especially when they are perceived as excessive, often contribute to the feeling of time pressure. The working world consists of numerous pressures, many of which are related to time constraints and deadlines. One who does not experience the pressure of such time demands may even have difficulties in social relations with those who are under time pressure.

Time pressure can have either positive or negative aspects. Some people are challenged by the demands of the pressure, enjoy it, use time relatively efficiently, stay productive, engage the challenge, have good time management skills, and don't waste energy on trivial matters. The negative effects of time pressure are common in that they prevent individuals from enjoying social activities, eating properly, and sleeping well, and can retard progress on projects. Some become unusually impatient, smoke, consume excessive amounts of alcohol, and so forth.

Causes

Time pressure is caused by the feeling that one must accomplish much with limited time. It causes stress in our daily lives, living conditions, working conditions, and society. It may also be contributed to by problems encountered in properly establishing priorities. Many live in a conflict between the urgent (regardless of importance) and the truly important, such that urgent matters demand and receive instant action and the really important are put off—to create additional tensions.

Treatment

When one experiences the negative effects of time pressure, one should learn to properly relax and learn **Time Management** skills that can be incorporated into one's life.

SEE ALSO:

Stress Management Methods
Time Management
Type A Behavior

BIBLIOGRAPHY

Gmelck, W. H. (1996, Sept–Oct). It's about time. *Academe, bulletin of the American Association of University Professors, 82,* 22–26.

Klein, G. (1996). The effects of acute stressors on decision making. In J. E. Driskell & E. Salas (Eds.), *Stress and human performance. Series in applied psychology* (pp. 49–88). Mahwah, NJ: Erlbaum.

Maule, A. J., Hockey, G., & Robert, J. (1993). State, stress and time pressure. In O. Svenson & A. J. Maule (Eds.), *Time pressure and stress in human judgment and decision making* (pp. 83–101). New York: Plenum.

Rastegary, H., & Landy, F. J. (1993). The interactions among time urgency, uncertainty, and time pressure. In O. Svenson & A. J. Maule (Eds.), *Time pressure and stress in human judgement and decision making* (pp. 217–239). New York: Plenum.

Steinmetz, J., Blakenship, J., Brown, L., Hall, D., & Miller, G. (1980). *Managing stress before it manages you.* Palo Alto, CA: Bull.

Tinnitus, Tonal

Description

Tinnitus (from the latin, "a jingling") is a ringing, roaring, hissing, or other sensation of noise in the ears. This unpleasant and disturbing experience may lead to adjustment problems ("stress") that can amplify the distress.

Causes

Organic causes can be several, such as disease of the middle ear. Researchers have found that **Stress** and **Depression** contribute to the loudness of tinnitus.

Treatment

Researchers at the University of Washington Medical School gave an antidepressant drug, nortriptyline, to 49 patients suffering from severe tinnitus, depression, and high levels of stress. After 12 weeks on the drug, the disabilities that scientists thought were permanent began to lift significantly more than they did in 43 people who received a placebo. People on the drug were able to sleep, concentrate, do their jobs, and enjoy social activities. This group also reported feeling less stress and greater decreases in the loudness of their tinnitus.

This study is among those that show that if one reduces one's depression and abnormal reaction to stressors, some associated disabilities decrease, even though the medical illness remains.

Less severe cases of tinnitus exacerbated by stress may respond to therapies such as **Biofeedback,** in attempts to control one's stress.

SEE ALSO:

Biofeedback
Depression
Stress, Defined

BIBLIOGRAPHY

Sullivan, M. (1994). Stress and tinnitus. *Archives of Internal Medicine, 10,* 28–35.
Schwartz, M. S. (1995). Tinnitus: Nothing is as loud as a sound you are trying not to hear. In M. S. Schwartz (Ed.), *Biofeedback: A practitioner's guide* (2nd ed., pp. 790–802). New York: Guilford Press.

Tobacco Use

Description

Smoking is often used as an attempt by an individual to cope with stressors. The individual may smoke to lower feelings of stress reactions, to increase the capacity to cope with the stress, and perhaps even to calm down.

Yet smoking itself is a source of stress in several different ways. One of these is that it affects the cardiovascular system by increasing the heart rate—cardiovascular reactivity is greater for those who smoke while experiencing stressors than for those who smoke while relaxing. Withdrawing from nicotine also causes stress reactions associated with smoking. Although smoking may be used for the relief of anxiety, each cigarette only relieves the withdrawal symptoms for a limited amount of time; then when a new environmental stressor occurs, the smoker's anxiety level increases.

Smoking is one of the six most dangerous contributing factors to atherosclerosis; the other five factors are high blood cholesterol, **High Blood Pressure,** lack of exercise, excess weight, and stress. There are also relationships with death and smoking, heredity, chronic bronchitis, and stress, such that the greater the extent to which these factors coexist, the higher the risk for death by lung cancer.

Causes

Nicotine is an addictive agent for smokers. The danger is that when feeling anxious, an individual may turn for relief to nicotine, but in doing so he or she incurs a physiological reaction, which may in turn cause more stress that is detrimental to health in general.

Treatment

Smoking cessation programs need to address the causes of anxiety and stress and to teach skills for coping with stress to those who are trying to quit. Those who successfully quit smoking are at risk for relapse even after abstaining for a period of months, so that ongoing maintenance counseling needs to be incorporated into the program.

S E E   A L S O :

Addictive Behaviors
Compulsive Behavior
Drug Abuse in the Workplace

Hypertension, Essential (High Blood Pressure)
Obsessive-Compulsive Behavior

B I B L I O G R A P H Y

Borgatta, E. F., & Evans, R. E. (Eds.). (1968). *Smoking, health, and behavior.* Chicago: Aldine.
Christensen, N. J., & Jensen, E. W. (1995). Sympathoadrenal activity and psychosocial stress: The significance of aging, long-term smoking, and stress models. In G. P. Chrousos, R. McCarty, K. Pacak, G. Cizza, E. Sternberg, P. W. Gold, & R. Kvetnansky (Eds.), *Stress: Basic mechanisms and clinical implications* (pp. 640–647). New York: New York Academy of Sciences.
Eysenck, H. J. (1991). *Smoking, personality, and stress.* New York: Springer-Verlag.
Fisher, E. B., Jr. (1996). A behavioral economic perspective on the influence of social support on cigarette smoking. In L. Green & J. H. Kagel (Eds.), *Advances in behavioral economics, Vol. 3: Substance use and abuse* (pp. 207–236). Norwood, NJ: Ablex.
Mears, G. N. (1990). *The Effect of a personalized multicomponent smoking cessation intervention on behavioral, physiological, and psychological parameters of cigarette smoking (stress management).* Philadelphia: Temple University.

Parrott, A. C. (1995). Stress modulation over the day in cigarette smokers. *Addiction, 90,* 233–244.

Pomerleau, C. S., & Pomerleau, O. F. (1987). The effects of a psychological stressor on cigarette smoking and subsequent behavioral and physiological responses. *Psychophysiology, 24,* 278–285.

Sheahan. S. L. (1990). *Stress, coping, and smoking among college students.* Lexington: University of Kentucky Press.

Swan, G. E., Denk, C. E., Perker, S. D., Carmelli, D., Furze, C. T., & Rosenman, R. H. (1988). Risk factors for late relapse in male and female ex-smokers. *Addictive Behaviors, 13,* 253–266.

Trauma

Description

The traumatic process often advances through different stages: the traumatic event itself; perhaps denial of the event; acceptance of the reality of the event; cognitive survival state (identification with an aggressor in some cases); a shock or acute phase; and trauma response onset.

Causes

Trauma has been defined as a response to an occurrence in a person's life that threatens the natural balancing system of the body and results in psychiatric symptoms. Events that may cause trauma range from the stressors of everyday life to crime, rape, family abuses, war, and holocausts; and they include both human and natural disasters. A difference between the ordinary effects of stressors and trauma is the fact that stressful responses may be anticipatory to the stressor event, while trauma typically occurs after-the-fact and is event-specific.

Treatment

In planning treatment for severely traumatized individuals the care giver should have a commitment to work with the patient through the entire process of recovery. This is important because trust in each other grows as important aspects of the trauma become disclosed to the therapist.

Because trauma often affects nearly every aspect of the person's life, treatment concerns both the internal mental processes and the key external environmental events with which the victim must interact. Treatment has been found effective when focused on the person's interaction with his or her family, work, and other social systems.

Significant issues in therapy concern power and trust. The traumatic experience may negatively impact how the trauma victim views and conducts personal relationships, as well as how the individual interacts with the social system in general. While working with victims of trauma, the therapist should be sensitive to issues of control, influence, and power within relationships, since these may cause the victim to go into panic or into primitive survival behavior.

Stress Management Methods can be beneficial therapy because trauma often involves an event out of the person's control and because it may put the individual back in self-control.

SEE ALSO:

Post-Traumatic Stress Disorder
Self-Operations Control
Stress Management Methods

BIBLIOGRAPHY

Everstine, D. S., & Everstine, L. (1993). *The Trauma response: Treatment for emotional injury.* New York: W. W. Norton.
Van der Kolk, B. A., McFarlane, A. C., & Weisaeth, L. (Eds.). 1996. *Traumatic stress: The effects of overwhelming experience on mind, body, and society.* New York: Guilford Press.
Wilson, J. P., & Raphael, B. (Eds.). (1993). *International handbook of traumatic stress syndromes.* New York: Plenum.

Type A Behavior

Description

Type A Behavior (TAB) is a complex behavior pattern in those who are chronically, incessantly struggling to achieve more and more in less and less time. TAB affects perhaps a majority of American males. This type of person is usually hard-driving, aggressive, energetic, ambitious, highly competitive, impatient, time-conscious, and overly tense. They seldom seem fatigued and usually have restricted awareness of others. He or she tends to regard characteristics of low self-disclosure, low emotional involvement, low display of feelings, high defensiveness, and high insensitivity as important for the acquisition of power and control. TAB has been referred to as a "coronary-prone behavior pattern" such that it often results in cardiovascular disease.

Causes

Cardiac researchers Maya Friedman and Ray Rosenman found, in the 1950s, that traditional coronary risk factors such as dietary cholesterol, blood pressure, and heredity could not sufficiently explain or predict coronary heart disease. More recent studies suggest that it is the aggressive tendency and anger of TAB (as opposed to time-consciousness, impatience, competitiveness, or workaholism) that provide an important link with heart disease. Such frenetic behavior causes the body to produce excessive adrenalin, which may damage the arteries and the heart. Both hereditary and learned behavior apparently interact in the development of TAB.

Treatment

Recent studies indicate that the TAB pattern can be modified. Primarily recommended are some of the **Stress Management Methods,** especially **Progressive Relaxation,** in which emphasis is specifically placed on identifying important priorities, scheduling time for high priorities, and minimizing time-wasting tasks (see also **Time Management**). **Exercise,** which helps control some of the physical symptoms of stress by lowering blood pressure and strengthening the heart, is also recommended.

SEE ALSO:

Cardiovascular Disease
Exercise, Benefits of
Progressive Relaxation

Stress Management Methods
Time Management
Time Pressure

BIBLIOGRAPHY

Friedman, M. (1996). *Type A behavior: Its diagnosis and treatment.* New York: Plenum.
Friedman, M., & Rosenman, R. H. (1974). *Type A behavior and your heart.* New York: Alfred K. Knopf.
McGuigan F. J. (1992). *Calm down: A guide for stress and tension control* (2nd ed.). Dubuque, IA: Kendall/Hunt.
Snel, J., & van Mechelen, W. (1995). Lifestyle and health from young adulthood to adulthood. In H. C. G. Kemper (Ed.), *The Amsterdam growth study: A longitudinal analysis of health, fitness, and lifestyle. HK sport science monograph series,* Vol. 6 (pp. 159–171). Champaign, IL: Human Kinetics.

Type B Behavior

Description

Although the Type A behavior (TAB) "coronary-prone personality" has been extensively researched and written about, people exhibiting the contrasting Type B Behavior (TBB) have served mainly as comparison groups against which the characteristics of TAB individuals were evaluated. Those with TBB speak less quickly, loudly, and explosively than TABs and describe themselves as less aggressive, active, hard-working, and achievement-oriented. Relative to TABs, TBB individuals regard themselves as more self-controlled and more satisfied with their work, life achievements, and marriages. Psychophysiological studies have usually found TBBs to be less autonomically responsive than TABs during aversive stimulation or exposure to a difficult problem-solving task.

Some studies have outlined several distinguishing features of the TBB relative to TAB: TBB individuals excel on tasks requiring deliberation and patience and are more likely to persist in problem-solving efforts in the face of highly salient feedbacks that these efforts are not succeeding. Finally, TBBs seem to have a broader focus of attention than TABs, and for this reason may outperform those with TAB on secondary tasks intended to distract attention from a primary task. All of these are characteristics of persons who are **Differentially Relaxed.**

There is, however, some considerable heterogeneity among the two classifications. That is, people who are classified as Type A differ considerably among themselves, as do people who are classified as Type B. Yet the distinction carries some valid notion of the distinction between, for example, a somewhat nervous person versus a more relaxed type of person. One simplistic way of characterizing the effectiveness of **Progressive Relaxation** is to change Type A individuals into Type B individuals.

In the original research validating the Type A/B distinction, nearly one-third of the men who developed coronary heart disease were classified as Type B. This may indicate that the Type B personality is by no means coronary-immune, merely less coronary-prone than the Type A. Furthermore, the description of the Type B personality in terms opposite to those used to characterize Type A may sometimes be misleading.

SEE ALSO:

Differential Relaxation
Progressive Relaxation
Type A Behavior

BIBLIOGRAPHY

Friedman, M. (1996). *Type A behavior: Its diagnosis and treatment.* New York: Plenum.

Freidman, M., & Rosenman, R. H. (1974). *Type A behavior and your heart.* New York: Alfred K. Knopf.

Houston, B. K., & Snyder, C. R. (Eds.). (1988). *Type A behavior pattern: Research, theory, and intervention. Wiley series on health psychology/behavioral medicine.* New York: Wiley.

McGuigan, F. J. (1992). *Calm down: A guide for stress and tension control* (2nd ed.). Dubuque, IA: Kendall/Hunt.

U Ulcers

Ulcers, Peptic and Duodenal

An ulcer is a lesion on the skin or mucous membrane (those membranes that line the passages and cavities of the body), in which surface tissue becomes pitted, allowing the underlying tissues to be damaged and inflamed. Ulcers are usually round, indented areas about ½ inch to more than 1 inch in diameter.

Peptic ulcers of the gastrointestinal tract are generally classified as "gastric" (located in the stomach) or "duodenal" (located in the first 9 or so inches of the small intestine). Duodenal ulcers account for about 75 percent of gastrointestinal ulcers. Duodenal and gastric ulcer pains are similar, though a duodenal ulcer may also be felt in the lower back if it is located on the back wall of the duodenum.

Gastric ulcers are thought to occur in up to 20 percent of the world population. Common symptoms are burning, gnawing pain in the upper abdomen and occasionally in the lower chest. The pain may begin soon after eating or not occur until hours later, and vomiting may help relieve pain.

Duodenal ulcers occur about seven times more often than do gastric ulcers. Young to middle-aged adult men are more likely than women to suffer from duodenal ulcers. About 10 percent of men develop duodenal ulcers at some time in their lives. Discomfort is usually noticed several hours after eating. Bleeding may occur, resulting in anemia. Sudden, heavy bleeding may result in vomiting of blood or fresh blood in the stool, in which case a physician should be seen immediately. In rare cases (perhaps 1 to 2 percent), the ulcer may progress though the wall of the duodenum and make an opening into the abdominal cavity, causing the very serious condition of peritonitis. (Peritonitis is characterized by sudden, intense pain and can lead to dehydration and shock; hospitalization and surgery are then required, since the intestinal contents are no longer contained.)

Causes

Three causes of ulcers are: (1) nonsteroidal antiinflammatory medications (sometimes called NSAIDs) such as ibuprofen and aspirin, which can be very irritating to the stomach, for some people, if taken on a regular basis—especially in high doses; (2) the excessive production of stomach acid, which can be exacerbated by inadequate coping with stressors; (3) the most common cause of ulcers is a type of bacterium, Helicobacter pylori, found in the stomach. One theory as to how bacteria cause ulcers is that the activity of the bacteria damages and weakens the barrier that protects the stomach and duodenum from acid, allowing acid to irritate the stomach and duodenum, eventually causing the ulcer. The bacterium is also a major cause of gastritis and may be related to gastric malignancy.

Contrary to most opinions, stress and spicy food do not cause ulcers, nor do special diets help to cure them. Stress, however, exacerbates ulcers. Smoking irritates ulcers and can also increase stomach acid, which further irritates the ulcer.

Duodenal ulcers are thought to be exacerbated by excessive hydrochloric acid and digestive enzyme secretions from the stomach, which erode the surface of the duodenum. Smoking and alcoholic beverages also contribute to this problem. Smoking is known to impede the healing of duodenal ulcers by reducing the acid-neutralizing secretions from the pancreas and allowing duodenal liquids back into the stomach. There is evidence of familial tendencies to oversecrete these products. Relatives (children and siblings) of ulcer sufferers are three times more likely to develop ulcers.

Recent research has convincingly shown bacteria to contribute to the appearance of gastric and duodenal ulcers. Increased susceptibility to bacterial infection may be due to malfunctioning of the immune system. Numerous research reports have shown that stress can lower immune system defenses to a variety of infections. Thus, while the consensus is that stress does not cause ulcers, it can make them worse, presumably by increasing the secretion of enzymes and acids. Stressors may trigger vagus nerve activity, which can cause hydrochloric acid and pepsinogen secretion. The vagus nerve is distributed widely throughout the body. Pepsinogen is an enzyme converted into pepsin for the digestion of protein. Tissues damaged by an excess of acid and enzyme are thereby susceptible to further damage.

Ineffective coping styles and strategies as well as one's personal relationships contribute to the incidence and severity of ulcers. During **Stressful Life Events** the normal, rhythmic movements of the gastrointestinal tract can be disturbed and the protective tissues lining this tract can become abraded. Muscular overtension can then suppress the body's immune system, retarding the healing process and increasing the chance for infection. Stress-related muscular tension is, therefore, a major reason for exacerbation of ulcers.

During stress, gastrointestinal peristalsis (rhythmic movement) becomes disturbed and the gastrointestinal lining may become abraded, "buckled," or even "broken." Once this happens, the hydrochloric acid can erode the wall behind the lining.

During stress, there can be an increase in gastric acidity that may ulcerate even a normal, intact mucinoid lining. During stress, the immune system seems to be suppressed so that healing is slowed, while the opportunities for infection increase.

Treatment

Patients with gastric or duodenal ulcers who are infected with H. pylori bacteria should be treated with antimicrobials regardless of whether they are suffering from the initial presentation of the disease or from a recurrence. The treatment for

H. pylori infection varies with the administration of different combinations of drugs, including Pepto-Bismol. Medication for the reduction of acid in the stomach is important because acid is not only bad for the ulcer but it can prevent the antibiotic from working effectively.

Ulcers can often be treated by relaxing the gastrointestinal tract. It is with reduced gastric activity, such as the reduction of secretion of hydrochloric acid, that the ulcer may be relieved. Clinical **Progressive Relaxation** provides the body an opportunity to heal itself.

Relaxed eating habits can also be helpful. Eating slowly and resting after each meal for about one-half hour are recommended. Eating numerous smaller meals instead of a few large meals is beneficial, since food in the stomach will tend to neutralize the digestive juices that can cause pain. Major changes in diet are no longer routinely recommended because dietary change itself may create stress, leading to increased acid production.

Discontinuing the use of alcohol and tobacco, along with the use of antacids, is also helpful. Prescription drugs are available to promote healing by coating the ulcer with a protective layer of protein. If ulcers do not respond, a physician should be consulted who may prescribe medication to reduce the production of hydrochloric (stomach) acid and/or provide a protective coating for the ulcer. Surgical treatment for the reduction of acid production may be used after an extended period without response to treatment, but this is rarely necessary.

SEE ALSO:

Gastrointestinal Disorders
Progressive Relaxation
Stressful Life Events

BIBLIOGRAPHY

Garrett, V. D. (1995). Gastrointestinal disorders. In A. J. Goreczny (Ed.), *Handbook of health and rehabilitation psychology. Plenum series in rehabilitation and health* (pp. 79–97). New York: Plenum.

Helicobacter pylori in peptic ulcer disease. (1994, Feb 7–9). *National Institute for Health consensus statement, 12*, 1–23.

Hernandez, D. E., & Glavin, G. B. (Eds.). (1990). *Neurobiology of stress ulcers. Annals of the New York Academy of Sciences* (Vol. 597). New York: New York Academy of Sciences.

V

Violence, Workplace

Violence, Workplace

Description

Our media are saturated with reports of workplace violence. Violence has found its way into the offices and corridors of fashionable, upscale office buildings; murder is now a major workplace health problem. According to the Centers for Disease Control (CDC), there were more than 750 workplace homicides in 1992, and the CDC thereby declared workplace homicide an epidemic. But murder is merely the tip of the violence iceberg. For every murder, there are scores of injuries, beatings, stabbings, suicides, shootings, rapes, near-suicides, psychological traumas, and mental health problems. From an economic perspective, violence disrupts productivity and costs business untold millions of dollars annually. Violence contributes to or is part of workplace **Drug** and **Alcohol Abuse, Absenteeism,** and many other factors that impede business operations and decrease productivity.

Treatment

There are a number of steps that employers can take to reduce workplace violence, especially applying **Stress Management Methods.** A few specific strategies include:

Threat assessment teams. When a threat is made, staffers from the human resources, security, health and safety, and legal departments convene to evaluate the problem, including the critical decision on when to notify law enforcement agencies.

Training for supervisors and managers. Supervisors and managers who know how to recognize aggressive behavior and mitigate its effects form a crucial front-line defense. Training includes how to recognize and respond to at-risk employees; conflict resolution and mediation; communication, and protocols for referring employees to suitable counselors.

Prevention planning when downsizing. Since job losses trigger so much workplace violence, companies planning workforce reductions must be more sensitive to the needs of those who will be affected. This means giving workers as much advance notice as possible, handling layoffs fairly, and providing reasonable severance benefits if feasible. If downsizing is mishandled, the potential exists for both guilt among survivors and anger among those terminated.

SEE ALSO:

Absenteeism	Drug Abuse in the Workplace
Alcohol Abuse in the Workplace	Stress Management Methods
Downsizing, Stress of	Workplace Stress

BIBLIOGRAPHY

Girdano, D. A., Everly, G. S., Jr., & Dusek, D. E. (1997). *Controlling stress and tension* (5th ed.). Boston: Allyn & Bacon.

Flannery, R. B. (1995). *Violence in the workplace.* New York: Crossroad.

Kinney, J. A., & Johnson, D. L. (1993). *Breaking point.* Chicago: National Safe Working Institute.

Vandenbos, G. R., & Bulatao, E. O. (Eds). (1996). *Violence on the job: Identifying risks and developing solutions.* Washington, DC: American Psychological Association.

W Water Intoxication– Worry

Water Intoxication and Stress

Description

Water intoxication, caused by disease, neurologic damage, or abnormal behavior, is characterized by a low concentration of solutes in the blood, meaning that osmotic activity of the blood and extracellular fluids is abnormally low. Headache, giddiness, and feelings of unreality often develop, accompanied by a bad-tempered, querulous disposition. In serious cases, neural and muscular excitability increase, leading not only to irritability and mental confusion but also to fibrillation (fine, rapid contractions of muscle fibers) and spasticity of muscles, convulsions and seizures, delirium, lethargy, coma, and even death.

Causes

This condition is considered to be caused in part by excessive loss of sodium from the body, by excessive water intake, or by a combination of both. When the body's sodium levels fall or water levels rise, one can become irritable and confused. A primary cause of these severe symptoms is the movement of water from the blood into the cells of the brain, causing them to swell and function abnormally.

Many types of neurologic damage—for example, meningitis, brain tumors, head trauma—can cause water intoxication. In many of these cases, water intake may be normal, but it is not excreted because of excessive levels of antidiuretic hormone (ADH), which causes water retention. ADH is produced in the hypothalamic region of the brain and is then transported to the posterior pituitary gland. From there it is released into the blood, finally exerting its action on the kidneys. When excessive ADH is present, water flows out of the collecting ducts of the kidneys into the blood, and concentrated urine is formed that contains very little water.

Because they influence the release of ADH, various states of emotional and physical stress can contribute to the development of water intoxication. It has been reported that water intoxication has been found in persons suffering from schizophrenia and manic-depressive psychosis. In these cases, the alleviation of psychotic symptoms has been observed to be associated with reduced levels of ADH and subsequent correction of a water overload.

Some persons suffering from water intoxication are classified as "compulsive drinkers," suffering from a condition called "psychogenic polydipsia." Polydipsia is one type of adjunctive behavior in which drinking water accompanies other responses produced by a stimulus. According to adjunctive schedules, organisms, including humans, can learn maladaptive drinking patterns. Individuals have been known to consume five to eight liters of water a day for no apparent reason. One survey of 27 cases of psychogenic polydipsia reported that 67 percent involved patients who were either schizophrenic or otherwise mentally disturbed, 18 percent involved alcoholics, and the remaining 15 percent included persons suffering from a variety of other disorders.

Treatment

Treatment for water intoxication varies according to its cause. When one's sodium level falls, a physician must consider that physiological condition and treat it, not just advise increased consumption of salt. If the cause is neurological damage, such as meningitis or brain tumor, neurological treatment is prescribed. If the cause is compulsive drinking behavior, a method of treatment might include **Systematic Desensitization.** Therapy for **Compulsive Behavior** may alleviate the condition. Further, since water intoxication may be caused by emotional and physical stress, **Stress Management Methods** may be appropriate. If the cause is polydipsia, the reinforcement schedule can be changed so that the individual can learn adaptive liquid consuming patterns rather than maladaptive ones.

SEE ALSO:

Compulsive Behavior
Stress Management Methods
Systematic Desensitization

BIBLIOGRAPHY

Bloch, G. (1985). *Body and self: Elements of human biology, behavior, and health.* Los Altos, CA: Wm. Kaufmann.
Catania, A. C. (1984). *Learning* (2nd ed.). Englewood Cliffs, NJ: Prentice-Hall.
Leadbetter, R. A., Shutty, M. S., Jr., Hammersberg. J. R., Higgins, P. B., & Pavalonis, D. (1996). Management of polydipsia and hyponatremia. In D. B. Schnur & D. G. Kirch (Eds.), *Water balance in schizophrenia. Progress in psychiatry, No. 48.* Washington, DC: American Psychiatric Press.

Workplace Stress

Description

Workplace stress arises from the interaction of people and their jobs when stressors disrupt efficient functioning. However, not all job stress is bad. Some stress is necessary in order for us to feel energetic and enthusiastic about our work; we call this positive stress (**Eustress**). But excessive stress (**Distress**) can be detrimental in many ways to the individual and contribute to an increase in employee sick days, lower productivity, and diminished performance; this translates to a smaller bottom line for those in management (which, in turn, is a stressor for them).

The symptoms associated with workplace stress are manifested both physiologically and psychologically. From a physiological perspective, early signs of workplace stress can be seen by the frequency and intensity in which the worker experiences colds or other minor infections. As stress builds up, the worker may begin to experience headaches, back pain, arthritis, insomnia, and skin disorders. In more severe cases, hypertension, cardiovascular disease, respiratory problems, gastrointestinal disorders, and even cancer have been implicated.

Psychologically, **Anxiety, Tension, Depression,** and chemical dependency (**Addiction**) may set in as the victim of negative stress experiences harder, more frustrating, and longer work hours. At some point, feelings of inadequacy may arise from frequent loss of concentration, difficulties in making decisions, and worry. This may cause the worker to become overly sensitive to insignificant disappointments or setbacks, often leading to frequent confrontations with fellow employees and alienation. The end result is often absenteeism and high employee turnover. In extreme cases, the overly stressed employee may lash out violently against fellow employees, employer, or even self.

Causes

Workplace stress takes many forms and has many causes, including unrealistic expectations or demands of superiors, financial pressures, career development concerns, required changes due to human and organizational obsolescence, and all the demands of life having a negative impact on the worker, the family, and other interpersonal relationships. Workplace stress can also be the result of the demands of specific tasks, time, overload and underload, roles, relationships, and physical factors. Much work stress can be the result of one's relationship with his or her superior. For example, a lack of recognition for a job well done and a feeling of being powerless in the ability to make changes necessary for the successful performance of a task can culminate in the introduction of excess stressors. The physical demands of vocations can include a variety of environmental factors such as noise, ventilation, temperature, humidity, illumination, and safety hazards.

Career development concerns can involve promotions, business opportunities and relocation, which can all contribute to increased stress. Relocation intensifies a family's emotional dependence on each other, often involves the loss of friends, and demands more training and many other adjustments. Family conflict due to workplace stress can be noted in the areas of marital relations, childbearing and child rearing, and family structure, with the family acting as either a place of refuge or a contributor to stress.

A significant factor contributing to stress in the workplace is the overall, ever-changing environment. The quest for profit in a global marketplace requires that change be implemented to secure a competitive advantage in one's industry. Implementing change does impact the working conditions, sometimes making work necessarily fast and excessive. Such demands at work ultimately cultivate excessive stressors.

Factors contributing to job stress don't necessarily originate at the workplace. There are many external influences that the individual experiences that affect the ability to perform at work, thereby inducing negative stress. Examples of these external influences include marital problems, financial difficulties, serious illness or death of a family member or close friend, troubled personal relationships, and the discord between residential location and individual well-being.

Treatment

Alleviating job stress can take place on both an organizational and individual level. From an organizational perspective, management can do well by ensuring a physical environment conducive to efficiency. This means making sure that there is good lighting, ample support material for work, and a reasonably comfortable setting—free from extraneous distractions such as excessive noise or odors.

Managers should also treat their people as valuable assets to the company, rather than as commodities to be used and discarded. Having a sense of purpose and communicating this to employees can reduce role ambiguities, eradicate poor working relationships, and cushion the demands of change necessary for a company to survive in a turbulent environment. Reward systems, including formal praise and monetary incentives, should be implemented and practiced continuously. This will instill a feeling of importance and loyalty among workers. Finally, managers should provide employee facilities and assistance and wellness programs to help workers prevent and deal with negative stress.

From an individual perspective, workers can engage in certain activities that will preclude and/or treat negative stress. These may include a variety of **Stress Management Methods.**

Biofeedback is a method by which people can learn to modify their behavior through observation of their internal responses (via instrumentation) and adjusting their physical activity accordingly. For example, by monitoring muscle activity through an electromyographic instrument (EMG), an individual can reduce muscle tension by relaxing. Workers might engage in some form of physical exercise at least three times a week for a minimum of 30 minutes each. Preferably, the activity should be of an aerobic nature such as bicycling, swimming, running, and the like. Exercise increases circulation to the brain, thereby increasing the availability of glucose and improvement in oxygen transportation, which may result in improvement in subjective feelings.

Progressive Relaxation is an effective, well-validated method for managing stress. Most people, when hit by a stress inducer, react immediately in an irrational fashion that does them in. Progressive relaxation involves relaxing the body in the face of stressful situations, momentarily assessing the situation, and developing a rational mode of behavior.

Progressive relaxation is based on the fact that when a stress inducer occurs, several reactions happen immediately. These include contraction of the skeletal muscles, followed by faster and deeper breathing, quickened heartbeat, and the halting of digestion in the stomach. Progressive relaxation operates under the premise that since excessive tension is a circular muscle-to-brain-to-muscle reaction, it is possible to interrupt the circuit by simply relaxing the skeletal muscles.

SEE ALSO:

Absenteeism	Eustress (Positive Stress)
Addiction	Executive Stress
Anxiety	Repetitive Stress Injuries
Burnout	Stress Management Methods
Depression	Tension
Distress (Negative Stress)	Violence, Workplace

BIBLIOGRAPHY

Cooper, R. K. (1991). *The Performance edge: New strategies to maximize your work effectiveness and competitive advantage.* Boston: Houghton Mifflin.

Klarreich, S. H. (1990). *Work without stress: A practical guide to emotional and physical well-being on the job.* New York: Brunner/Mazel.

Matteson, M. T., & Ivancevich, J. M. (1987). *Controlling work stress: Effective human resource and management strategies.* San Francisco: Jossey-Bass.

McGuigan, F. J. (1992). *Calm down: A guide for stress and tension control* (2nd ed.). Dubuque, IA: Kendall/Hunt.

Murphy, L. R., Hurrell, J. J., Sauter, S. L., & Keita, G. P. (Eds.). (1995). *Job stress interventions.* Washington, DC: American Psychological Association.

Sauter, S. L., & Murphy, L. R. (Eds.). (1995). *Organizational risk factors for job stress.* Washington, DC: American Psychological Association.

Worry

Description

Worry is nonadaptive behavior in which the worrier goes over and over a problem without achieving a solution. There is physiological activation that often disrupts performance. There may be emotional disturbance with difficulty of dismissing negative thoughts. Lack of control is a salient feature of the worry of intrusive thoughts. Worry is further characterized by high frequency, intensity, and disruption of attention and decision-making ability. There may be a relationship between worry and somatic aspects of anxiousness in which physiological events enhance worry.

Three levels of worry have been identified: One is about the everyday stressful events, one is about "life changes," and one is about worldly events. Usually, though, everyday events constitute the sources of worry for the individual.

Causes

Edmund Jacobson (1978) noted that life changes affect each individual, one way or another. An individual's adjustments to them add to the problems that have to be met, and this tends to increase extreme nervous tension. Contemplations of adjustments lead to reflections and worries that individuals may find difficult to eliminate. Further, contemplations of fear may also lead to worry.

Worry has contributed to a number of disorders and mood-related conditions identified in the Diagnostic and Statistical Manual of Mental Disorders (DSM-IV).

Treatment

As with **Anxiety,** behavioral methods help one to cope with daily living and with their long-term consequences, including the effects of worry on the human body. These effects can be focused on by a therapist specially trained to observe the small-muscle tensions that are present when a particular complaint is experienced. These are the muscle tensions that are activated when these unwanted acts of worry begin. By relaxing these tiny skeletal muscle components, the resultant neuromuscular tranquillity can eliminate the worry, phobia, or depression. It is **Progressive Relaxation** that deals effectively with ongoing worry. This method promotes healing by having the patient isolate the relevant muscular control signals during the act of worry. More specifically, the patient reports in detail to the clinician the mental imagery that accompanies the worry, along with the muscular tension sensations that are present during the process of worrying. By gaining control over these tensions that produce the worries, the patient can learn to control worry. Energy can then be saved, rather than wasted, if directed toward the effective accomplishment of goals.

SEE ALSO:

Anxiety
Progressive Relaxation

BIBLIOGRAPHY

Davey, G. C. L. (1994). Trait factors and rating of controllability as predictors of worrying about significant life stressors. *Personality and individual differences, 16,* 379–384.

Eysenck, M. H. (1996). Anxiety, processing efficiency theory, and performance. In W. Battrman & S. Dutke (Eds.), *Processes of molar regulation of behavior* (pp. 91–104). Scottsdale, AZ: Pabst Science.

Jacobson, E. (1978). *You must relax* (5th ed.). New York: McGraw-Hill.

McGuigan, F. J. (1992). *Calm down: A guide for stress and tension control* (2nd ed). Dubuque, IA: Kendall/Hunt.

Rapee, R. M., and Barlow, D. H. (Eds.) (1991). *Chronic anxiety: Generalized anxiety disorder and mixed anxiety depression.* New York: Guilford Press.

Schwarzer, R. (1996). Thought control of action: Interfering self doubts. In I. G. Sarason, G. R. Pierce, & B. R. Sarason (Eds.), *Cognitive interference: Theories, methods, and findings. The LEA series in personality and clinical psychology* (pp. 99–115). Mahwah, NJ: Erlbaum.

Y Yoga

Yoga

"Yoga" is a sanskrit word interpreted as "to meditate" and "to join," the latter implying that one connects oneself with a cosmic source. Yoga developed in Eastern religious environments. While there are many varieties of yoga, in general, they all have a purpose of helping individuals to achieve "higher levels of functioning." Classic yoga philosophy holds that worldly life is an illusion that must be overcome so that one can "become one with the universal spirit." When people learn yoga techniques, it is assumed that they become capable of functioning to extract those aspects from the surrounding world that can facilitate their inner development. Many people use some form of yoga as a stress management method.

SEE ALSO:

Stress Management Methods

BIBLIOGRAPHY

Corsini, R. J. (Ed.). (1987). *Concise encyclopedia of psychology.* New York: Wiley.
Girdano, D. A., Everly, G. S., Jr., & Dusek, D. E. (1997). *Controlling stress and tension* (5th ed.). Boston: Allyn & Bacon.
Patal, C. (1993). Yoga-based therapy. In P. M. Lehrer & R. L. Woolfolk (Eds.), *Principles and practices of stress management* (2nd ed., pp. 89–137). New York: Guilford Press.
Seaward, B. L. (1994). *Managing stress: Principles and strategies for health and wellbeing.* Boston: Jones & Bartlett.
Smith, J. C. (1993). *Understanding stress and coping.* New York: Macmillan.

INDEX